RENEWALS 458-4574

D0884525

Supply-Side Follies

Supply-Side Follies

Why Conservative Economics Fails,
Liberal Economics Falters, and
Innovation Economics Is the Answer

Robert D. Atkinson

ROWMAN & LITTLEFIELD PUBLISHERS, INC.
Lanham • Boulder • New York • Toronto • Plymouth, UK

ROWMAN & LITTLEFIELD PUBLISHERS, INC.

Published in the United States of America
by Rowman & Littlefield Publishers, Inc.
A wholly owned subsidary of The Rowman & Littlefield Publishing Group, Inc.
4501 Forbes Boulevard, Suite 200, Lanham, Maryland 20706
www.rowmanlittlefield.com

Estover Road
Plymouth PL6 7PY
United Kingdom

Distributed by National Book Network

British Library Cataloguing in Publication Information Available

Library of Congress Cataloging-in-Publication Data

Atkinson, Robert D.
  Supply-side follies : why conservative economics fails, liberal economics falters,
and innovation economics is the answer / Robert D. Atkinson.
     p.   cm.
  Includes bibliographical references and index.
  ISBN-13: 978-0-7425-5106-0 (cloth : alk. paper)
  ISBN-10: 0-7425-5106-7 (cloth : alk. paper)
    1. United States—Economic policy—2001-   2. Fiscal policy—United States.
  3. Supply-side economics—United States.   I. Title.
  HC106.83.A85   2006
  339.5'20973—dc22   2006005567

Printed in the United States of America

♾ ™ The paper used in this publication meets the minimum requirements of American
National Standard for Information Sciences—Permanence of Paper for Printed Library
Materials, ANSI/NISO Z39.48-1992.

Contents

Acknowledgments

Writing a book is not a task to be undertaken lightly, if for no other reason than the toll it can take in terms of time otherwise spent with one's family. As a result, I am immensely grateful to my wife, Anne-Marie, for her support and encouragement of this project. Her initial enthusiasm for this book helped me decide to take it on and sustained me during the many late nights and long weekends that went into producing it. I want to also thank my son, David, not only for his help as a research assistant and transcriber, but for his optimism and engagement in politics and policy.

I am also grateful to my friends and colleagues at the Progressive Policy Institute and the Democratic Leadership Council who have helped me over the past few years refine many of the ideas in this book. In particular, I would like to thank Ed Kilgore and Will Marshall. I would also like to thank the following reviewers for their insightful and helpful comments: Jared Bernstein, Steven Crolius, Alexander Field, Robin Gaster, David Hart, Joe Kennedy, Michael Mandel, David Moschella, Andrew Reamer, Andrew Sherry, Robert Weissbourd, and Howard Wial. Each of them offered unique insights that helped make this book clearer, more accurate, and hopefully more compelling. Finally, I would like to thank my editor, Christopher Anzalone, who from the beginning has had faith in this project and provided consistent support and helpful insights.

If any errors remain, they are my sole responsibility. Moreover, the views and positions expressed in this book are my own, and not necessarily those of the Information Technology and Innovation Foundation.

Part One

THE SUPPLY-SIDE REVIVAL

Chapter One

The Perfect Reagan Republican

Practical men, who believe themselves to be quite exempt from any intellectual influences, are usually the slaves of some defunct economist.

—John Maynard Keynes

In 1990, a young economist published a book defending the Reagan administration's supply-side economic policies of cutting taxes and limiting nondefense government spending. Supply-side economics offered a simple message that appealed not just to a new breed of conservative, but to the tens of thousands of wealthy individuals who bankrolled the Republican Party: the most important thing government can do to grow the economy is cut taxes, particularly on the top income tax rates and on savings and investments. After 260 pages of data and argument claiming to show that lower taxes boosted work, savings, and investment, the last chapter outlined a bold agenda on what should come after the Reagan revolution, which the author saw as just the first step of a radical change in Washington's economic policies. The first step was to preserve the hard-fought gains Reagan had achieved, especially keeping the top income tax rate from exceeding its then current 28 percent (down from 70 percent when Reagan took office in 1981).

But as the Robespierre of the supply-side revolution, the author wanted to extend the Reagan revolution and transform economic policy. To do this, he argued, Congress should slash the capital gains and dividends tax rates, eliminate the deductibility of state and local taxes, establish large tax-free individual savings accounts, abolish the inheritance tax, and privatize Social Security. He left his boldest proposal for last: replacing the seventy-five-year-old progressive income tax with a flat tax of just 19 percent on income that is earned and on savings not already sheltered from taxes. For a relatively academic text, the book gained a modest share of attention in the conservative community, receiving favorable reviews in publications like the *National Review* and *Forbes*.

If the author expected to see his bold economic program implemented anytime soon, he was to be disappointed. Much to the dismay of supply-siders, the president, George H. W. Bush, not only didn't extend the Reagan revolution, but reversed course, raising taxes in order to cut the budget deficit. And with his election in 1992, Bill Clinton's New Democrat formula of fiscal discipline and targeted public investments was, to say the least, a far cry from the author's hoped-for supply-side paradise.

THE CHAMPION EMERGES

The author was not deterred and patiently waited for a supply-side champion to bring the Reagan revolution to fruition. His patience paid off in 1999 when he found that champion, Texas governor George W. Bush. Unlike his father, the younger Bush was a new kind of Republican whose roots were in the 1980s' Reagan era, not the 1950s-to-1970s' Eisenhower/Nixon era. For these new Republicans, government and taxes were the problem, not the solution.

As a result, when Bush went looking for an economic policy adviser for his presidential campaign, he turned to Larry Lindsey, the author of that 1990 book, *The Growth Experiment: How a New Tax Policy Is Transforming the U.S. Economy*. Lindsey, a Harvard-trained economist with stints in the Reagan and first Bush White Houses, had become a prominent figure in the supply-side economics movement. And he had become extremely close to this Texas governor. Indeed, Bush himself provided a jacket endorsement for Lindsey's 1999 book, *Economic Puppetmasters: Lessons from the Halls of Power*, stating, "Anyone who cares about our economic future should read this book." When asked during the campaign about Lindsey's role, Bush replied, "Larry Lindsey, I think you know, I'm close to; I spend a lot of time talking to Larry."[1] This was, to put it mildly, an understatement.

After winning the closest presidential election since 1960, Bush announced that he was appointing Lindsey to head the National Economic Council, a White House–level body akin to the National Security Council, responsible for shaping and overseeing the administration's economic policy. The appointment of Lindsey and a host of other prominent supply-siders to administration posts should not have come as a surprise to anyone who had followed conservative politics. For by 2000, supply-side economics had become the Republican Party's de facto economic doctrine, and virtually all economic conservatives subscribe to the supply-side doctrine, even if they would not call themselves "supply-siders." Yet listening to the president's speeches and reading White House press releases would lead few people to this conclusion, for this administration seldom uses the term "supply-side economics," as it was tarnished after the experience of the 1980s, when supply-siders promised to cut taxes and raise revenues: instead, the budget deficit soared. Indeed, Ed Kilgore, vice president of the Democratic Leadership Council, states, "The Bush administration will not acknowledge the existence of this supply-side doctrine. It can't because George W. Bush owes his presidency in large part to the masterful illusion that he was a different kind of Republican from Newt Gingrich."[2] But while the Bush administration has consigned the term "supply-side economics" to the closet in Dick Cheney's bunker, the fact is that the guiding light for its economic policies is the supply-side economics doctrine that Lindsey so eloquently articulated sixteen years earlier. As a result, this could be, in the words of supply-side pundit and former Reagan administration official Larry Kudlow, "the most conservative GOP administration since Calvin Coolidge's victory in 1924."[3] And this is saying a lot, since, according to conservative columnist Robert Novak, Calvin Coolidge was "the father of supply-side economics."[4]

Once in the White House, the administration lost no time in implementing Lindsey's radical supply-side economics agenda. The first step was to roll back the 1993 Clinton tax increases on the wealthiest Americans. Claiming that the budget surplus was too high, Bush easily persuaded the Republican-controlled Congress to cut the top marginal tax rate from 39.6 percent to 35 percent. The next step was to cut taxes for business. Then, in 2003, as part of their plan to eliminate taxes on savings, they proposed and Congress approved cutting the tax rate on dividends and capital gains to just 15 percent. As a result, George W. Bush became the biggest tax cutter in U.S. history, far outstripping even Ronald Reagan. Not surprisingly, federal revenues quickly fell, from around 20 percent of GDP in 2000 to 16 percent in 2004, the lowest level since 1959.

The administration is not done though, for their goal is not just to cut taxes a few percentage points; it's to fulfill Lindsey's 1990 agenda of transforming the tax system along supply-side principles. And with Republicans in control of Congress and the White House for the first time in seventy years, their dream is being fulfilled. Indeed, as Grover Norquist, a key player in Republican politics and head of Americans for Tax Reform (more appropriately named "Americans for Radical Tax Cuts"), predicted,

> A second Bush term will see more tax reduction, greater expansion of the ownership society, allowing people to take some of their Social Security—FICA taxes—and put them into a 401(k) personal savings account. Separate from that, allowing people to have health savings accounts that will eventually, I believe, displace Medicare. . . . The same thing with more retirement savings accounts and lifetime savings accounts—two ideas the Bush people introduced in their first term.[5]

Norquist left out repealing the alternative minimum tax (a requirement that affects a small but growing number of taxpayers that requires them to pay an extra tax on top of the regular income tax), eliminating the estate tax on the wealthiest Americans, and making the tax cuts from the first term permanent. At the end of the day, this administration is shockingly bold, for it seeks nothing less than a return to the kind of economy and the kind of tax and governing system that prevailed before FDR's New Deal and the countless progressive reforms that followed it.

The Bush administration promises that this supply-side economics agenda will yield bounteous economic prosperity. The president recently remarked, "The American economy grows when the American people are allowed to keep more of their own money so they can save and they can invest and they can spend as they see fit."[6] While such a message sounds wonderful, as we will see, the supply-side economic agenda actually is a deficient economic growth strategy for the twenty-first century economy. The administration's supply-side economics agenda simply does not produce economic growth in the short term or the long term. This is not to say that it produces no growth; it leads to growing budget deficits and income inequality.

WHY SUPPLY-SIDE ECONOMICS?

So why has the Republican Party embraced supply-side economics lock, stock, and barrel? Why have they abandoned the fiscal discipline that characterized the GOP from its founding in 1854 to the late 1970s? Why do they see the answer to so many of the nation's problems in cutting taxes and reducing the size of government? To understand this, it's important to understand that many of today's supply-siders cut their teeth on economic policy during the Reagan era. In the fifty years before Reagan, most Republicans were resigned to living in the world defined by Democratic economics. Economic policy was grounded in another revolution in economics known as Keynesianism, after its intellectual founder, Englishman John Maynard Keynes. Under Keynesianism "demand-side" economics, keeping employment high was seen as the best way to grow the economy, and government's job was to stimulate spending for goods and services, particularly during economic slowdowns when consumers and businesses might be cutting back on their spending. Lacking an alternative growth theory, most Republicans became "conservative Keynesians" consigned to controlling occasional Democratic spending excesses.

Today, conservative Keynesians on the Republican side of the aisle are as endangered as the Florida manatee. In their place are small-government supply-siders. Where did they come from? Conservative supply-siders kept their heads down during the long progressive era that spanned from Franklin Roosevelt to Jimmy Carter. Not withstanding the widespread popularity of FDR's New Deal, Truman's Fair Deal, JFK's New Frontier, and LBJ's Great Society, there remained within the Republican Party a small but hardy contingent of diehards who saw these progressive reforms as fundamentally un-American and a threat to freedom. These conservatives were sustaining an intellectual tradition of supply-side economics that had characterized the Republican Party from William McKinley to Herbert Hoover and that held that lower taxes on the rich and on savings and investment boosted work, investment, growth, and even tax revenues.

Yet after the emergence of the New Deal in the 1930s, most mainstream Republicans adapted to the new postwar managerial economy and its big-government consensus, shedding their prewar supply-side doctrine in exchange for conservative Keynesianism. As a result, for most of the postwar period, the remaining conservative supply-siders were consigned to the minority of the minority party. Occasionally one of these conservative supply-siders would emerge, as Republican senator Barry Goldwater did in 1964 when he ran and lost in a landslide against Lyndon Johnson. His was a campaign seeking to resurrect the pre–New Deal past, as evidenced by his declaration, "Remember that a government big enough to give you everything you want is also big enough to take away everything you have." But for the most part they remained underground, taking intellectual sustenance from works like William Buckley's *National Review*, Ayn Rand's libertarian bible *Atlas Shrugged*, and Frederick Hayek's *The Road to Serfdom*.

As the new economy of the postwar era began to run out of steam by the early 1970s, Democrats seemed to run out of answers. Economic growth lagged while inflation and unemployment soared, something that was not supposed to happen in the Keynesian world. This breakdown of the old economy opened a political and intellectual space that enabled the pre–New Deal supply-siders to reemerge, trumpeting a revitalized supply-side anthem as the solution to all our economic problems.

While this supply-side message would have been universally rejected in the prosperous 1960s (including by most Republicans), by the troubled 1970s, it didn't seem so foreign. As a result, it began to gain a following among a new generation of conservative economists and politicians. Taking on Keynesian orthodoxy, these new supply-siders claimed that the slowdown of the 1970s wasn't due to lagging demand for goods and services, as the Keynesians demand-siders asserted, but rather stemmed from a lagging supply of labor and capital that was best kindled by cutting taxes.

This new theory found a receptive ear with Ronald Reagan, a Republican more out of the mold of conservative Republicans like Barry Goldwater and Robert Taft than of moderates like Richard Nixon and Gerald Ford. Reagan rejected the conservative Keynesian notion of raising taxes to balance the budget, arguing instead that tax cuts, especially on the wealthy, would stimulate growth while simultaneously enhancing government revenues. Reagan's supply-siders rightly recognized that the old economy's governing system of Keynesian economics, economic regulation, and welfare-state bureaucracy was no longer appropriate to the challenges facing a global, dynamic new economy. Reagan's proclamation that "government is not the solution to our problem, government is the problem" reflected the view of many, not just conservatives.

However, it wasn't until the Gingrich revolution in 1994 and the takeover of Congress by a new breed of conservative Republican that supply-side economics fully emerged as the de facto economic doctrine of the party. By 2000, these revitalized supply-siders reigned supreme. As a result, upon his election, George W. Bush was able to install only the most ideologically pure conservative supply-siders, promising that his economic team would "come from the belief that government ought to be limited, that we ought to continue to grow the economy by people having more money in their pocket."[7] Among the most ideologically pure was Bush himself. As *Business Week* political correspondent Rick Dunham writes, Bush is a "committed Reagan Republican who seeks revolutionary change."[8] Grover Norquist agrees, writing that

> people learn their politics at a young age, and tend to stick with it. George Herbert Walker Bush, the 41st president, brought his understanding of what the Republican Party was and what it stood for, pre-Reagan. It would not have occurred to him that the Republican Party was reflexively anti-tax. This came after he became a Republican. . . . When George W. Bush, the 43rd president, came of age and started focusing on politics, it was during the Reagan presidency—of course, you're against gun control, and for lower taxes, and less spending, and for the Strategic Defense Initiative. . . . George Herbert Walker Bush was almost the quintessential pre-Reagan elected official. His son is a perfect Reagan Republican.[9]

Indeed, what is remarkable is how unified the right is on the supply-side economic message. While three different, and sometimes conflicting, economic doctrines struggle for the heart and soul of the Democratic Party (the old economy Keynesian and redistributionist economics that focuses on boosting demand through government policies and programs; Rubinomics—named after Clinton treasury secretary Robert Rubin—that stresses fiscal discipline and paying down the debt; and the New Economy growth economics that puts boosting innovation first), Republicans are unified around one: the supply-side doctrine that lower taxes and less government are the royal road to growth. As a result, they are able to largely speak with one voice. The days of George Bush Senior calling supply-side policies "voodoo economics" are long gone.

Today most Republicans constantly tout the supply-side mantra. The conservative think tanks, talk shows, op-ed pages, and political campaigns all stay on the supply-side message. The Republican-controlled Joint Economic Committee of Congress tells us that "high marginal tax rates discourage work effort, saving, and investment, and promote tax avoidance and tax evasion."[10] The conservative Heritage Foundation says, "Lower tax rates will reduce this 'tax wedge' and encourage additional work, savings, investment, risk-taking, and entrepreneurship."[11] Don Evans, former Bush administration secretary of commerce, concurs, stating, "If you tax something less, such as work, you will get more of it."[12] Glenn Hubbard, former head of Bush's Council of Economic Advisers (CEA) states that "cuts in marginal tax rates are our most potent tax tools for raising the standard of living for all Americans."[13] Greg Mankiw, who followed Hubbard as CEA head, agrees: "In the long run, lower tax rates expand the supply side of the economy by enhancing the incentives for work, saving, and investment."[14] The *Wall Street Journal* editorial page, the house organ of the supply-side movement, claims that "the more money individuals get to keep, the greater the opportunities for growth."[15] Former Reagan administration budget official Larry Kudlow promises that "tax-cut incentives will promote capital formation, productivity, jobs, and growth."[16] They all sing from the same hymnal, and they all sing it loud and proud.

MUCH HAS BEEN PROMISED;
LITTLE HAS BEEN ACHIEVED

While supply-siders promise a promised land, what have been the results of the Bush supply-side agenda? In short, anything but promising. Indeed, as part 2 shows, supply-side economics is ineffective and even counterproductive at achieving its stated goal of boosting growth, and it has pernicious social and fiscal byproducts to boot. To start with, the Bush administration's supply-side tax cuts provided a massive tax break for the wealthiest Americans. While it's true that most households received a tax cut, the lion's share of the cuts went to the less than 1 percent of households making more than $200,000.[17] In 2004, a married couple making $500,000 would enjoy a tax cut of $17,486, while a household making $50,000 would pay just $744 less. These aren't just the political talking points of liberal pundits. While testifying before Congress shortly after he left the administration, Glenn Hubbard stated, "By cutting top individual income tax rates, phasing out the estate tax, cutting the corporate income tax, and expanding opportunities for tax-free saving, the 2001–2004 tax cuts on balance made the tax system less progressive. Measured as a share of income, the top tenth of one percent of taxpayers—that's one in one thousand—got tax cuts 18 times as large as the bottom fifth got."[18]

On top of this, the supply-side tax cuts blew a hole in the budget big enough to drive a Mack truck through. When President Bush took office, he inherited a surplus of $236 billion, but by 2004, the federal government took in $412 billion less than went out the door, $674 billion worse than what the Bush administration's first budget projected (a $262 budget surplus) (see figure 1.1). Brookings Institution economists William Gale and Peter Orszag estimate that the Bush tax cuts will reduce federal revenue by $1.9 trillion between 2001 and 2011, and if the tax cuts are made permanent, as President Bush calls for, the price will increase to $3.3 trillion. When increased interest payments because of the higher national debt are factored in, the net budget loss will be almost $4.5 trillion over the next ten years.[19] That amounts to $30,000 for every American worker. Even in Washington, that's a lot of money.

Even though these two results are not exactly heartening, supply-siders will argue that they are but a small price to pay for spirited growth. Unfortunately, growth has not been particularly spirited. In the short run, because the tax cuts were focused on wealthy taxpayers (who spend less of their tax cuts than would lower-income earners) and on savings, they produced relatively

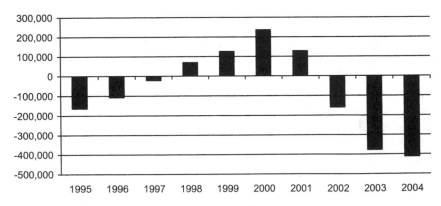

Figure 1.1   Federal Budget Deficit/Surplus ($ millions)

Source: Office of Management and Budget, *Budget of the United States Government, FY 2007.*

little spending and economic stimulus. This is certainly one reason why employment growth has been lackluster and why a smaller share of the working-age population is in the workforce today than in the 1990s (see figure 1.2). Lee Price of the Economic Policy Institute compared the current economic recovery to similar stages of past business cycles going back to 1948 and found that by almost every measure the current recovery has been lackluster.[20] For example, personal income has grown at almost half the rate of past recoveries (see figure 1.3). Only investment in residential housing has been above the average of past recessions. In the long run, as we will see in

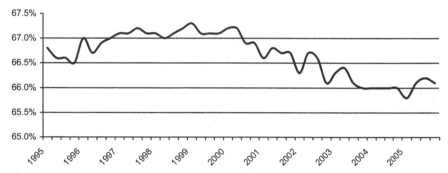

Figure 1.2   Percentage of Working-Age Americans in the Workforce
Source: Bureau of Labor Statistics.

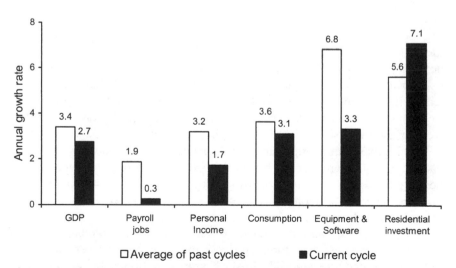

Figure 1.3   The Current Business Cycle Lags Past Cycles by Almost Every Measure
Source: Lee Price, Economic Policy Institute (analysis of Bureau of Economic Analysis and Bureau of Labor Statistics data).

part 2, supply-side tax cuts on individuals don't lead them to work, save, or invest more. The evidence that supply-side policies boost growth over the longer term is tenuous at best and in fact is contradicted by most careful economic studies.[21] In short, supply-side economics is not only unfair and fiscally irresponsible, but it is a failed growth strategy.

WHAT'S REALLY BEHIND THEIR COMMITMENT TO SUPPLY-SIDE ECONOMICS?

If the tax cuts have exacerbated growing income inequality, have blown a hole in the deficit, have provided a weak stimulus to jump-start the economy, and will hurt growth in the long run, why did George Bush stake his presidency on them? Like his motivation to invade Iraq, his motivations are complex and ultimately difficult to determine.

Perhaps part of the president's motivation was that he feared a repeat of his father's experience, where a poor economy helped cost him reelection in 1992. He may have reasoned that if he cut taxes enough, the economy would be so strong in 2004 that he would easily be reelected. But if this were the case, why pass tax cuts that were phased in over a period of years and that focused on wealthy Americans who didn't spend as much of them as average-income Americans would have? Besides, Bush began arguing for tax cuts in 1999, when the economy was moving, and he continues to argue for more now that the economy has begun to get moving again.

Perhaps he had learned another lesson from his father's experience, when after George H. W. Bush took the responsible path of raising taxes and limiting spending to help bring the budget deficit more under control, he incurred the wrath of the political right for breaking his promise of "Read my lips: no new taxes." Perhaps Bush was simply paying back his well-heeled campaign contributors, particularly the wealthy "Rangers" that pooled donations of at least $100,000. As *Tax Notes* author Martin Sullivan noted, "Conservatives love supply-side economics because it can be used to justify tax cuts for the wealthy and for business."[22] While keeping your political base and influential donors happy is surely important, simple pandering seems too easy an explanation. After all, why has Bush kept the tax-cutting pedal to the metal after he got elected to his second term? If this was just a cynical ploy to win election and curry favor among movement conservatives, he could have stopped after the second, or even the first, cut.

Perhaps it was because he wanted to "starve the beast," in other words, to use large budget deficits to force Congress and the public to accept large cuts in federal expenditures. Indeed, Grover Norquist has argued that tax cuts will force cuts in spending so that eventually the government will be so small that "we can drown it in the bathtub." Many conservatives don't just see progressive taxes and taxes on capital income as antigrowth and unfair; they see government spending itself—with exceptions like defense and law enforcement—as harmful to growth and personal initiative. Yet, while the Bush administration may hope that its huge tax-cut-induced budget deficits will eventually "starve the beast," they certainly have not shown any signs of putting the beast on a diet. In fact, in five years, the administration raised spending more than twice the amount Clinton did in eight years, boosting both defense and nondefense spending.[23]

A more compelling explanation of why this has been the most supply-side, economically conservative administration since Calvin Coolidge is that they actually believe in what they are doing. As a result, perhaps we should take them at their word as to why they have embarked on this agenda of serial tax cuts. This president and his team are disciples of tax cuts, tax cuts, and more tax cuts because they believe that they are the best way to grow the economy. In their view, high taxes reduce the incentives for people to work, save, and invest, and the best way to grow the economy is to restore these incentives by cutting taxes, particularly on the top rates and on capital income. Ever since the 1970s, having a compelling and easy-to-understand narrative of how to grow the economy has become a sine qua non of success in politics, and supply-side economics provides Republicans that narrative.

While the doctrine provides an easy-to-understand account of how government can grow the economy—cut taxes on individuals to free up workers, investors, and entrepreneurs—it's a fundamentally flawed strategy for growing the twenty-first-century economy. But its adherents easily overlook its flaws. As journalist Sidney Blumenthal states, supply-side economics serves as a utopian faith. He notes how

> supply-side economics has become premillennial miracle religion. Its catechism of tax cuts is granted magical powers to balance budgets . . . bring forth Republican unity, and erase doubts about the faith. The Reagan period is not seen as a refutation; instead deficits are explained as a sign of the incompleteness of the whole design, a shortcoming that only measures the level of belief and conversion. The insolvency of the plan actually produced is understood positively because it yielded a windfall of political profit . . . if only their crusade can compel universal belief, there will be a second coming of Reaganism—a true millennium.[24]

In short, they are believers in supply-side alchemy, where they can convert tax cuts into the golden fleece of a more prosperous economy and smaller federal government.

All of these factors—rewarding their political base, starving the beast, and growing the economy—help explain why the Bush administration has been on a single-minded mission to cut taxes. But at the end of the day, in order to understand what drives today's Republican Party to almost unanimously embrace supply-side economics, you have to understand an even more fundamental motivation. Modern conservatives, like pre–New Deal–era conservatives, see taxes, particularly higher tax rates on more affluent taxpayers and taxes to support anything beyond defense, justice, and a few other circumscribed areas, as theft. It's not just campaign rhetoric when President Bush says, "It's your money." He and most conservatives really believe it. This is why in the 2000 campaign, Bush argued that, "I think taxes are too high, I know it's a big issue in this campaign, I'm not getting off it. I don't give a darn what the polls say. People are paying too much in taxes."[25] Larry Lindsey agreed, warning that "the federal government now takes nearly 20 percent of GNP in total revenue, a figure undreamt of before the days of the income tax when most federal revenue was raised from tariffs and excise taxes."[26] What was undreamt of before the days of the income tax was Social Security; Medicare; America being the world's superpower; the interstate highway system; a federally funded science system second to none; unemployment insurance; a cleaner environment, safer workplaces, and a relatively safe food and drug supply stemming from federal enforcement of regulation; federal support for college enrollment; and a host of other initiatives. But even with all of these and other benefits that we as Americans collectively agree to support, many supply-siders see "the government" as an alien being that exists to limit their freedom and take their money. As former Republican congressional leader Dick Armey writes, "With every dollar government takes from you, it is taking more of your own power, independence, and dignity."[27]

In other words, conservatives see society as an aggregation of separate individuals, who, with the exception of cooperating to protect each other from foreign aggression or domestic lawlessness, have no higher purpose than simply satisfying their needs as consumers and family members. For them, private freedom trumps public interest, and one of the most vital aspects of freedom is the freedom to not have the state take "your money." Indeed, they see any effort to even advocate a public interest and employ the public sector to help achieve it, beyond the spheres of national defense and law enforcement, as a violation of liberty. As such, there is no goal, no "shining city on a hill" to aspire to, and no collective good, just the amoral workings of a free market where individuals get to "keep their money." If the president were to give John F. Kennedy's inaugural speech today, he might say something like, "Ask not what you can do for your country; ask what you can do for yourself." Indeed, in his 2004 Republican Convention speech, President Bush stated, "Government must take your side." For conservatives, limited government and enhanced "liberty"—avoiding centralizing decisions on the distribution of rights and resources—are ends in themselves, and the tax code should reinforce them.

It is in this context that we have to understand the power of supply-side economics on the Republican Party today. Supply-side economics provides conservatives with a valuable theory and doctrine to justify what they have long wanted: the system of lower taxes and smaller government that prevailed before the New Deal. Before Reagan, conservatives could gripe about the lack of freedom that activist government brought, but they couldn't make a compelling case as to why cutting taxes and government would improve the lot of the average person. Senator Robert Taft, leader of the anti–New Deal Republicans in the 1940s and 1950s, could only grouse:

> Today the interest of the people has come to center entirely in the field of economics . . . and the material welfare of the citizens. Programs are judged on the question of whether they give men more money, more bathtubs, more automobiles, and less time to work. Certainly no one can be against these economic objectives, but it is wrong to subordinate them to the need for greater morality, greater liberty of thought, and greater liberty of action.[28]

Today they can point to research (albeit much of it conducted by supply-siders) to bolster their case that tax cuts don't just make us freer; they make us more prosperous. To paraphrase Taft, tax cuts not only give us more freedom, but more mutual funds, hot tubs, and SUVs and more opportunity to work. What's not to like? The only thing not to like is that they don't give us more mutual funds, hot tubs, and SUVs and more opportunity to work, because supply-side economic policies do not generate more work, savings, or growth.

IT'S A NEW ECONOMY: WE NEED A NEW ECONOMIC POLICY

Supply-side economics fails precisely because it is a doctrine better suited to the realities of the economy of 1906 than to the economy of 2006. As I and a number of economic historians have argued, the U.S. economy has gone through distinct periods of transformation every fifty years or so, powered by new kinds of technology and production systems. Indeed, three great waves of technological change have broken over the United States in the last century, each leading to major transformations and the demise of one kind of economy and the emergence of another: the factory-based industrial economy from the 1890s to the 1940s; the corporate mass-production economy

from the 1940s to the 1990s; and now today's new entrepreneurial, knowledge-based economy. This series of transformations from one kind of economy and society to another has in fact been the dominant, if unappreciated,
story of America.[29]

It's this fact of economic (and social and political) transformation that is
the key to understanding both the resurgence of supply-side economics as the
Republican economic doctrine and why it's a failed doctrine. (As we will see
in chapter 10, it is also the key to understanding why the legacy liberal
demand-side economic policy held by most Democrats is also no longer an
effective economic doctrine.) As the old economy and its prevailing demand-
side economics doctrine deteriorated, conservative supply-siders sought to
resurrect the governing system that was in place the last time they were in
power, which was before the Great Depression. Indeed, their ideal era is one
before Franklin Roosevelt's New Deal; before Social Security and Medicare;
before federal departments of education, energy, and transportation; before
progressive income taxes; and before a broad role for the federal government
in solving pressing social and economic problems.

This deep connection with the pre–New Deal factory-era economy is why
supply-side economics has failed to deliver its promised land of economic
prosperity and a balanced budget. In that bygone era, the key to growth was
mobilizing capital. Large amounts of capital were needed to construct an
embryonic factory economy, and before the emergence of the kinds of
sophisticated global capital markets of today, most of that capital came from
wealthy tycoons. Today's supply-side economics still sees mobilizing capital
from wealthy individuals as the key to growth. But in the global twenty-first-
century knowledge economy, they are trying to stimulate the supply of an
item that the economy has enough of: investment capital. The problem is not
a lack of money but a lack of good investment opportunities here at home.
Therefore, not only are supply-side tax cuts not going to make much difference in the availability of capital, but even if they did, the supply of capital
is not the key factor driving growth.

The twenty-first-century knowledge economy requires a fundamentally
different approach to boosting growth than simply cutting taxes on the richest
investors. A small set of Promethean investors seeking to maximize their
portfolios might have powered growth in an industrial economy driven by
huge capital-intensive factories, but in a knowledge economy, it's the creativ-
ity, inspiration, knowledge, and risk-taking of all Americans that are the drivers of growth. Creative entrepreneurs, skilled workers, effective managers,
and cutting-edge researchers, all relying on a state-of-the-art social and physical infrastructure, are now the source of the wealth of nations. Tax cuts to
boost the supply of capital do little to support their efforts, and to the extent

that they reduce the ability of government to make investments in knowledge, research, skills, and next-generation infrastructure, they are actually injurious to growth. Our long-term economic problem is not too little investment capital; it's too little intellectual capital.

This disjunction between current realities and past inspirations is a key reason why scholarly research suggests that supply-side economics doesn't work. Supply-side economics promises to boost growth by reducing the disincentives to more work, savings, and investment. But while marginal tax rates above 90 or even 70 percent might dissuade work or savings (although as we will see in part 2, the evidence suggests that they didn't), the overwhelming consensus is that the lower tax rates in place in the 1990s had little or no effect on these supply-side motivations.[30] Even supply-siders admit as much. In *The Growth Experiment*, Larry Lindsey states that "the tremendous reduction in the top marginal tax rate in the United States, from 70 percent at the start of the decade to 33 percent at the decade's close has exploited most of the potential for improving incentives by rate cuts alone."[31] Former Bush Council of Economic Advisers chair Glenn Hubbard agreed: "In fact, the economic evidence seems to suggest that both labor supply and saving are relatively insensitive to taxes, so any efficiency gains are likely to be modest."[32] In other words, cutting taxes is likely to produce little or no growth, and by blowing a hole in the deficit (and raising interest rates) and leading to reduced funding for research, education, and infrastructure, the Bush tax cuts actually generate less longer-term growth. This is why the Congressional Budget Office found that the long-term effects of the Bush tax cuts would actually be to shrink economic growth.[33]

Luckily, a new economic strategy that fits the realities of the twenty-first-century global, technology-driven, knowledge-based economy is available: growth economics. Growth economics is based on the notion that only through actions taken by workers, companies, entrepreneurs, research institutions, and governments can an economy's productive and innovative power be enhanced. As a result, when examining how the New Economy creates wealth, growth economics is focused on a different set of questions: are entrepreneurs taking risks to start new ventures? Are workers getting skilled, and are companies organizing production in ways that utilize those skills? Are companies investing in technological breakthroughs, and is government supporting the technology base (e.g., funding research and the training of scientists and engineers)? Are regional clusters of firms and supporting institutions fostering innovation? Are research institutions transferring knowledge to companies? Are our trade policies working to ensure a level playing field and open markets for American companies? Are policy makers avoiding erecting protections for companies against more innovative competitors? And perhaps most importantly, are there policies supporting the ubiquitous adoption of advanced information and communication technologies and the broader digital transformation of society and the economy? In short, growth economics recognizes the fundamental insight that innovation takes place in the context of institutions. This shifts the focus of economic policy toward creating an institutional environment that supports technological innovation, entrepreneurial drive, and higher skills.

At the end of the day, supply-side economics and growth economics are based on fundamentally different notions of how the economy works, and as a result they lead to a set of fundamentally different choices for how to grow the economy. On the one side, the Bush administration's supply-side doctrine focuses on permanent tax cuts for the rich, huge deficits, and dramatically fewer public investments in the building blocks of growth. On the other side, growth economics focuses on increased public investments (including tax incentives for business to invest) in research, new equipment, and skills; the development and adoption of strategic policies to speed and extend the digital revolution, including widespread deployment of truly high-speed broadband communication networks and e-transformation of key sectors like health care; and a dramatically reinvented government, all in the context of fiscal discipline. While the Bush administration and its conservative supporters in Congress see an economy where wealth trickles down from the few, proponents of growth economics see one where wealth is generated by all Americans. Instead of blessing select corporate clients with protections and turning a blind eye to misdeeds, growth economics strives for a level and competitive playing field that drives the private sector to innovate. Instead of permanent tax cuts for the most well-off Americans even if it means a massive national debt, growth economics is grounded in fiscal discipline that keeps interest rates low to help boost investment. Instead of putting money in people's pockets by socking the next generation with the bill of a huge national debt, growth economics wants to put money in people's hands the old-fashioned way, by helping them earn much more of it through more productive jobs. Instead of trying to starve government, growth economics focuses on feeding knowledge and innovation. Instead of focusing on "getting government off people's backs," growth economics makes a reinvented and more efficient public sector a partner in helping all Americans achieve the American dream.

Because growth economics is based on the belief that smart public-sector action and strategic public-private partnerships are the key to growth, Democrats, because they see the promise of the use of public-sector action for public purposes, are the natural sponsors of growth economics. However, to date, they have not embraced it in a complete and enthusiastic manner, in large part because many on the left remain stuck in a worldview that places excessive emphasis on the demand side of the economic equation, rather than the supply side. Conservative supply-siders are right in one sense: robust economic growth depends on what happens on the supply side of the economy, although their particular tax-cutting strategy for boosting the supply side is flawed. Many on the left also let an important emphasis on fairness crowd out an equally important emphasis on innovation, productivity, and growth. Again, in this sense, supply-siders are also right: a focus on innovation, productivity, and growth is critical, since, to paraphrase John F. Kennedy, without a rising tide, it's hard to lift all boats. Finally, to the extent that Democrats, particularly moderate Democrats, have an answer for how to grow the economy, all too often the answer is balancing the budget. But while fiscal discipline helps, by itself it is not enough to grow the economy, especially one confronting serious competitiveness challenges from abroad.

At the end of the day, our long-term national welfare and prosperity calls for a new framework of economic policy based on growth economics. However, before articulating this growth economics agenda, we must first understand the supply-side economics agenda and where it came from. It's to that task that we now turn.

NOTES

1. Larry Kudlow, "W. Slams a Homer for Growth," *National Review Online*, 20 October 2000, www.nationalreview.com/kudlow/kudlow102100.shtml (accessed 21 November 2005).

2. Ed Kilgore, "Starving the Beast," *Blueprint Magazine*, June 2003, 44–46.

3. Larry Kudlow, "Coolidge Redux," *National Review Online*, 28 July 2000, www.nationalreview.com/kudlow/kudlow072800.shtml (accessed 21 November 2005).

4. Robert Novak, "Father of Supply-Side," *TownHall.com*, 1 September 2005, www.townhall.com/opinion/columns/robertnovak/2005/09/01/155310.html (accessed 21 November 2005).

5. Grover Norquist, interview on *Frontline*, 12 October 2004, www.pbs.org/wgbh/pages/frontline/shows/choice2004/interviews/norquist.html (accessed 21 November 2005).

6. George W. Bush, "President Discusses Strong and Growing Economy," Chicago, 6 January 2006, www.whitehouse.gov/news/releases/2006/01/20060106-7.html (accessed 31 January 2006).

7. Kudlow, "W. Slams a Homer."

8. Richard Dunham, Howard Gleckman, and Lee Walczak, "Gambling on Growth," *Business Week*, 17 February 2003, www.businessweek.com/magazine/content/03_07/b3820001_mz001.htm (accessed 21 November 2005).

9. Grover Norquist, *Frontline*.

10. Joint Economic Committee, "The Reagan Tax Cuts: Lessons for Tax Reform"

(Washington, DC: U.S. Congress, April 1986), www.house.gov/jec/fiscal/tx-grwth/reag txct/reagtxct.htm (accessed 21 November 2005).

11. Daniel Mitchell, "Reducing Tax Rates across the Board: A Cornerstone of Pro-Growth Tax Relief" (Washington, DC: Heritage Foundation, 2001).

12. Lyric Wallwork Winik, "Intelligence Report," *Parade*, 4 January 2004, 7.

13. R. Glenn Hubbard, "The Tax-Cut Debate," *Wall Street Journal*, 28 July 1999, www0.gsb.columbia.edu/faculty/ghubbard/Articles%20for%20Web%20Site/Wall%20 Street%20Journal/07.28.99%20The%20Tax-Cut%20Debate.pdf (accessed 21 November 2005).

14. Greg Mankiw, "Ask the White House," 8 October 2004, www.whitehouse.gov/ ask/20041008.html (accessed 21 November 2005).

15. *Wall Street Journal*, 2002.

16. Kudlow, "W. Slams a Homer."

17. William Gale and Peter Orszag, "Bush Administration Tax Policy: Summary and Outlook," *Tax Notes*, 29 November 2004, 1281.

18. R. Glenn Hubbard, "Tax Code Revision," testimony to Committee on House Ways and Means Committee, 8 June 2005, http://www0.gsb.columbia.edu/faculty/ghubbard/ speeches/6.8.05.pdf (accessed 21 November 2005).

19. Gale and Orszag, "Bush Administration Tax Policy: Summary and Outlook."

20. Lee Price, "The Boom That Wasn't" (Washington, DC: Economic Policy Institute, December 2005), www.epi.org/briefingpapers/168/bp168.pdf (accessed 3 February 2006).

21. For a good summary of the economic literature on tax cuts and growth, see Peter R. Orszag, "Marginal Tax Rate Reductions and the Economy: What Would Be the Long-Term Effects of the Bush Tax Cut?" (Washington, DC: Center on Budget and Policy Priorities, 16 March 2001), www.cbpp.org/3-15-01tax.htm (accessed 21 November 2005).

22. Martin A. Sullivan, "Do Economists Matter," *Tax Notes*, 15 January 2001, 280.

23. In 2000 dollars, federal spending as $1.68 trillion in 1993, $1.81 trillion in 2001, and $2.09 trillion in 2004. Source, Congressional Budget Office, "Historical Budget Data" (Washington, DC: Congressional Budget Office, 2005).

24. Sidney Blumenthal, "Seeking Insolvency: The Strange Career of Supply-Side Economics," *World Policy Journal*, 22 June 1997.

25. Kudlow, "W. Slams a Homer."

26. Lawrence B. Lindsey, *The Growth Experiment: How the New Tax Policy Is Transforming the U.S. Economy* (New York: Basic Books, 1990), 153.

27. Richard Armey, *The Flat Tax* (New York: Ballantine Books, 1996).

28. Russell Kirk and James McClellan, *The Political Principles of Robert A. Taft* (New York: Fleet Press Corporation, 1967), 54.

29. For a more detailed discussion of economic transformations, see Robert D. Atkinson, *The Past and Future of America's Economy: Waves of Innovation that Power Cycles of Growth* (Northampton, MA: Edward Elgar, 2005).

30. Indeed, relative to other nations, tax rates during the Clinton years were relatively low. Of the twenty-nine OECD countries in 1996, the United States had the twenty-fifth lowest ratio of taxes to GDP. Japan's ratio was 0.1 percentage point of GDP lower than the U.S. ratio, and only Mexico, Turkey, and Korea had lower ratios. Cited by William Gale, "Economic Growth Through Tax Cuts," testimony before the Joint Economic Com-

mittee, 4 March 1999, www.brookings.edu/views/testimony/gale/19990304.htm (accessed 21 November 2005).

31. Lindsey, *The Growth Experiment*, 235.

32. Hubbard, "Tax Code Revision," 6.

33. Congressional Budget Office, "An Analysis of the President's Budgetary Proposals for Fiscal Year 2004" (Washington, DC: Congressional Budget Office, March 2003).

Chapter Two

What Is Supply-Side Economics?

I am in favor of cutting taxes under any circumstances and for any excuse, for any reason, whenever it's possible.

—Milton Friedman

Many people equate supply-side economics with one claim, that tax cuts boost tax revenues. But supply-side economics is distinguished by at least ten key features (see table 2.1). First, supply-siders are more interested in boosting long-term growth than in managing the business cycle around a fixed growth trend, in part because they doubt that the business cycle can be managed.

Second, for many supply-siders, the ultimate gauge of economic well-being is not income, but wealth. Supply-sider Larry Kudlow states, "In the year 2000, wealth is more important than income."[1] When asked about slack

Table 2.1.   Ten Core Features of Supply-Side Economics

1. Growth, not managing the business cycle, should be the core focus.
2. Boosting wealth is more important than boosting employment.
3. Growth is best achieved by focusing on the supply-side of the economy.
4. Policies affecting micro-level incentives facing individuals are more important than policies affecting overall economic factors.
5. Reducing the top income tax rates provide the strongest incentive for individuals to change their behavior.
6. The supply of financial capital (savings) is the most important factor in growth.
7. Tax policy should focus on boosting savings, by lowering the top income tax rate and cutting taxes on saving and investment.
8. Tax policy should not be used to encourage any particular kind of behavior, therefore a simple tax system is better than one with complex deductions and credits.
9. Government spending distorts the economy and thereby should be as low as possible.
10. Some tax cuts, especially on the top rate and on savings and investment, are likely to produce even more revenues for the government.

job growth, former Bush administration Secretary of Labor Elaine Chao responded that "the stock market is, after all, the final arbiter."[2]

Third, instead of focusing on boosting consumer demand, supply-side economics focuses on boosting the productive capacity of the economy. Growth is achieved by encouraging workers to work more, entrepreneurs to take more risks and start more companies, and existing companies to invest more.

Fourth, unlike Keynesian economics that is focused on macro-level factors like overall spending, supply-side economics is focused on micro-level incentives facing individuals and companies. Arthur Laffer notes that supply-side economics "is a recognition that people change their behavior when marginal incentives change." One of the biggest incentives, supply-siders claim, is taxes. As a result, Larry Lindsey notes, "In its simplest form the supply-side claim has been 'Taxes matter.'"

Fifth, while all taxes matter, top marginal tax rates matter most. With a progressive tax system, the marginal rate is the rate paid on the next dollar earned, which for most taxpayers is higher than the rate paid on the first dollar earned. For example, the first $7,300 of an individual's taxable income is taxed at a rate of 10 percent, while the next dollar earned over $326,450 is taxed at 35 percent. Therefore supply-siders argue that while cutting the lowest rate could lead some earners to work and save more, it won't motivate higher earners, because any additional earnings will be taxed at the same higher rate. As a result, supply-siders believe that reducing top tax rates produces a more muscular incentive than cutting lower rates. A leading supply-side economist explains:

> The same 33 percent rate reduction will cut the bottom tax rate from 15 percent to 10 percent. Here take-home pay per $100 of additional earnings will rise from $85 to $90, only a 5.9 percent increase in the incentive to earn (compared to the 100 percent increase in the top bracket). Because cutting the 15 percent rate to 10 percent exerts only a small effect on the incentive to earn, the rate reduction has little impact on the tax base.[3]

Sixth, financial capital is the most important driver of growth. Larry Lindsey argues, "The key to economic growth and a rising standard of living is capital investment in new technology, equipment, and processes. But a society cannot invest more than it saves except by borrowing from abroad. America's savings rate is the lowest in the industrialized world and our tax system, though vastly improved since the late 1970s, is still biased against savings. But with only a very modest loss of tax revenue, the tax system can be reformed to substantially encourage the savings we need to sustain our investment in a more productive economy."[4] Supply-siders are "capital fundamentalists" who believe that it's the supply of capital, not the demand for it, that is at the heart of prosperity.

Seventh, because capital investment is the key to growth and more saving fuels capital investment, supply-siders believe that government should stimulate savings, and the best way to do that, they believe, is to boost incentives for individuals to save. Importantly, supply-siders focus more on boosting the supply of savings than on boosting the demand for savings (e.g., creating incentives for companies to invest), for they believe that investment is driven by the supply of savings. This is one of the main reasons why the lion's share of the Bush tax cuts has gone to individuals and not corporations. As former Reagan administration official Paul Craig Roberts notes, "cutting individual income tax rates seemed to me a more powerful vehicle [than cutting corporate rates] for a supply side policy."[5] But not all individual tax cuts are born equal; cuts on saving are most important. This is why the Bush administration cut the capital gains and dividend tax rates and seeks to expand tax-free savings and investment accounts. This focus on savings is another reason why the administration pushed so hard to reduce top marginal rates and why so many supply-siders from Dick Armey to Steve Forbes argue so passionately for a flat tax. Because richer people on average save a larger share of their income, supply-siders believe that cutting the top tax rates that high-income individuals face will boost private savings more.

Eighth, supply-siders seek to minimize the role of taxes in economic decision making because they believe that any taxes, especially tax preferences for particular kinds of activities, lead to costly distortions and to the greatest of all neoclassical economic sins: the misallocation of resources. In the view of one conservative think tank, "Every tax system distorts economic decisions and leads to less economic activity than otherwise would occur, resulting in what economists call 'deadweight loss.'"[6] They also believe this about much government spending, seeing it as distorting decisions by actors in the marketplace.

Because the market, not government, should make economic decisions, many supply-siders oppose using the tax system for anything other than raising revenue, including curbing economic downturns; redistributing income from higher-income individuals to lower-income ones; and providing incentives for people to act in the public interest, such as consuming less energy, getting more education, adopting a child, or buying more socially beneficial products such as environment friendly cars. Moreover, they fear that most tax breaks are the result of self-interested political pressure by interest groups, and so it's better for government to simply stay out of the business of targeted tax policies altogether. Lindsey complains that for decades the tax system "had been used heavily for other purposes as well: income redistribution, macroeconomic management, and social engineering."[7] Dick Armey promoted his flat tax proposal by promising that "throughout the nation's capital all the bureaucrats who have used the tax code as their blueprint of social engineering, for meting out rewards and punishments on private behavior, will sit quietly at their desks. America's economic decisions will be left to us, to the workers and earners and creators of wealth, the way it was always meant to be in the first place."[8] For supply-siders, tax policy shouldn't be used as a tool of "social engineers." People should be their own "personal engineers." It's this aversion that supply-siders have to using incentives to get people to behave in ways that are in the "public interest" that leads George Bush to state, "We don't believe in planners and deciders making decisions on behalf of Americans."[9] It's bad enough that the tax code is a means of taking people's property; it's even worse that it is also used as a means of limiting people's liberty by trying to control their actions by using tax incentives for things that the government decides are in the public interest. It's made even worse by the fact that government is captive to special interests who will distort decisions for their own self-interest. As a result, supply-siders ideally want a flat tax at the lowest level possible while still high enough to fund the basic necessities of government.

Ninth, while supply-siders view lower taxes as the key to growth, they also see lower spending, even if taxes were to remain the same, as a stimulus to growth. They believe that many government expenditures, including both direct spending and tax expenditures (targeted tax deductions targeted to particular activities, such as installing solar panels on a house), have a host of pernicious effects. Heritage Foundation economist Dan Mitchell actually asks, "Is spending hindering economic performance because of the taxes used to finance government? Would the economic damage be reduced if government had some magical source of free revenue?"[10] He concludes that even if somehow government programs could be implemented at no cost, they would still harm economic growth. He details a litany of purported harms from government, including its support of activities that displace more productive private-sector activity; that fund government agencies that harm the economy (e.g., regulatory agencies like the Environmental Protection Agency or the Securities and Exchange Commission); that lead to bad behaviors (e.g., unemployment insurance, since it leads to less work); that reduce personal saving (social supports make people save less); that lead to economic stagnation as people stop competing and rely on government programs; that boost inefficiency since government programs are inefficient; and finally, and perhaps most importantly, that distort the marketplace as government choices substitute for the free choices of individuals in competitive markets.

Mitchell is not alone. In a recent White House ceremony honoring conservative economist Milton Freidman, President Bush proclaimed that

> Milton Friedman has shown us that when government attempts to substitute its own judgments for the judgments of free people, the results are usually disastrous. In contrast to the free market's invisible hand, which improves the lives of people, the government's invisible foot tramples on people's hopes and destroys their dreams. . . . He has never claimed that free markets are perfect. Yet he has demonstrated that even an imperfect market produces better results than arrogant experts and grasping bureaucrats.[11]

Government redistribution, in particular, has, according to supply-siders, particularly pernicious effects on individuals. According to supply-siders, government programs that shelter individuals from risk only serve to reduce their willingness to work hard and be entrepreneurial. Glenn Hubbard objected that in the Clinton administration, "the new orthodoxy revolves around an economy of guarantees. In this view, for example, the objective of health policy is to 'guarantee' access to health insurance and medical care regardless of need, desire, or price. Alternatively, each worker must be endowed with a 'right' to a 'good job'—including a government-determined wage and guarantees of benefits."[12] What's wrong with giving Americans these kinds of supports and tools? According to Hubbard, "The orthodox mixture of costly guarantees and the tax burdens required to sustain them breeds as well a class-warfare mentality that undervalues the dynamism of the economy and handcuffs the ability to undertake beneficial, pro-growth policies."[13] This belief that reducing risk reduces initiative is why the Bush administration has cut programs to support laid-off workers, has opposed temporarily extending unemployment insurance benefits for workers who have exhausted their benefits, and has proposed reducing the tax that employers pay into the federal unemployment insurance trust fund. It's also why the Bush administration has opposed providing trade adjustment assistance for service-sector workers who lose their jobs when they are offshored to countries like India.[14]

More broadly, it's this belief by supply-siders that the market knows best that is behind their deep reluctance to use public means to assist in solving a whole host of pressing public problems, whether it's to ensure universal health care, address global warming, reduce dependence on foreign oil with a national energy strategy, boost broadband technology adoption, address the growing challenge to U.S. competitiveness, or respond proactively to any of the other issues in the long list of challenges our nation faces. Compounding the problems for supply-siders is their view that the risk of "political failure" is great and that government policies will be guided by self-interested "rent seekers" (the process by which an individual or firm seeks to profit through manipulation of the economic environment rather than through the production of added wealth) divorced from the public interest.

Tenth, some supply-siders believe in the Laffer curve—the notion that cutting taxes increases revenues. Even those supply-siders who scoff at true-blue Lafferites usually believe that tax cuts don't result in a dollar-for-dollar loss of revenue. Greg Mankiw is a case in point. In the third edition of his textbook *Principles of Macroeconomics*, he states,

> An example of fad economics occurred in 1980, when a small group of economists advised Presidential candidate, Ronald Reagan, that an across-the-board cut in income tax rates would raise tax revenue. They argued that if people could keep a higher fraction of their income, people would work harder to earn more income. Even though tax rates would be lower, income would rise by so much, they claimed, that tax revenues would rise. Almost all professional economists, including most of those who supported Reagan's proposal to cut taxes, viewed this outcome as far too optimistic. Lower tax rates might encourage people to work harder and this extra effort would offset the direct effects of lower tax rates to some extent, but there was no credible evidence that work effort would rise by enough to cause tax revenues to rise in the face of lower tax rates.[15]

The keyword is *enough*. Even a skeptic like Mankiw believes that tax cuts don't produce a one-to-one revenue loss, particularly if they are targeted at the rich. As a result, many supply-siders claim that some tax cuts like cutting top marginal tax rates and cutting taxes like the estate and capital gains taxes will produce more revenue than is lost. It's only when taxes are cut on working- and middle-class Americans, they say, that government loses money.

To be sure, not all supply-siders espouse all ten tenets listed here, but most believe most of them. What unites supply-siders is a belief that taxes are the most important component of government economic policy; that lower taxes are always better than higher taxes, especially on the rich and on saving and investment; and that the role for government in the economy should be minimized. Nor do you need to be a card-carrying conservative economist to be a supply-sider. Just as most Democratic politicians in the old economy had not read Keynes, most Republican elected officials in Washington have not read Jude Wanniski or Larry Lindsey. But they have absorbed the worldview and the message, as it fits their political needs and political orientation.

NOTES

1. Larry Kudlow, "Bush's Disappointment," *National Review Online*, 1 December 1999, www.nationalreview.com/kudlow/kudlow120199.html (accessed 21 November 2005).

2. Tom Raum, "Bush Economic Team under Fire over Jobs," *Associated Press*, 20 February 2004.

3. James D. Gwartney, "Supply-Side Economics," in *The Concise Encyclopedia of Economics*, www.econlib.org/library/Enc/SupplySideEconomics.html (accessed 21 November 2005).

4. Lawrence Lindsey, "A Tax Code for the Future: The Growth Experiment Revisited" (New York: Manhattan Institute, January 1995), www.manhattan-institute.org/html/research_memorandum_3.htm (accessed 21 November 2005).

5. Paul Craig Roberts, *The Supply-Side Revolution: An Insider's Account of Policymaking in Washington* (Cambridge, MA: Harvard University Press, 1984), 33.

6. Lawrence A. Hunter and Stephen J. Entin, "A Framework for Tax Reform" (Dallas: Institute for Policy Innovation, 14 January 2005).

7. Lawrence B. Lindsey, *The Growth Experiment: How the New Tax Policy Is Transforming the U.S. Economy* (New York: Basic Books, 1990), 10.

8. Richard Armey, *The Flat Tax* (New York: Ballantine Books, 1996), 4.

9. George W. Bush, speech in Scranton, PA, 6 September 2000.

10. Daniel J. Mitchell, supplement to "The Impact of Government Spending on Economic Growth" (Washington, DC: Heritage Foundation, 15 March 2005).

11. George W. Bush, "President Honors Milton Friedman for Lifetime Achievements," remarks by the president in tribute to Milton Friedman, Eisenhower Executive Office Building, May 2002.

12. R. Glenn Hubbard, "A Framework for Economic Policy," Ronald Reagan Presidential Library, 15 February 2002, http://www0.gsb.columbia.edu/faculty/ghubbard/speeches/2.15.02.pdf (accessed 21 November 2005).

13. Hubbard, "A Framework for Economic Policy," 13.

14. Laid-off programmers filed a class-action suit against the Department of Labor claiming that the agency has illegally denied 10,000 of them benefits under the Trade Adjustment Assistance Act. During the Bush administration, the Department of Labor has ruled that many software workers are ineligible because software and IT services do not qualify as products or "articles" under TAA guidelines. Only workers who made more tangible products, such as clothing and furniture, can get TAA benefits, the department has ruled. In contrast, the Clinton administration usually ruled in favor of such workers.

15. Greg Mankiw, *Principles of Macroeconomics*, 3rd ed. (Mason, OH: Thompson, 2004).

Chapter Three

A Brief History of Supply-Side Economics

Collecting more taxes than is absolutely necessary is legalized robbery.

—Calvin Coolidge

Liberal economist Paul Krugman once asked in frustration, "Why does supply-side economics have such durability?" The answer is simple. Supply-side economics is not some obscure branch of economics generated by a few disenchanted economists. It is the core economic doctrine guiding today's Republican Party. Moreover, in contrast to what its adherents would have us believe, supply-side economics did not magically appear over a series of dinners in a New York City restaurant in the 1970s (as the supply-side birth myth holds): it reflects a reemergence of an economic doctrine that guided most economists and most Republicans for over fifty years before the rise of Keynesian economics and the New Deal in the 1930s. Indeed, for today's conservative supply-siders, this was the period before the country was diverted from its true path: where government was small; taxes were few and regressive; and, in the words of Calvin Coolidge, the business of government was business. For, as we will see, modern-day supply-siders are simply parroting, with one key difference (the embrace of fiscal discipline), the economic doctrine that was the staple of Republican thinking in that era. During the 2000 presidential campaign, top Bush adviser Karl Rove compared the Bush campaign to that of Republican president William McKinley. Conservative commentator James Glassman agreed, stating, "Americans are returning to values and ideas associated with the Republican Party, which dominated political life from the 1880s to the early 1930s."[1]

Supply-side economics, like the conservative politics that has accompanied it, is a revival of a prior theory of how the government should relate to the economy. This practical theory of policy, predominant from around the 1880s to the early 1930s, was rooted in classical economics (with one key exception: classicalists were opposed to tariffs, whereas the Republican Party strongly supported tariffs during this period). It was grounded in the view that taxes and government spending distorted the natural workings of the market economy. As supply-side economist Martin Feldstein notes, "Much of our 'supply-side economics' was a return to basic ideas about creating capacity and removing government impediments to individual initiative that were central in Adam Smith's *The Wealth of Nations* and in the writings of the classical economics of the nineteenth century."[2] Norman Ture, a supply-side pioneer and Reagan administration official, noted that supply-side economics' "basic concepts predate Keynesians by a century and half."[3] Indeed, virtually everything the supply-siders hold is consistent with the economic doctrine that prevailed before the New Deal, even the notion that tax cuts pay for themselves.

So what did classical economics hold? One place to look is economist Alfred Marshall's famous *Principals of Economics* textbook, first published in 1890. Marshall held that classical economics was based on four key principles. First, economic freedom is the key. By this he meant that individuals should be free to make the legal decisions they want, without distortion by government, including taxes. Any effort by government to require or even entice individuals to act in the public interest is the worst kind of social engineering that violates individuals' freedom and distorts the free workings of the market.

Second, individuals act to maximize their own self-interest, and the pursuit of that self-interest leads to the public interest. Indeed, among the holiest of "conservative" scriptures is Adam Smith's *Wealth of Nations*, which puts forth the doctrine of "the invisible hand," which holds that the individual who "intends only his own gain" will, in the course of maximizing his needs, be "led by an invisible hand to promote . . . the public interest."[4] As a result, supply-siders hold as an article of faith that the private sector is efficient and promotes growth, while government is inefficient and retards growth.

Third, competitive markets force producers to innovate and become more efficient, and as long as markets are competitive, no economic interest can establish a monopoly position. Because individuals are free and pursue their own self-interest in near-perfect competition, economic welfare is maximized. Therefore, the proper role for government is to "let alone and let be." In other words, laissez-faire was to be the governing principle, and the proper role for government was a minimal one confined to defending the nation, enforcing contracts, and providing the few goods and services the market is incapable of providing.

Fifth, classical economics held that the business cycle was self-adjusting. According to Say's law, named after French classical economist Jean-Baptiste Say, production creates its own demand. For example, if inventory doesn't sell, the price is cut until it does. As a result, classical economics held that the normal tendency for the economy is to be in full employment. If there is excess unemployment, the market will bid down the price of labor until its buyers (businesses) purchase enough of it so there is no excess. As a result, classical economists looked askance at practices like the minimum wage, Social Security taxes, and income taxes, since they distorted the "natural" workings of the labor market. Say's law implies that there is no need for government to intervene in managing the business cycle, for by their very nature business cycles should be brief. In spite of the elegance—or some might say simplicity—of classical economic theory, the real world didn't quite work that way: from 1853 to 1953, the economy was in recession 40 percent of the time.

Classical economics assigned a special role to saving, and it's that role which plays such a central place in today's supply-side economics. When Adam Smith published *The Wealth of Nations* in 1776, he rightly argued against the prevailing mercantilist belief that a nation's wealth was a function of the amount of precious metals it possessed. Instead, he argued that wealth was determined by the amount and use of a nation's productive assets, including land; labor; and, for him most importantly, capital (e.g., machinery). This led Smith to emphasize the importance of a high rate of savings, for this would enable more productive assets. In fact, just as Say's law holds that the supply of goods creates its own demand, a corollary of Say's law holds that the supply of capital creates its own demand. In other words, for classical economists, not only do savings equal investment, but more savings produce more investment. If savings is "excessive," interest rates will be bid down until all the money is invested. It's largely on this basis that modern supply-siders put so much emphasis on boosting savings.

Finally, because of the emphasis on economic freedom and on savings, classical economics viewed taxation, particularly at levels beyond the minimum needed to fulfill the necessary but limited role of the state, with significant trepidation. Taxation was seen as siphoning money from consumers and business into less productive government uses. Sounding like a modern-day supply-sider, Say argued that "taxation is the taking from individuals a part of their property for public purposes." He went on to argue that taxation is theft with little purpose, for "the value levied by taxation never reverts to the members of the community, after it has once been taken from them; and that taxation is not itself a means of reproduction." As a result, argues Say, "it is impossible to deny the conclusion, that the best taxes, or, rather those that are least bad, are 1. Such as are the most moderate . . . ; 2. Such as are least attended with those vexatious circumstances, that harass the taxpayer without bringing any thing into the public exchequer; 3. Such as press impartially on all classes, and 4. Such as are least injurious to reproduction."[5] In other words, taxation is theft that provides few benefits to society and even fewer to taxpayers. As a result, the best tax is one that is low, easy to administer, applies equally to everyone, and is only levied on wage income and not capital income. There we have it, the supply-side formula in a nutshell, advocated by a nineteenth-century French economist.

Not only do "excess" taxes distort the economy and lead to lower growth, but classicalists also argued that at too high levels, taxation failed to raise revenues. Sounding like a nineteenth-century Arthur Laffer, Say argued, "Taxation pushed to the extreme has the lamentable effect of impoverishing the individual without enriching the state."[6] Likewise, Adam Smith warned that "high taxes, sometimes by diminishing the consumption of the taxed commodities, and sometimes by encouraging smuggling, frequently afford a smaller revenue to government than what might be drawn from more moderate taxes."[7] The only answer, according to Smith, is to lower taxes: "When the diminution of revenue is the effect of the diminution of consumption there can be but one remedy, and that is the lowering of the tax."[8]

The heyday of classical economics in America was in the factory-based industrial economy that emerged in the 1880s and extended through the 1920s. As this new economy emerged, political leaders searched for guidance on how to manage it. They did not have to look far, for classical economics provided the answers they were looking for. As a result, while the term "supply-side economics" was not coined until the 1970s, the economic policy embraced by most economists and most public officials from the late 1800s to the late 1920s was right out of today's supply-side playbook. In his 1897 inaugural address, William McKinley summed up the tenor of the time: "Economy is demanded in every branch of the Government at all times, but especially in periods, like the present, of depression in business and distress among the people. The severest economy must be observed in all public expenditures, and extravagance stopped wherever it is found, and prevented wherever in the future it may be developed."[9] President Taft concurred, stating that "a national government cannot create good times. It cannot make the rain to fall, the sun to shine or the crops to grow."[10] Calvin Coolidge agreed, noting that "it does not follow at all that because abuses exist, it is the concern of the federal government to attempt their reform."[11] Herbert Hoover argued that "self-government does not and should not imply the use of political agencies alone. Progress is born of cooperation in the community—not from governmental restraints."[12]

It's not surprising that modern-day conservatives look with favor at that golden era of small government. There was no national income tax, and, notwithstanding the increased role of the federal government in regulating interstate commerce, protecting the food and drug supply, and enforcing antitrust laws, the government remained relatively small. Most conservatives, and the classical economists who provided intellectual support for their economic policies, opposed government intervention in the economy, such as a minimum wage, unemployment insurance, government-funded pensions, and other supports.

Even though most elected officials believed that the government's role should be limited, by the 1910s it became clear that an emerging industrial nation required some modest expansion of government in areas such as worker safety and incomes, product regulation, controlling monopolies, and regulating banking and the money supply. To help pay for this expansion, Congress and President Woodrow Wilson enacted the income tax in 1913. Initially, the rates were quite modest. But with the entrance of America into World War I, Congress raised the top rates to 73 percent, with the idea that the wealthiest Americans should pay a bigger burden of defending the nation. With the election of Republican Warren Harding in 1920 and, after his death in 1923, the assumption to the presidency of his vice president, Calvin Coolidge, coupled with the control of Congress in Republican hands, there was significant pressure to reduce the top rates. The leader of that effort was Andrew Mellon, Coolidge's secretary of the treasury and a wealthy tycoon in his own right, who stridently opposed high tax rates. As a result, three major tax cuts reduced the top marginal tax rate from 73 percent in 1921 to 25 percent in 1926, to about the prewar levels.

Republicans used the same arguments made by supply-siders today to push for lower taxes on the wealthy. Coolidge proclaimed, "I am convinced that the larger incomes of the country would actually yield more revenue to the government if the basis of taxation were scientifically revised downward."[13] He went on to state that, "if the price is too high, the taxpayer, through the many means available, avoids a taxable income and the Government gets less out of a high tax than it would out of a lower one." Sounding like the editorial page of today's *Wall Street Journal*, the *New York Times* wrote in support of the Mellon tax cuts because the cuts provided an incentive "to put more money into enterprises and industry and less into tax-exempt securities."[14] One of the motivations for cutting taxes was not just a supply-side one of boosting incentives for work and investment; it was to push for smaller government. Calvin Coolidge railed against "big government" in 1924, calling the 5.3 percent of GNP that the federal government collected in taxes (compared to around 17 percent today) a "stupendous sum," and as result he called on the government "to be unremitting in their efforts to reduce expenditures."[15]

Andrew Mellon even wrote a book, *Taxation: The People's Business*, to make the case for lower taxes. Bearing a striking resemblance to the arguments used by present-day supply-siders, he wrote,

> The history of taxation shows that taxes which are inherently excessive are not paid. The high rates inevitably put pressure upon the taxpayer to withdraw his capital from productive business and invest it in tax-exempt securities or to find other lawful methods of avoiding the realization of taxable income. The result is that the sources of taxation are drying up; wealth is failing to carry its share of the tax burden; and capital is being diverted into channels which yield neither revenue to the government nor profit to the people.[16]

While Mellon succeeded in getting tax rates down, he must not have gotten them low enough, for he was later prosecuted for tax evasion, and while he was found innocent, he had to pay a $400,000 fine for "mistakes" he had made in his favor.

Today's supply-siders sound like Roaring Twenties economists, not just when it comes to taxes, but on most economic issues, because by and large they are singing from the same hymnal. For example, compare Calvin Coolidge's statement "Under this republic the rewards of industry belong to those who earn them" to George Bush's "It's your money," or Calvin Coolidge's "The method of raising revenue ought not to impede the transaction of business; it ought to encourage it" to Bush's "Our economy can grow best when we give people their own money back." Likewise, Coolidge warned that "the method of raising revenue ought not to impede the transaction of business; it ought to encourage it," while Bush stated that "the complexity of the tax code is a tremendous burden on small businesses." Both then and now, they have argued that cutting taxes won't lose very much revenue. Coolidge was "opposed to extremely high rates, because they produce little or no revenue," while Larry Lindsey argued that, "because rich people change their behavior in a high tax environment, higher rates don't necessarily yield substantial amounts of tax revenue." Likewise, then and now, they have claimed that progressive taxes hurt growth. Coolidge proclaimed, "We cannot finance the country, we cannot improve social conditions, through any system of injustice, even if we attempt to inflict it upon the rich. Those who suffer the most harm will be the poor." Echoing this sentiment, Bush has argued that, "by dropping the top rate from 39.6 percent to 33 percent, we understand this fact—the role of government is not to create wealth, but an environment in which the entrepreneur or small business person can flourish." So the solution is less government. As Warren Harding stated, "I speak for administrative efficiency, for lightened tax burdens, for sound commercial practices, for adequate credit facilities, for sympathetic concern for all agricultural problems, for the omission of unnecessary interference of Government with business." Bush agreed, stating that he had "a plan to [continue our prosperity]. Less regulation. Less litigation. Lower taxes. . . . If America pursues limited government, low taxes, free and fair trade and free markets, our country will be prosperous." It's highly unlikely that Bush's speechwriters were combing through presidential speeches from the early 1900s looking for oratorical nuggets. These statements are so strikingly analogous because Republicans then and now hold similar views of the economy and the role of government. While the pre–New Deal Republicans were not called supply-siders, the reality is that both they and present-day Republicans embrace the classical economic view of the world.

THE GREAT DEPRESSION AND THE EMERGENCE OF THE KEYNESIAN CONSENSUS

Until 1929, classical economics prevailed. However, just as the exhaustion of the corporate, mass-production economy in the mid-1970s exposed the limitations of Keynesian economics, so too did the exhaustion of the old factory economy in the 1930s, sparking the Great Depression, expose the fundamental limitations of classical economics.

As the Depression began, Herbert Hoover and most elected officials and business leaders assumed that it would be short-lived and would naturally correct itself as past downturns had. In the face of an economy in free fall, Hoover's Secretary of the Treasury, Andrew Mellon, could only bellow, "Liquidate labor, liquidate stocks, liquidate the farmers, liquidate real estate. . . . It will purge the rottenness out of the system. . . . People will work harder, live a more moral life. Values will be adjusted, and enterprising people will pick up the wrecks from less competent people."[17] But as the crisis deepened, it became clear to many that something was seriously wrong. Yet classical economics could only claim that in the long-run growth would reemerge if government would just get out of the way, to which Keynes quipped, "In the long-run we are all dead."

However, as the old factory-based economy exhausted itself and transformed into a mass-production, managerial corporate economy, a fundamentally different type of national economic policy was required. Yet, so committed were they to the belief that "markets know best," these neoclassical economists could not simply imagine a new approach. Indeed, as the Depression worsened, so too did their despair at having no answers.

As a result, crafting a new economic doctrine that more closely fit the new conditions was up to someone not wedded to the classical synthesis. In this case, it was Englishman John Maynard Keynes. Keynes's 1936 magnum opus, *The General Theory of Employment*, revolutionized economics and economic policy, for it challenged the prevailing classical economics paradigm. Indeed, the book ushered in what became known as the Keynesian revolution, for it changed how economists and public officials thought about the economy, particularly about the role of the government in managing the business cycle.

Keynes's key contribution was to show that the economy had changed in fundamental ways that made the classical model anachronistic. For example, with the rise of labor unions, wages became what economists called "sticky" and did not fall as much as classical economics theory would predict when unemployment went up. With the rise of large corporations that possessed some market power, prices did not necessarily fall in slowdowns. Indeed, these new corporate titans favored cuts in production rather than competitive price warfare.

As a result, instead of asking, as the classical economists did, if prices of goods, labor, and money (e.g., interest rates) would fall enough to permit investment, Keynes asked a different question. Did ample and profitable opportunities exist for investment? Keynes argued that wary consumers and investors might not spend or borrow, even at low interest rates. To break this impasse, Keynes said that government had to "prime the pump," ideally by temporarily boosting federal spending. Indeed, the essence of Keynesianism is its conclusion that national income and employment are determined by the level of total demand (by consumers, investors, and governments) and that during slowdowns, demand can be stimulated by government spending or temporary tax cuts, particularly on low-income individuals who are most likely to spend the tax cuts. In short, while classical economists focused on supply, Keynesians focused on demand.

Moreover, while classicalists focused on microeconomics and studied factors like the profitability of firms; return on investment; and decisions of individuals and firms at the margins to work, save, and invest, Keynesian economists focused on macroeconomics—the study of the entire economy in terms of total amount of goods and services produced, income earned, and the level of employment of productive resources.

Just as supply-side economics gave a resurgent Republican right an economic rationale for their inclinations to cut taxes and limit government, Keynesianism gave a resurgent Democratic left an economic rationale for increasing the size and scope of government and, once the Depression ended, for boosting taxes. For, according to this new doctrine, government wasn't a necessary evil as classicalists conceived it to be, but rather a key player in ensuring that the economy stayed on an even keel and kept growing. As a result, the implications of Keynes's work went far beyond just helping end the Depression; they went to the heart of the role of government in the economy and society. Now for the first time, worker's wages and government spending were the centerpiece of economic policy. By the 1940s, Keynesianism reigned supreme, and the classicalists were either in retreat or had been captured and converted. For in the words of economist Seymour Harris, Keynesianism had become "the New Economics." In his 1946 book that sought to stem the Keynesian tide, classical economist Henry Hazlitt grudgingly agreed, stating, "There is no more persistent and influential faith in the world today than the faith in government spending. Everywhere government spending is presented as a panacea for all our economic ills."[18]

Keynesianism was only one aspect of the changes transforming the American economy and society. More broadly, as the factory economy of the early 1900s began to exhaust itself by the early 1930s, the public philosophy of limited government and reliance on private action became an increasingly poor compass with which to guide social progress. In response to the exhaustion, Hoover tried to save the system of self-control. But he failed, and voters turned to Franklin Roosevelt, who after much experimentation fundamentally reordered government's relationship with society and the economy.

Building on this recognition of the need for a new governing system, the new macroeconomics quickly became the guiding force for a revitalized Democratic Party. And while Franklin Roosevelt only met with Keynes once and surely did not fully understand Keynesian economics, he knew enough to know that the old order was giving way to a new one that required a more activist role for the federal government. As FDR stated in his second inaugural address, "Instinctively we recognized a deeper need—the need to find through government the instrument of our united purpose to solve for the individual the ever-rising problems of a complex civilization. Repeated attempts at their solution without the aid of government had left us baffled and bewildered."[19] In a direct attack at the Republican classical economic doctrine, he went on to state, "We refused to leave the problems of our common welfare to be solved by the winds of chance and the hurricanes of disaster. We have always known that heedless self-interest was bad morals; we know now that it is bad economics."

Indeed, the entire economy and society was being transformed. Thus, while the economy of 1929 looked very much like the economy of 1909 (albeit larger and with some new products and innovations), it looked dramatically different from the economy of 1949. The new national corporate mass-production economy of the 1940s and 1950s represented a turning point from the old smaller-firm, regionally based manufacturing economy of the first half of the century. Indeed, that "mixed economy" was so different from the one that preceded it that an October 1955 issue of *Fortune* magazine featured stories on the "New Economy."[20]

By the beginning of the 1950s, a new economy driven by corporate reorganization had emerged. Big corporations had become a way of life, and Americans had grown used to them. Professional managers ran corporations, so much so that the period became known as the era of managerial capitalism. A new technology system based on electromechanical and chemical technologies and mass-production techniques was cranking out a dizzying array of consumer goods, from cars to toasters to televisions. A network of transportation and communication now linked together formerly disparate regions into a unified national economy. Finally, what had largely been a production economy trying to provide the basic needs of a toiling working class transformed into a consumption economy designed to meet the wants of a growing middle class.

Politics was transformed as well. While small businesses and their affiliated organizations remained firmly in the classical economics camp and continued to support conservative Republicans, by the 1940s, large corporations were increasingly making their peace with Keynesianism, big government, organized labor, and the Democratic Party. Big business accepted a larger role for government, not just to smooth out the excesses of capitalism but also to lend stability to the entire economic system. The Committee for Economic Development (CED), a new organization of leading U.S. corporations, played a particularly important role in this change of attitude by publicly announcing its support for these new "interventionist" measures. The prestigious 1958 Rockefeller Palen Report on economic policy also supported the new order, stating, "Public expenditures in support of growth are an essential part of our economy. Far from being a hindrance to progress, they provide the environment within which our economy moves forward." Because of the strong perceived role of government in keeping up aggregate demand, people spoke of a "mixed economy" with both government and industry playing important roles.

At the same time, by the 1940s, the Republican Party had come around to the new realities, as even the Grand Old Party (GOP) platform supported an extension of Social Security and important labor safeguards such as the right to collective bargaining. Indeed, as one modern conservative complained, "The GOP was mostly dominated by FDR wannabes like Thomas Dewey and Wendell Willkie. . . . Both parties essentially accepted the New Deal precept that modern society . . . was too complex to be left to its own devices."[21] As the Eisenhower administration and a new Republican Congress took power in 1953, Republican hard-liners were hoping for a return to the kind of conservatism that was popular before FDR. To their disappointment, Eisenhower supported the expansion of Social Security, unemployment insurance, internationalism, and free trade. As former *Los Angeles Times* Washington Bureau chief William Donovan noted, "To many Republicans who had sincerely believed that the return of the party to power in 1952 would bring back the good old days of Coolidge and Hoover or maybe even McKinley, Eisenhower seemed like just a typical Democratic President."[22] (Interestingly, many liberal Democrats hoped that Bill Clinton would bring back the glory days of JFK and LBJ, but ended up saying much the same about Clinton, that he seemed like a typical Republican president.)

Yet, while most Republicans accepted the new realities and saw any efforts to resurrect the pre–New Deal economy as not only impossible but politically disadvantageous, the conservative wing of the party was less disposed to adapt. Indeed, it suffered from the same unwillingness to accept the new reality of mass society, with its big government, big unions, and big corporations and the accompanying New Deal institutions, as do many liberals today in accepting the new global economy. As a result, conservative Republicans were in a constant state of frustration, not understanding that the world had changed in such fundamental ways as to make their governing ideology outmoded. Perhaps the person who best epitomized this opposition was Senator Robert A. Taft, son of President William Howard Taft and Republican leader of the Senate. As conservative author Russell Kirk noted, "In 1939 Senator Robert Taft set out to rebuild his enfeebled party upon a foundation of principle, as an instrument of resistance to the New Deal."[23] Taft argued,

There is an underlying philosophy in the principal measures of the New Deal which desires to effect a complete revolution in the whole American business and constitutional system under which this country has prospered for 150 years. Against that philosophy and the measures which attempt to carry it out, the Republican candidates must be wholeheartedly and violently opposed. That policy is one of a planned economy.[24]

As Donovan noted in a statement that might be applied to liberal Democrats today,

Any attempt to arrive at an understanding of the Republican predicament must begin with a recognition that in a period of revolutionary change both in this country and around the world the party has not kept pace. When the old order collapsed, late in the 1920s, they were unprepared for it. As the new order began to take root, they still clung to the old. In a time of such tremendous revolutionary changes as the last twenty-five years have produced, institutions that do not keep abreast falter and

decline. The Republican party must fight being erroneously labeled as the party
which is against change and new ideas.[25]

Perhaps the Republican leader other than Taft who was most clearly identi-
fied with the old order was Republican senator and 1964 presidential candidate Barry Goldwater. Looking back to the factory-based-economy era of the
early 1900s, Goldwater declared, "[I have] little interest in streamlining government or making it more efficient, for I mean to reduce its size." In his
1960 book, *Conscience of a Conservative*, Goldwater made it clear that he
aimed to return to the old economy governing system by downsizing the federal government, opposing unions, scrapping the welfare state, and rolling
back the progressive income tax.

However, while some backward-looking conservatives railed against the
changes, as the new mass-production, corporate economy emerged from the
wreckage of the Great Depression, a consensus emerged among most elected
officials from both parties that the autonomic forces of the market and
individual-firm decisions were no longer adequate to manage a complex
corporate economy. Harvard sociologist Daniel Bell argued that "the fundamental political fact in the second half of the twentieth century has been
the extension of state-directed economies. In the last quarter of the century
we now move on to state-managed societies. And these emerge because of the
increase in the large scale social demands (health, education, welfare, social
services) which have become entitlements for the population."[26] Because of
the governing philosophy that emerged to address the new postwar corporate
economy, politics became defined not by the laissez-faire prewar notions but
by the new welfare-state model. It would not be until the 1970s that this doctrine would be effectively challenged.

However, while public officials, including many Republicans, recognized
that the new economy required a new governing system, Keynesianism did
not immediately take hold. In fact, just as the supply-siders did not really
form a unified force until the election of George W. Bush, Keynesians didn't
get their hands on the levers of power until the election of John F. Kennedy
in 1960. Just as George Bush surrounded himself with true-blue "second-
generation" supply-siders, Kennedy surrounded himself with tried-and-true
disciples of Keynes, including John Kenneth Galbraith, Walter Heller, Walt
Rostow, Robert Solow, and James Tobin. It had taken that long for Keynesians who were trained in the 1940s to move up in their careers and displace
the classicalists. As a result, people now spoke of the "new economics" in
the Kennedy administration to reflect this newly emboldened Keynesianism.

One of the signal economic policy acts of the Kennedy administration was
its push for a major tax cut. When Kennedy took office in 1961, the economy

was barely recovering from recession. Kennedy's advisers, in classic Keynesian fashion, advised spending increases and tax cuts. As a result, JFK proposed a series of tax cuts, including cutting income taxes and providing tax incentives for business investment. Today, the motivation for these tax cuts is in great dispute, with Keynesians and supply-siders wanting to lay claim to Kennedy. Because Kennedy, a Democrat, cut taxes, including cutting the top income tax rate, supply-siders are desperate to call him one of their own. See, they say, even Democrats support supply-side economics. Supply-side guru Jude Wanniski argues, "In a real sense, the Reagan Revolution did not begin with Reagan, or Kemp, but with President Kennedy's 1962 proposal to get the country moving again by slashing the top rate on personal income to 65% from 91%."[27]

There's only one problem with this interpretation: it's wishful thinking. Larry Lindsey admits that Walter Heller, chairman of JFK's Council of Economic Advisers and the architect of the tax cut, was "a leading proponent of demand side responses."[28] Heller himself argued that, with regard to the growth that followed the tax cut, "the record is crystal clear that it was its stimulus to *demand* [his emphasis], the multiplied impact of its release of over $10 billion of consumer purchasing power and $2 billion of corporate funds that powered the 1964–65 expansion and restored a good part of the initial revenue loss."[29] Arthur Okun, one of Kennedy's economic advisers, stated that "the Revenue Act of 1964 was aimed at the demand, rather than the supply, side of the economy."[30] As historian David Greenberg notes, the statements that supply-siders use to claim that the Kennedy cuts were inspired by supply-side motivations came from a speech JFK gave to business leaders. As he notes, "It is from this December 1962 speech that the supply-side appropriators of the Kennedy mystique usually cull their quotations. They skirt the ample documentary evidence showing the pro-business rhetoric of the Economic Club speech was largely strategic."[31]

THE 1970s–1980s KEYNESIAN BREAKDOWN

As evidenced by President Nixon's statement "I am now a Keynesian," as late as the early 1970s, most conservatives and liberals shared the postwar economy policy consensus. In the heyday of the postwar economy, Republicans did not fundamentally challenge the demand-side consensus. Presidents Eisenhower, Nixon, and Ford all believed in government spending to manage the economy; they just believed in spending a little less than Democrats. Supply-sider Larry Kudlow tells a story of speaking at a Republican event in 1986:

I was collecting my papers, feeling kind of lonely, when Dick Cheney came up to me to chat. By then the Wyomian was Republican Whip in the House. He told me that he really enjoyed my talk and agreed with me that the Reagan tax cuts worked successfully. We were standing alone drinking coffee when President Ford walked over. Cheney told Ford, "You know, Mr. President, Kudlow here is right." Ford responded by looking me straight in the eye saying, "Kudlow, you're my favorite supply-sider. But I don't believe a word of it."[32]

Yet, no sooner had virtually everyone embraced the demand-side model than the exhaustion of the corporate, mass-production economy led to the unraveling of the Keynesian consensus that only a few years before had seemed unassailable. By the mid-1970s, Keynesian "fine-tuning" of the economy no longer seemed to work. The emergence of high unemployment with high inflation, coupled with a dramatic slowdown in productivity growth, soon led many to question the prevailing economic doctrine. The exhaustion of the old economy and its resultant economic stagnation created the political opening for a wide-ranging and fundamental critique of the demand-side economic doctrine. What became the supply-side economics movement filled that void.

What happened? In a word, stagflation. Under Keynesian economics, there was assumed to be a trade-off between unemployment and inflation. Known as the Phillips curve, the notion was that as unemployment went down, it put pressure on prices, so inflation rose, and vice versa. Thus, if inflation was too high, policy makers implemented restrictive fiscal and monetary policies, slowing the economy and increasing unemployment while restraining inflation. If unemployment was too high, policy makers loosed monetary policy and cut taxes or increased spending. For forty years, liberals sided with lower unemployment and were willing to tolerate a bit more inflation, while conservatives wanted to err on the side of less inflation and were willing to tolerate a bit more unemployment. So the best that economic policy makers could achieve was a kind of tenuous balance that got low enough unemployment without triggering too much inflation. But the rise of stagflation—low growth and high inflation—challenged that paradigm. Things got so bad that Jimmy Carter termed the sum of the unemployment rate and inflation rate the "misery index." On top of this, productivity growth began to slow after 1973, leading to stagnant wages and incomes. Moreover, by the late 1970s, America's economic competitive position began to weaken as Europe and Japan challenged America in a host of industries.

Keynesianism had no apparent answer to these new challenges. If policy makers loosened fiscal and monetary policy to reduce unemployment, inflation would get even higher. If they tightened policy to control inflation, unemployment would get even higher. But the problems with Keynesian economics went even deeper. In the depth of the Great Depression, at its heart Keynesianism was not a growth theory. It had surprisingly little to say about how to grow the economy. Rather, its raison d'être was to help manage the business cycle. As leading Keynesian economist James Tobin described it, "The high year-to-year rates of increase of economic activity and real Gross Domestic Product during such business-cycle upswings reflect the re-employment of idle resources, both workers and industrial capacity. This additional output growth is the essence of prosperity."[33] In other words, according to Keynesians, the best that could be expected was for economic policy to keep recessions to a minimum. They couldn't do much, if anything, about boosting the long-term growth trend of the economy.

Many academic economists continued to offer policy advice from a Keynesian perspective but did not have new ideas to deal with stagflation. Harvard economist John Kenneth Galbraith counseled increased spending to lower unemployment and wage and price controls to limit inflation. But just as wage and price cuts weren't a viable solution in the 1930s, spending increases and wage and price controls were not a viable solution in the 1970s. And while by the mid-1970s, some Keynesians did begin to talk about the importance of supply and not just demand, it was too little, too late.

Just as classical economics was left behind by the 1930s' breakdown of the old factory economy, Keynesianism was left behind by the mid-1970s' breakdown of the old corporate, mass-production economy. As conservative economist Henry Hazlitt stated in 1979, "Keynesians and New Dealers seem to be in slow retreat. Conservatives, libertarians, and other defenders of free enterprise are becoming more outspoken and more articulate. And there are many more of them."[34] As Keynesian demand management failed to deliver the goods, classical economics made a comeback in the form of supply-side economics and its calls for smaller government, lower taxes, and higher private savings. Keynesianism had no satisfactory answers. Washington was ready for something different.

As a result, by the mid- to late 1970s, new strains of classical economics enjoyed revivals, including rational expectations, public choice economics, monetarism, and of course supply-side economics. They all shared one thing in common: distrust of government and belief that the market can do it all and that managing the economy is an oxymoron. And supply-side economics was about to find its political champion.

NOTES

1. James K. Glassman, "Secular Politics," *Washington Post*, 22 August 1995, A18.
2. Martin Feldstein, "Supply Side Economics: Old Truths and New Claims" (working paper 1792, Cambridge, MA, National Bureau of Economic Research, January 1986).

3. David Roboy, "Norman B. Ture on Supply-Side Economics," *Enterprise*, June 1980, 18.

4. Adam Smith, *The Wealth of Nations* (New York: Penguin Classics, 2000), 32.

5. Jean-Baptiste Say, *Treatises of Political Economy*, bk. 3, ch. 8, par. 11, www.econlib.org/library/Say/sayT41.html (accessed 21 November 2005).

6. Say, *Treatises of Political Economy*, bk. 3, ch. 8, par. 15.

7. Smith, *The Wealth of Nations*, bk. 5, ch. 2, v. 2.178.

8. Smith, *The Wealth of Nations*, bk. 5, ch. 2, v. 2.178.

9. William McKinley, "First Inaugural Address," 4 March 1897.

10. William Howard Taft, "The Anti-Trust Law," Beverly, MA, 1 October 1912, Authentic History Center, www.authentichistory.com/audio/1900s/19121001_William_H_Taft-The_Anti-Trust_Law.html (accessed 27 November 2005).

11. Fred Seigel (undated) sums up the conservative worldview: "The GOP, a largely Protestant party, looked upon itself as the manifestation of the divine creed of Americanism revealed through the Constitution. To be a conservative, then, was to share in a religiously ordained vision of a largely stateless society of self-regulating individuals." Houghton Mifflin, "The Reader's Companion to American History, Conservatism" (Boston, MA: Houghton Mifflin), http://college.hmco.com/history/readerscomp/rcah/html/ah_019700_conservatism.htm (accessed 28 November 2005).

12. Herbert Hoover, "Inaugural Address," 4 March 1929.

13. Calvin Coolidge, "State of the Union Message," 3 December 1924.

14. Quoted in Paul Craig Roberts, *The Supply-Side Revolution: An Insider's Account of Policymaking in Washington* (Cambridge, MA: Harvard University Press, 1984), 16.

15. Calvin Coolidge, "Address before the National Republican Club at the Waldorf-Astoria," New York, 12 February 1924.

16. Andrew Mellon, *Taxation: The People's Business* (New York: Macmillan, 1924), 13.

17. Ron Chernow, *The House of Morgan* (New York: Simon & Schuster, 1990), 322.

18. Henry Hazlitt, *Economics in One Lesson* (1946; repr., New York: Arlington House Publishers, 1979).

19. Franklin Delano Roosevelt, "Second Inaugural Address," 1937.

20. Robert D. Atkinson, *The Past and Future of America's Economy: Long Waves of Innovation that Power Cycles of Growth* (Northampton, MA: Edward Elgar, 2005).

21. Glenn Garvin, "He Was Right: Looking Back at the Goldwater Moment," *Reason Online*, October 2002, www.reason.com/0203/cr.gg.he.shtml (accessed 29 November 2005).

22. William Donovan, *The Future of the Republican Party* (New York: New American Library, 1964), 32.

23. Russell Kirk and James McClellan, *The Political Principles of Robert A. Taft* (New York: Fleet Press Corporation, 1967), 129.

24. Kirk and McClellan, *The Political Principles of Robert A. Taft*, 129.

25. Donovan, *The Future of the Republican Party*.

26. Daniel Bell, *The Cultural Contradictions of Capitalism* (New York: Basic Books, 1976), 24.

27. Jude Wanniski, "SSU Spring Lesson #7: The Kennedy Tax Cut," www.wanniski.com/showarticle.asp?articleid=4213 (accessed 22 November 2005).

28. Lindsey, *The Growth Experiment*, 3.

29. Walter Heller, "The Kemp-Roth-Laffer Free Lunch," *Wall Street Journal*, 12 July 1978, 20.

30. David Greenberg, "Tax Cuts in Camelot?" *Slate*, 16 January 2004, www.slate .com/id/2093947/ (accessed 22 November 2005).

31. Greenberg, "Tax Cuts in Camelot?"

32. Larry Kudlow, "Cheney the Supply-Sider," *National Review Online*, 24 July 2000, www.nationalreview.com/kudlow/kudlow072400.html (accessed 21 November 2005).

33. James Tobin, "Fiscal Policy: Its Macroeconomics in Perspective" (discussion paper 1301, Yale University, Cowles Foundation for Research in Economics, New Haven, CT, May 2001).

34. Hazlitt, *Economics in One Lesson*.

Chapter Four

Supply-Side Economics: From Ronald Reagan to George W. Bush

My plan reduces the national debt, and fast—so fast, in fact, that economists worry that we're going to run out of debt to retire.

—President George W. Bush, radio address, February 24, 2001

With the election of Ronald Reagan in 1980, the revival of classical economics known as supply-side economics got its first champion in the White House since the 1920s. President Reagan did not have to rediscover a long-forgotten doctrine; he had the benefit of being able to rely on the work of proponents of supply-side economics who had spent much of the prior decade developing it and honing the arguments. Where exactly did the revival come from? Each "revolution" has its own creation myth. In the case of supply-side economics, there were several supposed creations. One is said to have occurred over a series of dinner conversations in New York in the mid-1970s. Three of the regulars were Jude Wanniski, Robert Mundell, and Arthur Laffer. Wanniski was a senior editor for the *Wall Street Journal* editorial page. Mundell, a Columbia University economist, was best known for his work in international economics, which was to win him a Nobel Prize in 2001. And Laffer was an economist at the University of Southern California who had worked for the Office of Management and Budget during the Nixon administration.

Another creation is said to have occurred earlier in 1974 in Washington when Laffer was having dinner with Donald Rumsfeld, Gerald Ford's chief of staff, and Dick Cheney, his chief of staff, in the Two Continents Lounge atop the Hotel Washington. The economy was in recession, and so the Ford administration was looking for new ideas. Laffer is supposed to have drawn two perpendicular lines and an arc on a napkin to show that government could cut taxes and still boost revenue. Thus was born an icon of the supply-side movement: the famous Laffer curve.

The term "supply side" was purportedly first used in a paper presented by Herbert Stein in 1976.[1] Stein, a former economic adviser in the Nixon administration, used the term "supply-side fiscalists" to refer to the fact that this doctrine focused on only a specific aspect of the supply side: the fiscal aspects, and in particular the tax aspects. Later that year, Jude Wanniski simplified it to "supply-side economics." Wanniski had discovered the budding supply-side movement in Congress in the mid-1970s and quickly became its St. Paul. While supply-side economics did not become highly visible until the election of Ronald Reagan, the 1970s were a period of fertile growth. Indeed, in the mid-1970s the *Wall Street Journal* worked to popularize the theory and was extremely influential in having this new, unorthodox doctrine adopted by political leaders.

Wanniski was so taken by this reemergence of classical economics that he wrote what became the bible for the budding movement, his 1978 book, *The Way the World Works*. In an article for *Policy Review*, the journal of the conservative Heritage Foundation, listing the top twenty most important conservative documents of the twentieth century, George Nash lists *The Way the World Works* as one of the "most important and influential works advancing conservative ideas in the last 20 years."[2] So influential was it that Nash argued that two decades after Wanniski's bible was published, "tax cuts remain at the core of conservative Republicanism."

But there were other thinkers behind the budding movement. One was conservative writer George Gilder. As Nash states, "If Jude Wanniski was the most ardent propagandist for supply-side economics, writer George Gilder has been called its theologian." Gilder, in his best-selling 1981 book, *Wealth and Poverty*, stated, "A successful economy depends on the proliferation of the rich."[3] Moreover, in a direct attack at the prevailing notions of the importance of the welfare state, he argued that successful entrepreneurs were the "heroes of economic life," and "regressive taxes help the poor" because "the poor need more of the spur of their poverty." Moreover, "to help the poor and the middle classes, one must cut the taxes of the rich." Now, instead of government being the driver of growth, the rich were.

Drawing on this intellectual conservative ferment, a handful of elected and appointed officials began to be more outspoken advocates of this new economic and social doctrine. One was President Ford's Treasury Secretary William Simon. Simon was a supply-sider in all but name only. A believer in small, unobtrusive government, Simon believed that "free competitive markets are the most effective way to provide for increased output."[4] As Paul MacAvoy notes, Simon "felt that savings had to increase and therefore the personal income tax needed to be reduced and double taxation of dividends as both personal and corporate income had to be limited." Simon also believed that the capital gains tax should be eliminated and taxes on savings reduced. The only major difference between Simon and today's supply-siders is that Simon took fiscal discipline seriously. When testifying before the Senate discussing President Ford's economic plan, he said, "You will recall that he said on October 6 that he [Ford] would consider a tax cut unacceptable without a corresponding expenditure limitation."[5]

The combination of a declining economy and energized policy entrepreneurs allowed supply-side economics to effectively challenge Keynesian economics. As Lindsey notes, "The supply-side challenge of that year [1981] was the greatest challenge to a reigning economic dogma since the overthrow of classical economics in the 1930s."[6] And the key to understanding supply-side economics is that it represented a revival, or perhaps more accurately a reemergence, of classical economics.

While intellectual movements come and go, what made the supply-side classical revival significant was that it found an eager audience in an insurgent group of Republican officials. While the Keynesian orthodoxy was being challenged in the 1970s, so too was the reigning Republican Party orthodoxy. Since the emergence of the New Deal, Republicans had been the minority party in both branches of Congress for most years. As such, when it came to fiscal policy, they saw their role as being the champions of fiscal discipline and of limiting the spending excesses of Democrats. In this role, they could not justify large tax cuts, for that would only boost deficits. Indeed, they often supported tax increases to avoid large budget deficits. Given that Democrats controlled the Congress and were not going to cut government, Republicans could only fume. However, by the end of the 1970s, it began to dawn on some that it was time to stop fuming and stop worrying about deficits, or as some said, to stop being the revenue collector for the welfare state.

Moreover, the slow economic growth of the 1970s provided Republicans with an opportunity to effectively charge the Democrats with mismanaging the economy. But to capitalize on the Democrats' vulnerability, they needed an alternative economic strategy, and supply-side economics provided that alternative. After forty years in the political wilderness, by the mid-1970s a small group of conservatives began to argue that if the Democrats were going to push for spending, it was time for Republicans to push for tax cuts.[7] As a result, Republicans turned away from a losing strategy of supporting a balanced budget and instead embraced a "let 'er rip" tax cut strategy. One of the leaders of this insurgent movement was Jack Kemp, a former NFL quarterback turned Republican congressman from Buffalo, New York. Starting in the mid-1970s, Kemp worked to persuade the Republicans to "stop worshipping at the altar of the balanced budget." Because inflation and unemployment were high, these supply-side insurgents wanted to combat both problems by expanding the economy's ability to produce more. As a result, they offered a strategy that they claimed would lower unemployment without boosting inflation and reduce taxes without boosting the deficit, all the while limiting the role of government. Unlike Keynesians, who saw tax cuts as potentially inflationary, supply-siders claimed that tax cuts would boost work and savings, which would in turn expand supply, leading to the promised land of growth without inflation.

Kemp proceeded to introduce legislation to provide an across-the-board 30 percent cut in income tax rates. The idea is purported to have come from Paul Craig Roberts, then Kemp's staff economist and an early supply-sider. Senator William Roth (R-DE) proceeded to introduce a companion bill. Yet Kemp-Roth quickly became stalled, for it was opposed not just by most Democrats but also by powerful Republicans, who cared about fiscal discipline and had no use for untested economic theories drawn on napkins and opined about in the *Wall Street Journal*. In fact, one of the biggest opponents of Kemp-Roth was Oklahoma Senator Henry Bellmon, the ranking Republican on the Budget Committee, who favored deficit reduction over tax cuts. It was to take the election of a president who rejected conservative Keynesianism in favor of supply-side economics for Kemp-Roth to become a reality.

THE REAGAN REVOLUTION

On January 20, 1981, Ronald Reagan was elected the fortieth president of the United States. The first president since Calvin Coolidge to campaign actively against the federal government, Reagan was swept into office against Jimmy Carter. Reagan owed part of his success to Carter's disastrous foreign policy, but it was the widespread economic malaise gripping the nation that led many voters to risk voting for this new kind of Republican.

Reagan won because the politics of the nation were changing. The 1970s brought a widespread dissatisfaction with taxes and government itself. The antitax movement began to gain political legs in the mid- to late 1970s because high inflation rates were pushing middle-class households into higher income tax brackets. Moreover, local antitax movements, like California's 1978 Proposition 13, added fuel to the fire. Antitax movements gained support as incomes stagnated. If people couldn't raise their standard of living through higher wages, at least government could boost their after-tax incomes by cutting taxes. More broadly, the old New Deal coalition (voters whose economic interests were aligned with redistribution) began to change. The blue-collar voters that supported the New Deal were having kids who were joining the middle class, and even the upper middle class. Finally, large corporations that now confronted global competition began to abandon Keynesianism and saw the kind of antitax, antiregulation agenda proposed by Republicans as eminently attractive.

Indeed, the prevailing faith in the welfare-state, big bureaucratic governing model that had been developed after World War II was now being questioned by many Americans. By the 1970s, many public problems were seen as too complex and government's ability to solve them too limited. Not surprisingly, just as the political consensus around limited government fell apart as the factory economy broke down in the 1930s, the old economy political consensus around big government began to unravel around this time. By the early 1970s, the perceived failure of government to solve problems in areas such as crime, poverty, pollution, transportation, and the economy had tarnished the image of planning and managerial government, and had belied the notion that government could be made to work if it just brought in the "best and brightest" experts. While government was able to solve what some called "tame" problems like putting a man on the moon, it failed to solve "wicked" ones like revitalizing decaying urban areas, reducing crime, and getting the economy growing.

Hence, the complaint, "If we can put a man on the moon, surely we can fix the cities," became commonplace. Yet as the old economy continued to disintegrate, by the 1970s this reformist hope gave way, with the help of a reenergized conservative Republican party, to a pessimistic rejection of government and an inclination to leave problem solving to the market and civil society. Many believed that government had overreached and had to set its sights lower. Indeed, the public's trust in government to effectively do the right thing declined from a high of 76 percent in 1964 to 21 percent in 1994.[8] Budget cuts stemming from slower economic growth just exacerbated the trend toward smaller government. As a result, the watchwords of the day became *deregulation, devolution, privatization,* and *retrenchment.*

As this realization set in, politics rapidly pitted liberals, who sought to preserve the New Deal and Great Society consensus and its related governing apparatus, against conservatives, who sought to destroy that governing framework, arguing that it, like the underlying economic structure, had run its course. Goldwater's conservative views of a reduced federal government, states' rights, and hostility to unions had little chance of taking hold in the 1960s, as they were sowed during the heyday of the old economy when big government was the dominant paradigm. It took the decline of the old economy and emerging cracks in the bureaucratic model before the small-government market model could be considered viable by more than the most hardcore ideologues.

Republicans, led by Ronald Reagan, now articulated a forceful critique of the old economy governing system and politics. Many voted for Reagan and later for George H. W. Bush and their smaller-government philosophy not because they rejected government, but because they instinctively felt that big bureaucratic government's time had passed.

As a result, a key component of the Reagan platform was its endorsement of Kemp-Roth. As soon as he took office, Reagan proposed a 25 percent across-the-board tax cut as well as indexing tax rates for inflation. Unlike past tax cuts undertaken during recessions, Reagan and his team did not sell this on Keynesian grounds that the tax cuts would boost spending and employment in the short term. Rather, they used a supply-side rationale, with Reagan arguing, "To those who called for more government planning, more regulations and even more taxes, we said that in a nation, as in a man or a woman, economic success is not a matter of bricks, mortar, balance sheets or subsidies. No, if a national economy is to soar, first the inventive, enterprising, pioneering, dreaming entrepreneurial spirit of the nation's people must soar. And that meant not more regulations, but fewer. Not more government direction, but less. And yes, not higher taxes, but lower taxes."[9] Instead of talking about the role of government in boosting growth—as Keynesians had for a generation—Reagan talked of nurturing "the strength and vitality of the American people by reducing the burdensome, intrusive role of the Federal government."[10]

Notwithstanding the embrace of supply-side economics by the president, mainstream economists were more reluctant to jump on board. In the early 1980s, of the American Economics Association's eighteen thousand members, only twelve called themselves supply-side economists. In fact, many establishment economists saw supply-side economics as some kind of sideshow. As Larry Lindsey wrote, supply-side economics is "the story of the clash between an economic orthodoxy in decline and a challenger from the fringes of economic thought."[11]

So why did Reagan endorse this maverick view? The chief reason is that at its heart, supply-side economics is a revival of the classical economics that the Republican Party embraced until the New Deal. Reagan was not a Keynesian Republican in the mode of Eisenhower, Rockefeller, Nixon, or Ford. He was a Taft and Goldwater Republican in the mold of McKinley, Harding, and Coolidge. Supply-side economics gave Reagan a program that fit with his ideology of small government and lower and less progressive taxes. As William Niskanen, a member of Reagan's Council of Economic Advisers, notes, "Views that were once regarded as those of right-wing extremists became the views that would elect a president."[12] Ed Meese, Reagan's aide and then attorney general, said, "Reagan was a supply-sider long before the term was invented."[13]

With the administration's leadership, Congress passed the Economic

Recovery Tax Act (ERTA), which cut the highest marginal rate on unearned income from 70 percent to 50 percent and lowered income taxes across the board.[14] The administration later worked with Congress to pass the Tax Reform Act of 1986, which lowered tax rates even more, reducing the top rate from 50 percent to 28 percent and reducing the five-bracket schedule to just two, 15 and 28 percent. In exchange, a wide variety of corporate and individual tax loopholes were closed.

Perhaps the most controversial aspect of Reaganomics was its claim that the tax cuts would pay for themselves. Reagan and his team sold the cuts in part by claiming that they would result in even more revenues because the economy would grow and there would be fewer tax loopholes and tax manipulation. Yet as the budget deficits exploded in the 1980s, some Americans came to suspect that they had been sold a bill of goods. In fact, even today many conservative economists criticize supply-side economics for its claim that tax cuts would pay for themselves. As a result, supply-siders are actively engaged in an effort to airbrush out this part of the doctrine. Some argue that the budget deficit was not a result of tax cuts but other factors, such as lower inflation and higher spending. But, as we will see in chapter 7, the tax cuts did indeed contribute the largest share to the exploding budget deficit.

Others argue that the Reagan administration never claimed that tax cuts would pay for themselves. But the tax cuts were sold on this basis. For example, in selling the ERTA to budget hawks in the Republican Party, the administration promised that the tax cuts would pay for themselves, or at least a significant portion of the loss, in increased tax revenues. President Reagan stated, "I know the tax portion of our package is of concern to some of you. Let me make a few points that I think—feel have been overlooked. . . . Probably the most common misconception is that we are proposing to reduce government revenues to less than what the government has been receiving. This is not true."[15]

While the Reagan administration succeeded in enacting its supply-side agenda, it's easy to forget how difficult a task that was. Unlike today, when the Republican Party is virtually unified around supply-side economics, during the early 1980s there was anything but unanimity. Many Republicans looked askance at this strange doctrine. Indeed, George H. W. Bush famously quipped in 1980 that supply-side economics was "voodoo economics." Even within the Reagan administration, supply-siders were in the minority, with the budget cutters and deficit hawks in the majority. Many were "Rockefeller Republicans," moderates who didn't bear any special animus toward the federal government but who generally wanted it to be a bit smaller and a bit better run. Others were "deficit hawks," who worried (correctly) that huge tax cuts would blow a hole in the deficit. For example, in 1982, Alan Greenspan, then chairman of President Reagan's Economic Policy Advisory Board, warned Reagan about the risk of budget deficits. Likewise, Martin Feldstein, head of Reagan's Council of Economic Advisers, advocated cutting the deficit in order to "lower interest rates and accelerate the recovery."[16] Indeed, reading accounts of Reagan administration supply-siders is to read their consistent frustration with how their supply-side plans were being opposed by others in the administration, including budget director David Stockman, and within Congress.

The election of George H. W. Bush in 1988 demonstrated supply-side's still tenuous hold on the party. Running in 1988 and desperate to assure the conservative base of his fealty toward Ronald Reagan, Bush famously promised, "Read my lips: no new taxes." Yet Bush was not the ideological supply-sider that his son, George W., would be; he was an old-line Republican pragmatist from Connecticut. As a result, because of the rising budget deficits, Bush and the Democratically-controlled Congress agreed on the Omnibus Budget and Reconciliation Act in 1990. The act boosted the top income tax rate to 31 percent, raised the income level at which taxpayers paid the Medicare tax, and instituted a lower phaseout of personal exemptions. Conservatives howled at the betrayal of Reaganomics and consequently did little to help Bush's reelection campaign in 1992. So, while the act helped put the government's finances on a sounder footing, it put Bush's electoral fortunes on a footing of quicksand.

THE CLINTONOMICS INTERLUDE

When Bill Clinton took office in 1993, he was confronted with a budget mess worse than the Bush administration had let on. With his cabinet made up of budget hawks on one side and Keynesians on the other, Clinton sided with Bob Rubin, then head of the National Economic Council, and the other budget hawks and worked to restrain spending growth while also raising taxes. Under the Omnibus Budget and Reconciliation Act of 1993, the administration pushed through by one vote in the Senate a tax increase that added new tax brackets of 36 and 39.6 percent and eliminated the wage cap on the Medicare tax. The administration intended to use most of the money to pay down the national debt, stating, "The favorable long-term budget results in these projections can be realized only with prudent policy—choosing continuing reductions in outstanding debt, rather than expensive tax cuts or spending increases."[17] The move paid off as the federal government finally began running surpluses by 1998, rising to $236 billion in 2000. Certainly credit for the surplus has to also be given to the budget deal cut between the Clinton administration and the Republican-controlled Congress, which put in place strict budget rules regarding increases in federal spending.

However, the tax increases were apostasy to the growing supply-side movement. Supply-siders were convinced the sky would fall. *Forbes* magazine warned of a market crash. Senator Phil Graham (R-TX) warned that the tax increase would cause the greatest recession since the Great Depression. House Republican leader Newt Gingrich threatened, "I believe this will lead to a recession next year. This is the Democratic machine's recession and each one of them will be held personally accountable."

The economy proceeded to take off, enjoying the longest expansion in American history, creating over twenty million new jobs, driving poverty rates to all-time lows, and seeing a revival of productivity growth. While tax increases can't be credited with causing the boom, surely they can't be blamed for having a deleterious effect on growth, in contrast to what supply-siders would have us believe. However, when the economy finally slowed in 2001, supply-siders were quick to finally blame the Clinton tax increases. Larry Lindsey argued that "very high personal taxes were clearly one factor that helped choke off the expansion."[18] Brian Wesbury, a leading supply-sider, wrote, "The recession of 2001 was at least partially caused by these tax hikes and the movement of more people to higher rates as their incomes went up."[19] By this logic, it took seven years for the pernicious effects of the tax increases to take effect, while the tech bust and the 9/11 terrorist attacks were minor blips.

While Clinton and his team were not supply-siders, they were also not Keynesians. In fact, Clinton's economic policies marked a signal change from the kind of economic policies adopted by Democratic administrations of the previous sixty years. When confronted with an economic slowdown upon taking office, Clinton proposed a modest stimulus plan along Keynesian lines, but he also proposed reducing the budget deficit. The administration focused on helping private-sector growth, in part through fiscal discipline to keep down interest rates, but also with new public investments in infrastructure, education and training, and research and development to help companies become more productive and innovative.

By 1994, in part because of the tax increases, Republicans gained control of both chambers of Congress. This was a very different group of Republicans from those who controlled the Senate just twelve years earlier. Instead of the deficit-hawk business Keynesians being in the majority, the small-government supply-siders were. When Newt Gingrich assumed the role of speaker of the House in 1995 and initially laid out a new strategy to put a balanced budget ahead of tax cuts, he was quickly vilified by conservative members of his caucus. Gingrich soon got with the supply-side program, arguing that, "every year, I want to shrink the government and lower taxes and increase economic growth." He proceeded to call for elimination of 280 federal programs; abolition of the departments of energy, commerce, and education; and deep cuts in taxes. House Republican leader Dick Armey was an even more ardent supply-sider. Armey, a former economics professor, promoted a 17 percent flat tax that would have meant deep cuts in government. He would have gone for an even lower rate if he thought it would pass. In his book extolling the wonders of the flat tax, Armey argued, "In Dick Armey's America, the income tax could never rise above 10 percent. . . . My 'model' for this belief . . . is the biblical tithe. I've always thought that if 10 percent is sufficient for God, it ought be sufficient for government. I know it won't seem a compelling argument to fellow economists, but, well, it's a good enough model for me."[20]

Even budget-hawk stalwarts like Bob Dole, who was once referred to as the tax collector for the welfare state, got supply-side religion, making a 10 percent cut in income taxes the centerpiece of his failed presidential campaign. Indeed, in his 1996 campaign, Dole was singing the supply-side song, repeating that "the top rate now stands at almost 40 percent. High marginal rates discourage work, reduce the rewards of entrepreneurship, and encourage tax avoidance."[21] *Business Week* wrote, "For more than a decade, Dole has been telling a joke about a bus full of supply-siders. The good news: The bus went off a cliff. The bad: There were three empty seats. Now, Dole seems to have climbed aboard and grabbed hold of the wheel. The question is: Will his plan take the nation down the road to prosperity—or over that precipice?"[22]

THE GEORGE W. BUSH ADMINISTRATION

The election of George W. Bush represented a signal turning point in American politics. For the first time in seventy years, the Republicans controlled the White House and both chambers of Congress. Equally important, for the first time in seventy years, Republicans were relatively unified in their economic beliefs. Twenty-five years of relentless work by conservative academics, think tanks, and elected officials had paid off: most national-level Republicans, including the president, sang from the same song sheet of classical supply-side economics.

As a result, upon taking office, Bush didn't appoint officials from a wide variety of economic backgrounds; he appointed a team of true-blue supply-siders. Let's go down the list. To the extent Karl Rove, Bush's longtime political adviser, has any guiding economic philosophy, it is straight from supply-side economics. In a recent speech to the New York Conservative Party, Rove repeated the mantra, "Conservatives believe in lower taxes; liberals believe in higher taxes. We want few regulations; they want more. We believe in curbing the size of government; they believe in expanding the size of government."[23]

The rest of Bush's economic team, from Larry Lindsey to Alan Hubbard, the current head of the National Economic Council, to Glenn Hubbard and Greg Mankiw, who headed up the president's Council of Economic Advisers, are dedicated supply-siders. Indeed, virtually all of the president's key economic advisers have been longtime advocates of supply-side economics, many in fact influential in the scholarly debates over it. Moreover, cabinet secretaries have all toed the supply-side party line, and the one that didn't, Treasury Secretary Paul O'Neill—a conservative Keynesian—was quickly shown the door.

Moreover, unlike the Reagan presidency when George H. W. Bush didn't see eye-to-eye on Reagan's supply-side economics, Vice President Dick Cheney is a committed supply-sider.[24] Larry Kudlow stated, "Look for Cheney to not only press for Bush's initial tax-rate reduction plan, but also to push even broader and more powerful tax-cut programs later on."[25] This goes a long way in explaining why Bush has been able to be effective in driving his agenda. As Grover Norquist argues, "Reagan could move in bursts, using his political capital from the 1980 and 1984 elections to push through key reforms, but then the Democratic majority in the House would slow or stop most other initiatives. The Bush administration can plan over an eight-year period, moving various initiatives. . . . One sees this longer time horizon not only in the annual tax cuts that move slowly toward a flat rate income tax."[26]

When then governor Bush began campaigning in 1999 for his party's nomination for president, he had made up his mind that he would not make his father's mistake of raising taxes and alienating the conservative base, a group that had only gotten stronger during the 1990s. Indeed, in his tough primary battle, particularly with Senator John McCain (R-AZ), Bush was determined not to lose the support of the right-wing party faithful, and tax cuts were the key to that. Bush understood that in the Republican Party of the late twentieth century, supply-side economics had become the party's de facto economic doctrine. Yet, while Bush's supply-side fervor appealed to the conservative base, it would be a mistake to characterize Bush's commitment to supply-side economics as simply a political tactic. Unlike his father, George W. Bush embraced supply-side economics as the best way to grow the economy.

However, in campaigning in the midst of an unprecedented economic boom, Bush couldn't very well argue that we needed to cut taxes and shrink government to get the economy growing. Plus, the administration didn't want to show its cards and explain the real reason it wanted to cut taxes—to shrink government and limit its ability to expropriate individuals' property. Moreover, because the supply-side brand had lost its luster in the 1980s, they couldn't very well lay out their supply-side credentials. They realized that they needed new bottles for that old supply-side wine. As a result, they seldom mentioned the term (a search of the term "supply side" on the White House website yields just three hits, none of which refer to their economic philosophy).

As the campaign struggled to hone their message, they grasped the only straw available to them: the budget surplus was too high. When Bush began campaigning, the efforts of the Clinton administration were paying off, not only in booming economic growth, but also in the first budget surpluses in almost thirty years, which were going to pay down the national debt.

So, in his stump speeches, Bush argued that big tax cuts were needed because, "If there's any excess money in Washington, it's not the government's money, it's the people's money."[27] He even explained to the people why the surplus existed: "You see, the growing surplus exists because taxes are too high and government is charging more than it needs. The people of America have been overcharged and on their behalf, I'm here asking for a refund."[28] In the month before the election, Bush again repeated his desire for tax cuts, stating, "I want to send some of that surplus back to you. But that's no big deal, it's your money to begin with." He reiterated that rationale a year later at the White House ceremony signing the tax cut legislation, proclaiming, "Today, we start to return some of the Ramos' money—and not only their money, but the money of everybody who paid taxes in the United States of America. . . . The message we send today, it's up to the American people; it's the American people's choice. We recognize loud and clear the surplus is not the government's money. The surplus is the people's money and we ought to trust them with their own money."[29]

The conservative establishment sang the same tune. In a 1999 op-ed in the *Wall Street Journal*, Glenn Hubbard argued, "What about Mr. Clinton's suggestion that the Republican tax bills are too expensive? Would a large tax cut put the nation's fiscal house and economic expansion out of order? The simple answer is no. Referring to the 'cost' of a tax cut in the present circumstances is a bit like the management of a public company referring to dividends to shareholders as a cost. Just as we expect mature firms with large positive free cash flows to return those surpluses to shareholders, taxpayers have a claim on projected budget surpluses."[30]

There was only one problem. If the surplus is the "people's money," does this then mean that the national debt is the "government's debt?" When Bush signed his tax cut bill in 2001, the federal government still owed debtors over $5.7 trillion. It's as if the breadwinner of a family with huge credit card debt said we're no longer going to pay off our debt because the money is ours and the debt is the credit card company's.

Not content to rely just on the argument of "it's your money," the Bush campaign threw in an additional rationale: supply-side tax cuts as recession insurance. In a 1999 Iowa campaign speech, Bush contended,

> I hope for continued growth—but it is not guaranteed. A president must work for the best case, and prepare for the worst. There is a great deal at stake. A recession would doom our balanced budget. It would leave far less money to strengthen Social Security and Medicare. But, if delayed until a downturn begins, tax cuts would come too late to prevent a recession. Putting more wealth in the hands of the earners and creators of wealth—now, before trouble comes—would give our current expansion a timely second wind.[31]

Never mind that no Keynesian economist would ever counsel cutting taxes during an economic boom just to make sure that there was no slowdown. Never mind that supply-side doctrine holds that government does a poor job responding to recessions. Bush wasn't deterred by these facts; he was pulling out all the stops to make the case for lower taxes. But Lindsey made clear their real views: "The tax proposal was designed to be sound, incentive-oriented tax policy regardless of economic circumstances."[32] In other words, no matter what the ailment, boom or bust, the medicine is the supply-side elixir of "Tax Cuts." While it's true that short-term tax cuts focused more on lower- and middle-income Americans would have been good medicine in 2001 and 2002 to stimulate short-term growth, long-term supply-side tax cuts on the wealthy were not.

While Bush won the closest presidential election since 1960, he still had to convince Congress to pass tax cuts that would essentially repeal the Clinton tax increases. While Republicans controlled both houses of Congress, their majority in the Senate was razor thin. Indeed, it was not at all a sure thing that Bush would prevail. Not only were most Democrats skeptical of a large permanent tax cut, but a few Republicans who still cared about fiscal discipline worried whether the nation could afford it.

In fact, as the economy started to slow after Bush's election, the projected budget surplus declined, making it less likely that the nation could afford tax cuts. But the administration was not deterred and decided to make lemonade out of the budgetary lemons. Now large permanent tax cuts that were inspired by supply-side economics were sold on the basis that they were needed to stimulate a slowing economy. In essence, the Bush administration became supply-siders in Keynesian clothing. The new president argued, "It is not hard to see the difficulties that may lie ahead if we fail to act promptly. The economic outlook is uncertain. Unemployment is rising, and consumer confidence is falling. Excessive taxation is corroding our prosperity."[33] A few months later, as the economy deteriorated even further and as the president was justifying his tax cuts and trying to gain support for even more the next year, he used the same rationale:

> Given the economic news of the day, the tax cut was—looks more and more wise. I mean, after all, there's a new report out that shows over the last four quarters, economic growth has been slow. It hasn't been up to standard. The economy is puttering along. It's not nearly as strong as it should be. And what the tax cut does by sending money back to the American working people, it provides an incredibly important boost to economic vitality and economic growth.[34]

These statements are nothing if not bold. The president is saying that we must cut taxes permanently, even though a temporary tax cut would also stimulate the economy but without running up the deficit. He also failed to mention that most of the tax cuts would go to high earners, the very folks least likely to spend the money to get a slow-growing economy moving again.

It was in this environment that conservatives, from the *Wall Street Journal* to virtually every conservative think thank and of course the administration and its supporters in Congress, put on a full-court press for Bush's 2001 across-the-board tax cuts. Many conservatives relied on the standard supply-side logic: tax cuts on individuals would spur work and investment. But many supporters used arguments that were even more dubious. Using any and all claims to counter the argument that before taxpayers reward themselves with tax cuts they should first pay down a substantial part of the national debt, conservatives came up with the far-fetched claim that unless the government immediately implemented large tax cuts, the federal government would end up owning much of the private economy.

And once they got on this message, they repeated it relentlessly. The conservative Heritage Foundation argued that without immediate tax cuts, "politicians would be able to seize control of a large share of the U.S. economy."[35] Not to be outdone, Glenn Hubbard and American Enterprise Institute economist Kevin Hassett warned that, "projecting forward, the U.S. government could own about one-fifth of all domestic equities by 2020."[36] They were referring to the notion that the government would soon be retiring its debt faster than it was coming due. Indeed, by the late 1990s the government stopped issuing thirty-year bonds because they were bringing in more money than they needed. As bonds were reaching maturity, the government was paying off bondholders. But what if the government started collecting even more money than was coming due in debt? In this case, it would have to put the money somewhere, and, the claim went, government would end up buying stock in U.S. corporations, thereby nationalizing the economy. The right began to spin a story that by 2009 (eight long years from then) the federal government would have more money than it needed and would have to use it to buy stocks or bonds, and in so doing would exert political control over the economy.

This, however, was simply not true. First, as we have found out the hard way, the surpluses were by no means assured. Moreover, even if the government has more surplus revenues than were coming due in bonds, it could have paid a small premium to bondholders to have them sell the bonds to the government before they matured. Or it could have invested the money in bank debt, in blind index funds, or even in foreign equities, all of which would have avoided the supposed problem the right warned of. If these conservative Chicken Littles were really worried about the "nationalization" issue, they could have proposed that if in eight years time the surpluses became a "problem," taxes could be cut then. But of course, this was all a smoke screen. The goal was to cut taxes now, and supply-siders were willing to use any argument that would advance the goal, no matter how illogical.

As the supply-siders began to gin up support for tax cuts, disturbing signs began to emerge that the rosy budget projections might not be so rosy. The Congressional Budget Office reported that the projected budget surpluses were not the sure thing that tax cutters were portraying. So eager for their tax cuts, supply-siders dismissed such reports. The Heritage Foundation noted,

> Some politicians who oppose tax cuts continue to reject Chairman Greenspan's endorsement of tax reduction on the grounds that surplus projections are unreliable. These policymakers commonly assert that current economic growth levels (which determine the tax base and therefore tax collections) are unsustainable or that Congress will increase spending to absorb future revenues. Both demographic analysis and historical review, however, indicate that neither of these assertions is valid.[37]

Heritage went on to argue that the budget surpluses projected at the end of the Clinton administration were actually not in doubt. Really?

One reason the Bush administration and the conservative message machine put on such a full-court press was that most Americans didn't want to spend the surplus on tax cuts. Poll after poll showed that Americans would rather have used the budget surplus to ensure the solvency of Social Security, or as Bill Clinton had put it, to "save Social Security first." As a result, to sell his tax plan, Bush had to promise that it wouldn't significantly cut into the budget surplus, claiming, "We will use half of the surplus to strengthen Social Security and pay down debt—national commitments that we must keep. We will make important investments in Medicare, education, the environment, and national defense. And we will return about one fourth of the surplus to the American people."[38] He went on to say, "My tax cut plan for American people . . . reserves all the surplus for Social Security itself." As we will see, this also turned out to be untrue, and even after it became clear that the tax cuts ate into the Social Security surplus, Bush continued to push for making his tax cuts permanent and for new ones on top.

It's not clear how important the arguments from conservative think tanks were in convincing members of Congress to vote for the Bush tax cuts. But if there was one argument that was convincing, or I should say, one person who made an argument that was convincing, it was Federal Reserve chairman Alan Greenspan. For it is not too much of an exaggeration to say that if there was one person other than George Bush who with a single word before Congress could have stopped the tax cuts in their tracks, it was Greenspan. He had the stature that would give skittish politicians the cover needed to oppose the tax cuts. They could go back home and tell their constituents, "I had to vote against the budget-busting tax cuts because Chairman Greenspan concluded that the tax cuts were irresponsible at this time."

So when Alan Greenspan went to the Hill on January 25, 2001, to testify about the economy and the tax cuts, all eyes were on him. And he proceeded to provide an argument as weak as most of the other ones proffered by other supply-siders. First, Greenspan predicted—in what was either a mistake of enormous magnitude or a cynical ploy—that surpluses were adequate to allow for a huge tax cut. Then he testified, "If long-term fiscal stability is the criterion, it is far better, in my judgment, that the surpluses be lowered by tax reductions than by spending increases."[39] Since when did surpluses become a problem? Did he forget that while the government was running surpluses, it also owed over $5 trillion to bondholders and was paying over $200 billion a year in interest payments and that as the baby boom generation started retiring in just ten years, the pressure on the budget would be even greater?

What Greenspan worried about was that the surplus would be spent, and, being a conservative supply-sider, he reasoned that it would be better to cut taxes than boost spending. But this was a false choice. He could have used his considerable influence to strongly advocate for paying down the national debt.

Finally, the coup de grace. Greenspan's argument got even stranger—or even more cynical—when he claimed that Congress should cut taxes now, since paying off the debt would have made it difficult to manage monetary policy. This was a variant of the argument above. Only this time the argument was that if the Federal Reserve Bank couldn't go in the market and buy or sell treasury bills, its ability to manage the economy would be limited. Greenspan went on to caution, "Some holders of long-term Treasury securities may be reluctant to give them up, especially those who highly value the risk-free status of those issues. Inducing such holders, including foreign holders, to willingly offer to sell their securities prior to maturity could require paying premiums that far exceed any realistic value of retiring the debt before maturity"[40] Yet, according to President Bush's Council of Economic Advisers, two-thirds of the entire national debt was held in bonds that matured in less than five years, and 38 percent matured in one year.[41]

Again, even if this were a real problem, why not wait until 2009, when this "problem" would appear, and then stop paying off the debt? The reason, as economist Joseph Stiglitz points out, is that "Greenspan did not see fit to explain why it was desirable to cut taxes far in advance of this improbable catastrophe rather than wait for the peril to become a little bit more imminent—and for good reason; there was no reason."[42] If Greenspan had really been concerned about this issue and was not using it simply as a smoke screen to justify supply-side tax cuts, he could have advocated cutting taxes five years hence, or tax cut triggers that would automatically repeal the cuts if the projected budget surpluses didn't materialize. But he didn't.

With Greenspan's blessing, the floodgates opened, and hesitant members of Congress in both parties no longer had a crutch to fall back on. Congress cut the top rate from 39.6 percent to 35 percent for those making $297,350 and more a year, while also cutting the rates for other taxpayers. It also increased the limits of contributions that could be made to Individual Retirement Accounts and reduced the estate tax, provisions that largely benefit higher-income taxpayers. Finally, it allowed firms to take accelerated depreciation on new investments over the subsequent three years.

So why did Greenspan give such ill-advised advice? Maybe he just made a mistake—a $5 trillion mistake. But it's not likely that one of the keenest economic minds of our time would make such a fundamental error. A more cynical view is that he wanted to be reappointed to one more term as Federal Reserve chairman, and he knew that if he was not a loyal soldier for tax cuts, Bush would send him packing. This is certainly possible, but Greenspan had been known to stand up to presidents before. Why would this be any different?

The most plausible reason for Greenspan's blessing of these budget-busting tax cuts is that, like Bush, Greenspan is a dyed-in-the-wool supply-sider, not in the sense of believing that all tax cuts pay for themselves, but in the sense of believing that lower taxes significantly boost work, savings, and growth. Indeed, when he was younger, Greenspan was a close disciple of libertarian Ayn Rand, who advocated unfettered capitalism as a social and economic philosophy. In several chapters in Rand's 1964 book *Capitalism: The*

Unknown Ideal, Greenspan made it clear that he did not believe in any significant role for government. In dismissing the need for antitrust policy, he stated that "the hidden intent, and the actual practice of antitrust laws in the United States have led to the condemnation of the productive and efficient members of our society *because* they are productive and efficient."[43] In defending the gold standard, he argued that "deficit spending is simply a scheme for the 'hidden' confiscation of wealth. Gold stands in the way of this insidious process. It stands as a protector of property rights."[44] His writings on regulation were equally libertarian. For him, regulation "is an act of expropriation of wealth created by integrity." In fact, regulation's "sole 'contribution' is to substitute force and fear for incentive as the 'protector' of the consumer. . . . The basis of regulation is armed force. At the bottom of the endless pile of paper work which characterizes all regulation lies a gun."[45] Moreover, society doesn't even need business regulation because, "What collectivists refuse to recognize is that it is in the self-interest of every businessman to have a reputation for honest dealings and a quality product" (note to Enron CEO Ken Lay). Greenspan also opined, "All taxes are a drag on the economy. It's only a question of degree."[46] So if you believe that all taxes are a drag on the economy and George Bush wants to cut taxes, you get to work.

At the end of the day, Bush and his conservative supporters used virtually every conceivable argument (including some that were contradictory) to push through his large, budget-busting, supply-side tax cuts in the Economic Growth and Tax Relief Reconciliation Act of 2001 (EGTRRA). If the economy was booming, we needed tax cuts. If it was sputtering, we needed tax cuts. If the budget was in surplus, we needed tax cuts. If it was in deficit, we needed tax cuts.

But the administration was not deterred; more tax cuts were in the offing. This time they used new rationales to convince Americans that they needed even more tax cuts. Since government was now running growing budget deficits, the administration couldn't very well argue that it was preventing the problem of budget surpluses from rearing its ugly head. Instead, they reminded us of the terrorist attacks of September 11, with the president arguing, "We need to counter the shock wave of the evildoer by having individual rate cuts accelerated."[47] President Bush also told us, "It's your money," and "we need to update our tax code. It needs to be easier to understand and more simple."[48]

With Republican control of both houses of Congress, the administration succeeded in pushing through even more of its supply-side agenda. The Job Creation and Worker Assistance Act of 2002 reduced taxes for new business investments. The Jobs and Growth Tax Relief Reconciliation Act of 2003 accelerated the phase in of the 2001 law while cutting the tax on dividends to either 5 or 15 percent. (Prior to that, dividends were taxed at the same rate schedule as ordinary income.) Capital gains tax rates were lowered from 10 and 20 percent to 5 and 15 percent, depending on how long the assets were held. The ill-named American Jobs Creation Act of 2004 replaced explicit export subsidies with a mishmash of expensive and poorly focused tax cuts for business. These tax cuts, inspired by supply-side doctrine, were sold on Keynesian grounds as ways to get a weak economy going. In all, Bush's $1 trillion in tax cuts, the largest in American history, were bigger than even the Reagan tax cuts of 1981.[49]

What contributed to the administration's dramatic success was that, unlike congressional Republicans who after 1994 sought to achieve their supply-side paradise of radically lower and flatter taxes in one fell swoop, the Bush team realized that their agenda would have to be implemented step by step. As Grover Norquist, a key player in Republican politics and head of Americans for Tax Reform (more appropriately named "Americans for Radical Tax Cuts"), wrote,

> The Bush administration—wisely—has not proposed fundamental tax reform in a single piece of legislation. But the president has been taking deliberate steps toward such reform with each tax cut. There are five steps to a single-rate tax, which taxes income one time: Abolish the death tax, abolish the capital gains tax, expand IRAs so that all savings are tax-free, move to full expensing of business investment rather than long depreciation schedules and abolish the alternative minimum tax. Put a single rate on the new tax base and you have Steve Forbes and Dick Armey's flat tax. Each of the Bush tax cuts, past and proposed, moves us toward fundamental tax reform. The step-by-step annual tax cut avoids the problem that faced Bill and Hillary Clinton's too ambitious effort to nationalize health care in one gulp: It is easy to stop oversized reforms.[50]

Bruce Bartlett, a former Reagan administration official and prominent figure in the supply-side movement, agreed, referring to a five-easy-pieces supply-side tax strategy, stating,

> We can now see that Bush has had a strategy all along that conforms exactly to the five easy pieces. . . . By Bush's second term, it is possible that we will have made enough incremental progress toward a flat rate consumption tax that we may finally see fundamental tax reform fully enacted into law. If so, it will be testament to a very clever, yet bold strategy that was initially invisible even to people like me, who study such things for a living. I am impressed.[51]

As Bush entered his second term, more tax cuts and "reform" were on the agenda. Most importantly, the administration continues to work to make his tax cuts permanent. But it also wants to go further. The president proposed partial privatization of Social Security, with individuals being able to pay less in Social Security taxes and instead put the money in their own retirement accounts. While the administration sold this proposal in part on solvency grounds,[52] their true motivation was twofold. On the one hand, as Larry Lindsey wrote in his 1990 book, they believed that this would boost private savings. But they also believed that individuals should be in charge of their own retirement assets, not the state. In pushing for personal accounts, the administration even had the audacity to claim that we needed personal accounts because otherwise the Social Security surplus would be spent, which is exactly what the Bush administration has done.[53] However, widespread public opposition to the proposal appears to have led it to an early grave. The administration was not deterred. In its quest to exempt most interest and capital gains from taxation, they proposed overhauling retirement savings accounts such as Individual Retirement Accounts (IRAs) and 401(k)s. The administration's proposal would eliminate existing IRAs and replace them with Retirement Savings Accounts (RSAs), which would work just like today's Roth IRAs: there's no upfront tax deduction for contributions, but savings can grow tax free. The proposal would also eliminate the Roth IRA income eligibility cap and liberalize the annual contributions limit to $15,000 per couple (ballooning to $45,000 for taxpayers who take advantage of special loopholes). Finally, the administration has sought to permanently and completely repeal the inheritance tax and continues to work to make its tax cuts permanent.

AND THE WINNER IS?

While Bush and his supporters have made an assortment of promises regarding the supply-side-inspired tax cuts' salutary effects, the most basic has been that the tax cuts were needed to ensure that the economic slowdown was brief. According to Greg Mankiw, the economy has done better in the short term with the recent tax cuts than it would have without. Mankiw stated, "If we had left taxes exactly as they were when the President took office, many, many more people would be unemployed today. What I'm saying is sort of standard textbook economics."[54] Mankiw relied on Keynesian economics to justify supply-side tax cuts, claiming, "One can view the short-run effects of these tax cuts from a classic Keynesian perspective. The tax cuts let people keep more of the money they earned. This supported consumption and helped maintain the aggregated demand for goods and services."[55]

While technically true, the statement is ironic because supply-siders have long argued that short-term stimulus doesn't work. But the other problem with this statement is that it compares the Bush tax cuts to doing nothing. Of course tax cuts were needed to help spur economic recovery. The real question is what kind of tax cuts were best. As a result, the proper comparison is to another kind of stimulus, including short-term temporary tax cuts more focused on people who will spend them or on government spending/investment. Indeed, as a short-term stimulus measure, the Bush tax cuts were quite ineffective. First, they were phased in, with most of the tax cuts coming later, when the economy had recovered. Moreover, they targeted the wealthy, who were least likely to spend the money on goods and services.

Indeed, of all the tax cuts that could have been implemented, the Bush tax cuts had about the lowest stimulative impact. Using a "bang-for-the buck" estimate of how much growth is produced per dollar of revenue lost, the Congressional Budget Office concluded that bangs for the buck were "small" for accelerating the president's (EGTRRA) tax rate cuts and cutting taxes on capital gains, and "medium" for temporary investment incentives. The largest ratios were found for tax cuts geared toward low- and middle-income households.[56] Mark Zandi, head of the economic forecasting firm Economy.com, came up with similar results, estimating that the president's tax proposals had a bang for the buck of about 0.70 by 2003 (for every dollar in tax cuts, the economy would expand by seventy cents), with the dividend tax cut generating just nine cents on the dollar.[57] The programs with the largest "bang for the buck" would have been those that target low- and middle-income households, including the child tax credit rebate (1.04), the acceleration of the 10 percent bracket (1.34), providing aid to state and local governments (1.24), and extending unemployment insurance (1.73).[58] Larry Lindsey, however, didn't agree, stating that "unemployment checks do not grow the economy."[59] Perhaps this is why the administration opposed extending unemployment insurance and providing aid to state governments.

Not only did the tax cuts do little to grow the economy, but they exploded the deficit. While Bush promised that his tax cuts would preserve the Social Security surplus, in fact they did nothing of the kind. When he took office, the federal budget enjoyed a surplus of $236 billion, and Bush claimed that the budget surpluses would be so big ($5.6 trillion over ten years) that he could protect Social Security and Medicare, add a prescription drug benefit, expand the military, and pay off the national debt, and "with the money left over still fund large tax cuts."

But in actuality, in FY2006 the deficit will be over $420 billion, with deficits projected at $3.1 trillion between 2004 and 2013. As a result, the national debt will rise from $3.9 trillion in 2003 to $7.1 trillion in 2013.[60] To make matters worse, just after the national debt balloons to gigantic proportions, in 2017 the Social Security trust fund will start running a deficit as baby boomers retire in droves. This double deficit—triple when the approximately $4 trillion that U.S. debtors will owe lenders in other nations is included—is a huge burden we are bequeathing to the next generation. By 2014, when a child in the fifth grade today turns twenty-one, his or her graduation present will not be a savings bond or a down payment for a car; it will be a bill of $82,000 for this generation's excesses and fiscal irresponsibility. As baby boomers retire, the bill will go up even more.

Brookings economists Peter Orszag and William Gale estimate that the Bush tax cuts will reduce revenue by $1.9 trillion between 2001 and 2011, and if the tax cuts are made permanent as Bush has called for, the price will increase to $3.3 trillion. When increased interest payments (because of the higher national debt) are factored in, the net budget loss will be almost $4.5 trillion.[61] Moreover, because the tax cuts are phased in in later years, by 2014, the annual budget costs will equal $583 billion. Gale and Orszag point out that over the next seventy-five years, the revenue loss from the tax cuts, if they are made permanent, will be as large as the Social Security shortfall and the Medicare Part A (hospital insurance) trust-fund shortfall. In other words, without the Bush tax cuts, there would no shortfall in Social Security and a much smaller shortfall in Medicare.

Now that the budget deficit is back with a vengeance, are supply-siders experiencing a change of heart or second thoughts? The short answer is no. Before the 2000 election, they sounded more flexible, arguing that if the budget numbers headed south, then the tax cuts would, or at least should, be rethought. Greg Mankiw wrote,

> Consider how much the budget changes if you alter a few assumptions. According to an optimistic scenario, Congress lives within the spending caps and the economy continues to boom, resulting in a ten-year budget surplus of more than $5 trillion. In a pessimistic scenario, Congress abandons the caps, and the economy reverts to slower growth. In this case, the surplus quickly dissipates and turns into a ten-year budget deficit of $3 trillion. It's easy to imagine an even more pessimistic scenario in which—believe it or not—the U.S. economy actually experiences a recession once again, together with the usual adverse effects on the budget.[62]

He went on to ask, "So should the next President aim to enact a tax cut, and if so, what size? This question will dominate the Presidential campaign. But it's not a very relevant one. More vital than choosing a President with the right tax plan is electing a President with the political courage to change course when events demand it. If we have learned anything from the past decade of fiscal history, it's that we shouldn't look too hard into any budget forecaster's crystal ball."[63] Finally, he stated, "whatever tax plan the next President adopts, he may have to rethink it in a few years."[64]

Did President Bush have the political courage to change course when the deficit exploded? No, he pushed and continues to push for even more tax cuts. Did Greg Mankiw call for a change of course once he joined the administration? No. In fact, in a *Washington Post* op-ed in the midst of an expected budget deficit of $475 billion for 2004, he called for even more tax cuts, stating, "A number of tax policy issues also need to be addressed, including the sunset of the tax cuts already enacted and the growing number of people subject to the alternative minimum tax. Moreover, the tax code can be improved. The president's budget calls for such action, including his proposal to simplify and expand the use of tax-preferred savings accounts."[65]

While their overriding belief in supply-side tax cuts may have hindered their ability to view the problems of the deficit objectively, there is more to it than that. Many supply-siders didn't worry about the tax cuts blowing a hole in the deficit because they believed, or at least they said so publicly, that the tax cuts would increase tax revenues. Lafferism was back, or more accurately, it never went away. Kevin Hassett and Glenn Hubbard argued for the first Bush tax cuts so that we wouldn't have that pesky budget surplus to deal with. But then they went on to claim that "if supply-side arguments are correct, then the marginal-rate reductions proposed by Mr. Bush will eventually increase tax revenues and surpluses, presenting us once again with the quandary of what to buy."[66] In other words, tax cuts will produce even more taxes, leading to an even greater surplus that the government will be stuck with. Why not argue for higher tax rates, since according to their logic that's the only way to produce *less* revenue?

Finally, overall economic performance has been mediocre at best. It's true that productivity growth has been high during the Bush administration, although much of this is due to the continuing diffusion of the information technology revolution of the 1990s throughout the economy. However, employment growth has been anything but robust. Job growth in the fifteen months after the president's 2003 tax cuts was the worst for that point in any economic recovery of the last fifty years.[67] When President Bush took office, there were 111.6 million private-sector jobs. After losing 3.7 million private-sector jobs, it was not until May of 2005 that the economy finally got back to 2001 levels. A lower share of working-age Americans were in the workforce at the end of 2005 than at the end of 2000. Finally, income growth has fared even worse, as inflation-adjusted median income is actually lower today than when President Bush took office. The administration tries to make lemonade out of these economic lemons by touting the fact that "the Administration helped raise real after-tax income per person by 7 percent while the President has been in office—making a real difference for America's families."[68] They fail to point out that since pretax median income is down since 2000, the only reason after-tax income is up is because Bush has cut taxes so much. It's a bit like a family saying their income is up 7 percent as they take out home equity loans to boost their "income."

Ronald Reagan once quipped that the Democrat's view of the economy was, "If it moves, tax it. If it keeps moving, regulate it. And if it stops moving, subsidize it."[69] Today, the Republican view of the economy could be summed up as follows: "Cut taxes, no matter how big the deficit; eliminate regulation, no matter how egregious the abuse; and cut nondefense funding, no matter how great the national need." Unfortunately, as we will see in the next section, this supply-side agenda is not an effective growth strategy for the twenty-first-century knowledge economy.

NOTES

1. Cited in Kent Hughes, *Building the Next American Century: The Past and Future of Economic Competitiveness* (Washington, DC: Woodrow Wilson Press, 2005), 56.

2. George T. Nash, "Modern Tomes," *Policy Review* 84, no. 6 (July–August 1997), www.policyreview.org/jul97/thnash.html (accessed 22 November 2005).

3. George Gilder, *Wealth and Poverty* (New York: Bantam Books, 1981), 188.

4. Paul MacAvoy, "Treasury Secretary W. E. Simon and Congress on the Business Cycle," in *A Tribute to William E. Simon* (Rochester, NY: William E. Simon Graduate School of Business Administration, 2001), 13.

5. Susan L. Averett, Edward N. Gamber, and Shelia Handy, "William E. Simon's Contribution to Tax Policy," *Atlantic Economic Journal* 31, no. 3 (September 2003): 233–42.

6. Lawrence B. Lindsey, *The Growth Experiment: How the New Tax Policy Is Transforming the U.S. Economy* (New York: Basic Books, 1990), 5.

7. This ignores the fact that even with the Democrats in charge, deficits as a share of GDP were relatively small.

8. Marc Hetherington, *Why Trust Matters: Declining Political Trust and the Demise of American Liberalism* (Princeton, NJ: Princeton University Press, 2004).

9. Cited in Robert T. Gray, "President Reagan's Call for Continuing the Free-Enterprise Revolution," *Nation's Business* 76, no. 7 (July 1988): 63.

10. Ronald Reagan, "White House Report on the Program for Economic Recovery," 18 February 1981, www.reagan.utexas.edu/archives/speeches/1981/21881c.htm (accessed 22 November 2005).

11. Lawrence Lindsey, *The Growth Experiment*, 5.

12. William Niskanen, *Reaganomics: An Insider's Account of the Policies and the People* (New York: Oxford University Press, 1988), 15.

13. Ed Meese, *With Reagan: The Inside Story* (Washington, DC: Regnery Gateway, 1992), 121.

14. While the highest marginal tax rate in 1980 was 70 percent, it didn't kick in until $108,300, which was equivalent to $275,000 in today's dollars.

15. Ronald Reagan, "Economic Recovery Program" (speech delivered 28 April 1981), www.townhall.com/documents/recovery.html (accessed 22 November 2005).

16. In the last five years, Greenspan appeared to see his role as giving his blessing to continuous tax cuts, while Feldstein has joined the supply-side choir.

17. U.S. Office of Management and Budget, *FY 2002 Economic Outlook, Highlights from FY 94 to FY 2001, FY 2002 Baseline Projections* (Washington, DC: Office of Management and Budget, 16 January 2001), 27.

18. Lawrence B. Lindsey, "Why We Must Keep the Tax Cut," *Washington Post*, 18 January 2002, A25.

19. Brian S. Wesbury, "Taking the Voodoo Out of Tax Cuts," 2 June 2003, www.econ lib.org/library/Columns/y2003/Wesburytaxcuts.html (accessed 22 November 2005).

20. Richard Armey, *The Flat Tax* (New York: Ballantine Books, 1996).

21. Cited in Armey, *The Flat Tax*, 106.

22. *Business Week*, "Dole's Gamble," 19 October 1996, www.businessweek.com/1996/34/b34891.htm (accessed 22 November 2005).

23. Larry Kudlow, "The Supply Side of Karl Rove," *National Review Online*, 29 July 2005, www.nationalreview.com/kudlow/kudlow200507290839.asp (accessed 21 November 2005).

24. Arthur Laffer, one of the original supply-side prophets from the 1970s and 1980s, vouched for Cheney's belief, stating, "Cheney can lay claim to being one of the original supply-siders, in favor of lower marginal tax rates to create work and investment incentives that spur economic growth. . . . Dick Cheney is unabashedly for tax cuts." In Larry Kudlow, "Cheney the Supply Sider," *National Review Online*, 24 July 2000.

25. Kudlow, "Cheney the Supply Sider."

26. Grover Norquist, "Step-by-Step Tax Reform," *Washington Post*, 9 June 2003, A21, www.washingtonpost.com/ac2/wp-dyn?pagename = article&contentId = A32629-2003 Jun8&notFound = true (accessed 21 November 2005).

27. Larry Kudlow, "Bush's Walk on the Supply-Side," *National Review Online*, 21 February 2000, www.nationalreview.com/kudlow/kudlow022100.html (accessed 22 November 2005).

28. Cited in Larry Kudlow, "W. Holds His Ground," *National Review Online* www.na tionalreview.com/kudlow/kudlow022801.shtml (accessed 23 November 2005).

29. George W. Bush, "Remarks by the President in Tax Cut Bill Signing Ceremony," 7 June 2001.

30. Glenn Hubbard, "The Tax Cut Debate," *Wall Street Journal*, 28 July 1999.

31. George W. Bush, "Speech in Green Bay, Wisconsin," 28 September 2000.

32. Lawrence Lindsey, "Remarks by Dr. Lawrence B. Lindsey at the Federal Reserve Bank of Philadelphia" (Washington, DC: White House, 19 July 2001), http://www.white house.gov/news/releases/2001/07/20010719-4.html (12 February 2006).

33. George W. Bush, "A Blueprint for New Beginnings: A Responsible Budget for America's Priorities," message to Congress, White House, Washington, DC, February 2001.

34. George W. Bush, "Remarks by the President to Future Farmers of America," July 2001.

35. Peter B. Sperry, "Growing Surplus, Shrinking Debt: The Compelling Case for Tax Cuts Now" (Washington, DC: Heritage Foundation, 7 February 2001).

36. Kevin Hassett and R. Glenn Hubbard, "Where Do We Put the Surplus?" *The Wall Street Journal*, 29 January 2001, 26.

37. Peter B. Sperry, "The Compelling Case for Tax Cuts Now: Growing Surplus, Shrinking Debt," *Capitalism Magazine*, 12 February 2001, www.capmag.com/article.asp ?ID = 306 (accessed 22 November 2005).

38. George W. Bush, "President Discusses Economy and Tax Relief in North Carolina" (Washington, DC: White House, 5 December 2005).

39. Alan Greenspan, "Testimony before Committee on the Budget, U.S. Senate," 107th Cong., 1st Sess., 25 January 2001, www.federalreserve.gov/BoardDocs/Testimony/2001/209010125.htm (accessed 22 November 2005).

40. Greenspan, "Testimony."

41. Council of Economic Advisers, *2005 Economic Report of the President* (Washington, DC: Government Printing Office, 2005), Table B-88.

42. Joseph Stiglitz, *The Roaring Nineties: A New History of the World's Most Prosperous Decade* (New York: W. W. Norton & Company, 2003).

43. Alan Greenspan, "Antitrust," in *Capitalism: The Unknown Ideal*, ed. Ayn Rand (New York: Signet, 1964), 171.

44. Alan Greenspan, "Gold and Economic Freedom," in *Capitalism: The Unknown Ideal*, ed. Ayn Rand (New York: Signet, 1964), 101.

45. Alan Greenspan, "The Assault on Integrity," in *Capitalism: The Unknown Ideal*, ed. Ayn Rand (New York: Signet, 1964), 118.

46. Quoted in R. Glenn Hubbard, "A Framework for Economic Policy," Remarks at the Ronald Reagan Presidential Library, 15 February 2002, http://www0.gsb.columbia.ed u/faculty/ghubbard/speeches/2.15.02.pdf (accessed 22 November 2005).

47. George W. Bush, "Remarks by the President to the Employees of the Department of Labor," Washington, DC, 4 October 2001, www.yale.edu/lawweb/avalon/sept_11/president_052.htm (accessed 21 November 2005).

48. George W. Bush "President Bush Closes the White House Economic Conference," 16 December 2004, www.whitehouse.gov/news/releases/2004/12/20041216-8.html (accessed 21 November 2005).

49. This is the cost of the tax cuts from fiscal years 2001 to 2006. Joel Friedman and Aviva Aron-Dine, "Extending Expiring Tax Cuts and AMT Relief Would Cost $3.3 Trillion through 2016" (Washington, DC: Center on Budget and Policy Priorities, 2006).

50. Grover Norquist, "Step-by-Step Tax Reform," *Washington Post*, 9 June 2003, A21, www.washingtonpost.com/ac2/wp-dyn?pagename = article&contentId = A32629-2003Jun8&notFound = true (accessed 21 November 2005).

51. Bruce Bartlett, "Bush Is Laying the Foundation for Fundamental Tax Reform," Dallas, National Center for Policy Analysis, 2003, www.ncpa.org/edo/bb/2003/bb020503 .html (accessed 21 November 2005).

52. Social Security privatization would have no effect on solvency. It is true that if payroll taxes were invested in the market stock, equity prices would rise in the short run as the demand for stocks increases. However, as soon as baby boomers begin to retire and start selling their stocks to pay their mortgages, medical bills, and other expenses, stock prices would fall as the number of sellers exceeds buyers. As this happens, the real return to the stocks will fall, and the supposed miracle will have evaporated. Moreover, net savings would remain unchanged since money that was going to the Social Security trust fund would now be going to equity markets.

53. See Chuck Blahous, "Ask the White House," 8 June 2005, www.whitehouse.gov/ask/20050608.html (accessed 24 January 2006).

54. Cited in William G. Gale and Peter R. Orszag, "Bush Administration Tax Policy: Short-Term Stimulus," *Tax Notes*, 1 November 2004.

55. Gregory Mankiw, "Remarks at the Annual Meeting of the National Association of Business Economists," Atlanta, GA, 15 September 2003, http://post.economics.harvard.-edu/faculty/mankiw/columns/nabe.pdf (accessed 22 November 2005).

56. The CBO reports similar rankings of the president's and other policies. Congressional Budget Office, "Economic Stimulus: Evaluating Proposed Changes in Tax Policy" (Washington, DC: Congressional Budget Office, January 2002).

57. Mark Zandi, "The Economic Impact of the Bush and Congressional Democratic Economic Stimulus Plans," Economy.com, February 2003.

58. Mark Zandi, "Testimony before the Subcommittee on Economic Policy, Senate Banking, Housing and Urban Affairs Committee," 22 May 2003.

59. Lawrence B. Lindsey, "Why We Must Keep the Tax Cut," *Washington Post*, 18 January 2002, A25.

60. In fact, under reasonable political assumptions, the national debt, which hit a near-term low of 33 percent of GDP in 2001, is projected to grow from 38 percent of GDP in 2004 to 46 percent in 2013, and then to skyrocket to economically untenable levels (approaching 100 percent of GDP) as the baby boom generation continues to flow out of the workforce into retirement.

61. William Gale and Peter Orszag, "Bush Administration Tax Policy: Summary and Outlook," *Tax Notes*, 29 November 2004, 1280.

62. N. Gregory Mankiw, "Candidates Need Clues, Not Tax Plans," *Fortune*, 20 March 2000, http://post.economics.harvard.edu/faculty/mankiw/columns/mar00.html (accessed 22 November 2005).

63. Mankiw, "Candidates Need Clues, Not Tax Plans."

64. N. Gregory Mankiw, "Bush Is a Leader the Economy Can Trust," *Fortune*, 13 November 2000, http://post.economics.harvard.edu/faculty/mankiw/columns/nov00.html (accessed 22 November 2005).

65. N. Gregory Mankiw, "Deficits and Economic Priorities," *Washington Post*, 16 July 2003, http://post.economics.harvard.edu/faculty/mankiw/columns/washpost.pdf (accessed 22 November 2005).

66. Kevin A. Hassett and R. Glenn Hubbard, "Where Do We Put the Surplus?" *Wall Street Journal*, 29 January 2001.

67. Gene Sperling, "Bush's Job Record Belies Much-Touted Recovery," *Bloomberg News*, 13 August 2004.

68. White House, "President Bush's Agenda for Job Creation and Economic Opportunity," 6 January 2006, www.whitehouse.gov/infocus/economy (accessed 24 January 2006).

69. Ronald Reagan, "Great Quotes from President Reagan," The Reagan Information Page, www.presidentreagan.info/speeches/quotes.cfm (accessed 22 November 2005).

Part Two

LET'S LOOK AT THE EVIDENCE

Supply-siders and their conservative supporters embrace supply-side economics because they believe it is the best way to grow the economy. They tell us that supply-side tax cuts boost work, savings, investment, and tax revenues (or at least don't lead to a one-for-one reduction in tax revenues), leading to faster economic growth with little or no increase in income inequality. Are these claims true? If so, under what circumstances? And if the supply-side program does produce more work, savings, and growth, is it the best way to get these benefits?

Unfortunately for the supply-side claim, both real-world results and scholarly research suggest that these claims are at best vastly overstated, and in most cases, simply wrong. It turns out that supply-side economics is not only a program that is fiscally irresponsible and economically unfair, but it's an ineffectual approach to growing the economy. To see why, let's start by examining the logic, real-world experience, and scholarly evidence for its most basic claim: tax cuts boost work.

Chapter Five

Do Lower Taxes Boost Work?

Every day I get up and look through the *Forbes* list of the richest people in America. If I'm not there, I go to work.

—Robert Orben

As unemployment began to increase in the late 1970s, a key selling point of the supply-side program was that lower taxes would spur more work. Supply-siders claimed that high tax rates discouraged people from working more because each additional hour of work was taxed at the taxpayer's highest marginal rate. Indeed, Ronald Reagan reflected on his experience as an actor when the top marginal tax rate exceeded 90 percent, saying that once he made a certain amount of money, he wouldn't make any more movies that year since he would pay almost all of the additional income in taxes. Reagan noted,

> At the peak of my career at Warner Bros., I was in the ninety-four percent tax bracket; that meant that after a certain point, I received only six cents of each dollar I earned and that the government got the rest. The IRS took such a big chunk of my earnings that after a while I began asking myself whether it was worth it to keep on taking work. If I decided to do one less picture, that meant other people at the studio in lower tax brackets wouldn't work as much either; the effect filtered down, and there were fewer jobs available.[1]

Larry Lindsey summed up the president's story by saying that "very high tax rates make a life of leisure look even more attractive to such people as it might otherwise."[2] This argument was not a new one. Pre–New Deal supply-siders used it extensively. Andrew Mellon argued that, "where the Government takes away an unreasonable share of his earnings, the incentive to work is no longer there and a slackening of effort is the result."[3]

Like all successful arguments, this one certainly seems plausible. As Lindsey asks, "Does it make sense to believe that taxes have no effect on behavior or that they have the kind of effect demonstrated by economic studies?"[4] On

---

Why Don't Tax Cuts Boost Work?

1. Lower taxes could actually lead people to work less since they have more after-tax income.
2. Most people, especially full-time workers, have little choice in how much they work.
3. Since the 1980s, the top marginal tax rate has been relatively low.
4. Many taxpayers are not aware of the marginal rates they pay.
5. Many of the richest taxpayers paying top rates are not motivated by after-tax income.

---

first glance, it seems he's right. After all, if I was Ronald Reagan and my next movie's proceeds were to be taxed at 90 percent, I might not make that movie either (although the movie would probably still be made, but with a different actor). But on the other hand, if I wasn't making as much as Reagan the actor and my taxes went up, I might actually work more since my after-tax income would have gone down and I needed more money.

In fact, economists have long noted that there are two possible behavioral effects from changes in tax rates: substitution effects and income effects. Ronald Reagan demonstrated the substitution effect: in the face of higher taxes, he substituted work with leisure. If I worked more to make up for the lost income of higher taxes, this would be the income effect. Notwithstanding the fact that economic theory has no way of predicting which of these effects will be larger, supply-siders claim that the substitution effect vastly outweighs the income effect. In contrast, Keynesians argue that the income effect is also important and that these effects are likely to be offsetting.[5]

Before discussing the economic research, it's worth looking at the logic and real-world situation for most people. It's true that some people, like Ronald Reagan, might have been able to choose how much they work, but most people, including most wealthy people, don't have much choice: they work forty-plus-hour-a-week jobs, fifty weeks a year. When the Bush tax cuts reduced my taxes, I couldn't very well go to my boss and say, "Now that I will be paying fewer taxes, I would like to give up a week of vacation and work more. But I will need a commensurate salary increase." In fact, very few people think about how much they work in relation to changes in tax rates.

Even many highly paid workers, such as managers and CEOs who might be expected to be more likely to adjust their work due to lower tax rates, have relatively little choice in how much they work, in part because most are already working very long workweeks and work years. Lower taxes are not likely to get them to work sixty-five instead of sixty hours a week. In the face of this logic, some supply-siders have come around to admitting that the case for more work from lower taxes is a bit thin. Gregory Mankiw admits that all but young workers are "locked into jobs that give them little choice about how much they work."[6] Larry Lindsey agrees, stating that "males in their prime earning years tend to be quite unresponsive to wage changes [resulting from tax changes]."[7] But that doesn't stop supply-siders from continuing to endlessly repeat the claim that lower taxes boost work.[8]

If taxes don't affect how much most salaried and hourly-wage workers work, they could affect independent professionals like actors, doctors, and other independent self-employed workers. However, many of these workers might still choose to work the same amount even if their taxes go down because of social pressures, the status attached to pretax income levels, or other factors. Keeping up with the Joneses' Corian countertop and new Cadillac means that, for many, working less is not a serious option. Indeed, studies find that many workers who work more do so not because of changes in tax rates, but because growing consumerism leads them to want more income and also because in the New Economy, working more is what's expected of them.[9]

What about wealthy individuals facing the highest marginal tax rates? Surely they will work more if their tax rates go down. In fact, it appears that many of the highest-income workers are motivated more by boosting their pretax income levels. One reason is that, beyond a certain level of wealth, it's hard to imagine how one could spend it on nondurable goods for one's enjoyment. Above a certain income, wealthy people are not working harder for the consumption that the money brings, but for other factors, such as status, power, enjoyment, and the desire to make a difference. In essence, pretax income is a way of judging success and attaining high social status.[10] Classical economists long understood this. Adam Smith stated that "it is not economic motivation that prompts a man to work, but status, respect, esteem, moral mettle, qualities which would enable him to be a man of worth and dignity." Likewise, John Stuart Mill once wrote, "Men do not desire to be rich, but to be richer than other men." More recently, billionaire Howard Hunt quipped, "Money's just a way of keeping score. It's the game that matters."[11] In other words, a "capitalist spirit" model may best explain why the rich save so much and earn more than they "need." As a result, cutting their taxes is likely to have little effect on how hard they work.

REAL-WORLD RESULTS

If the logic behind the supply-side claim that lower taxes boost work is questionable, real-world impacts on work from changes in tax rates provide even less support. History suggests that, if anything, lower taxes are associated with less, not more, work. A century ago, those in the bottom 10 percent of income worked six hundred hours a year more than those in the top.[12] Indeed, one of the benefits of being at the top was that you could enjoy more leisure. In contrast, top earners today are the ones putting in long hours, working four hundred hours more per year than low earners. Yet top earners' income taxes went up over 35 percentage points (there was no income tax in 1900). According to supply-side theory, their work hours should have gone down, especially compared to lower-income workers. Perhaps higher taxes spurred the top earners to work more to make up lost income.

Production workers, as opposed to managers and professionals, also worked more even as tax rates went up. Between 1948 and 2004, there was a very strong (0.9) positive correlation between tax rates and the work hours of production workers. In contradiction to supply-side theory, lower taxes were associated with fewer hours worked. Supply-siders might argue that since most production workers don't face the highest marginal rate, this is misleading. However, there was also a strong positive correlation (0.66) between the lowest marginal tax rate and hours worked. Lower rates were associated with less work.

Still, supply-siders will counter that surely work must have increased during the Reagan administration when the maximum income tax rate was cut from 70 percent to 28 percent. Those lower rates must have provided a big incentive for people to work more, since work was taxed less. Yet, if there were effects, macroeconomic changes overwhelmed them. During those eight years, the labor force grew just 13 percent, compared to 20 percent in the previous eight years. Average annual work hours for production workers (including overtime) decreased by 2.3 percent. And the percentage of adult males in the workforce fell by 1.2 percentage points. It's true that the share of women who worked increased during the Reagan years (by 5 percentage points), but their growth rate actually slowed when compared to the prior eight years (7 percentage points) (see figure 5.1). In short, the Reagan tax cuts appeared to have no positive effect on work effort.

If lower taxes didn't spur more work in the 1980s, the increase in the top rate to 39.6 percent in 1993 surely must have led people to work less, with well-heeled CEOs cutting back to four days a week and unemployed people sitting at home instead of looking for a job. Actually, the opposite happened, with almost twenty-three million jobs created during the Clinton administra-

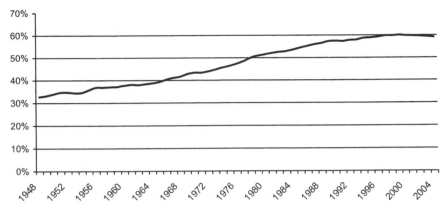

Figure 5.1　Percentage of Working-Age Women in the Workforce

Source: Bureau of Labor Statistics.

tion, compared to almost sixteen million during the Reagan years, despite slower population growth during the Clinton years. Moreover, average work hours (including overtime) for production workers went up (1 percent), reversing the 1980s' slide.

In contrast, the Bush tax cuts have coincided with a period of very slow job growth. Since the first tax cuts were passed in 2001, just fifty thousand net jobs per month were added (until November 2005), the most anemic employment expansion since the feds started to track the data after World War II. Moreover, for the first time since the government recorded the data, women's workforce participation has declined.

Finally, even if cutting the top tax rate did boost work effort, which it does not, the impact would be very limited. According to the Congressional Budget Office (CBO), less than 1 percent (0.8 percent) of taxpayers face the top two rates of 33 and 35 percent.[13] For the sake of argument, let's assume that tax cuts spur them to work an additional 5 percent more. In this case, the economy would experience a one-time boot of a minuscule 0.04 percent. This is not to say that there are no government policies that serve as a disincentive to work. Clearly the welfare system had these effects before it was reformed to encourage work. But arguing for fixing government programs to ensure that they encourage work is a far cry from claiming that tax cuts spur more work.

In sum, if tax rates matter to work, we certainly do not see the results in looking at employment performance over the last forty years. However, supply-siders will correctly argue that taxes are just one variable affecting employment and that to accurately assess the impact of changes in tax rates, more-careful studies are needed that control for a wide variety of different variables. But, as we will see, those studies provide equally weak support for this supply-side claim.

ECONOMIC STUDIES OF TAXES AND WORK

Academic economists have conducted numerous studies on the impact of changes in taxes on work. The consensus is that tax rates have little or no impact on work among men and single women. For married women, older studies found the same impact, but newer studies have found that higher taxes on married women, particularly those born after 1950, actually are associated with more, not less, work. This literature, known as the new tax responsiveness (NTR) literature, examines tax returns to explore the relationship between income and taxes, with the assumption that income is a proxy for work effort.

It's true that a few studies have concluded that tax cuts boost work. But most of these were conducted by supply-siders themselves who were looking for this very result. Yet, even with their predilection for finding a significant positive effect of lower taxes on work, supply-siders have not been able to find large effects. Lindsey claims that the Reagan tax cuts raised work by about 2.5 percent from 1981 to 1985. But even this modest effect is likely overstated because Lindsey simply assumes that a 10 percent cut in taxes leads a secondary earner (e.g., a person married to a full-time breadwinner) to work 10 percent more. In other words, Lindsey's model assumed that the Reagan tax cuts induced married women whose family earned $40,000 per year (in 1982) to increase their workweek from 40 hours to 47.2 hours. Does anyone know of a woman who actually did this?

The reality is that the increase in women's labor-force participation over the last thirty years had little to do with taxes. Before the Reagan tax cuts, the labor-force participation rate of working-age women grew 0.6 percentage points per year from 1948 to 1980, but at about half that rate (0.3) from 1980 to 2004.[14] The increased share of women in the workforce had much more to do with social factors (the women's movement; declining wages for many working men, which made it necessary for women to enter the workforce; the rise of less physically demanding service-sector jobs; etc.) than it did with taxes. Even Lindsey admits that this is largely a demographic trend, stating, "We have been working harder lately, mostly because of changes in demography. The biggest surge in work effort has come from increased female labor-force participation."[15]

Several other studies found positive effects from tax cuts, although modest in scope. Martin Feldstein, chair of President Reagan's Council of Economic

Advisers, found that after the 1986 tax reform, which lowered top rates from 50 percent to 28 percent, the incomes of the very rich rose the most, just as supply-side theory would predict. Randall Mariger, an economist at the Federal Reserve Board, found that the 1986 tax cuts increased labor supply between 1985 and 1986, but by less the 1 percent.[16] When looking at the tax cuts of the 1980s, economists Jonathan Gruber and Emmanuel Saez found only "modest effects on income of the tax cuts," and they suggest that their measures are on the higher side.[17]

Many of these studies, however, suffer from several serious limitations. First, while it may have been true in the 1980s that many married women were "secondary earners" whose work depended in part on how much their husbands made and on their household's marginal tax rates, this no longer seems to be the case. At least two studies have found that married women's wage elasticity (the degree to which their work hours respond to their real wage, including their after-tax earnings) has actually been going down since the mid-1980s and has been either zero or negative since then.[18] In other words, lower taxes lead married women to work less, not more. And this effect is stronger for younger women born after 1950. The explanation appears to be pretty clear: many more women today view work the way men do, as a career that they follow. As one study explains, "A married woman cannot be treated as a 'secondary worker' anymore, because informally speaking, she lives on her own income, which implies she is a separate 'primary worker.' Thus, when younger cohorts make up a higher percentage of working women, aggregate behavior changes."[19] In other words, the pillar of supply-side economics—that tax cuts boost more work, especially among married women—is no longer true. In fact, the opposite appears to be true, as the income effect takes hold, if anything, married women appear to cut back work hours if taxes are cut. Thus, it's not surprising that the share of women in the workforce went down after the Bush tax cuts.

A second limitation of these studies is that most do not measure hours worked (because the data are difficult to obtain). Instead, they measure taxable income (taxable income is less than total income) and assume that it is a good proxy for work effort. Indeed, Lindsey asserts that "the best summary measure of the behavioral response of taxpayers is taxable income."[20] Yet taxable income is actually not a very good measure. Increases in taxable income can be a result of either more work (the supply-side response) or of tax-shifting strategies to boost deductions, and hence more after-tax income. In the short run, workers can shift income forward or back a year. In the longer run, workers can increase the share of income that is paid to them in the form of tax-free or tax-deferred fringe benefits (like health care benefits, pensions, and company perks). They can convert ordinary income to capital gains income (which is taxed at a lower rate) by getting paid through stock options. They can shift their investment portfolio more toward tax-exempt investments (such as municipal bonds). They can buy more expensive houses and write off the mortgage interest. They can and do increase charitable donations.[21] Importantly, studies find that this kind of flexibility in the form of pay is significantly higher for the highest earners, precisely the group supply-siders claim are most responsive to changes in tax rates. As a result, as a CBO study concluded, "Thus, even though a substantial body of empirical evidence suggests that overall hours of work are not very sensitive to wage rates, and hence to changes in marginal tax rates, taxable income may still be very sensitive to changes in tax rates."[22] Goolsbee agrees, noting that "high tax rates need not induce people to work less. Instead, they need only lead people to shift their income out of taxable form."[23]

As a result, a finding that tax cuts boost after-tax income doesn't mean that they boosted work. For example, Feenberg and Poterba studied the richest 0.5 percent of taxpayers following the Tax Reform Act of 1986 and found that their share of national income increased from 8 percent in 1985 to 11 percent in 1989.[24] But the authors conclude that the growth in incomes was likely not a result of more work but rather was a result of growth in income that formerly was reported as nontaxable income but now was reported as taxable income.

There is a second problem with using income as a measure of work effort. CBO tax policy experts Sammartino and Weiner argue that "a fundamental objection to these studies is they do not adequately control for the many factors, other than tax changes, that have influenced the shape of the income distribution over the sample period."[25] One of the most important of these is the growing share of incomes going to the wealthy. As Goolsbee notes, trends in income inequality potentially bias studies equating tax cuts of the 1980s with higher earnings. He argues that the backbone of the NTR studies is the assumption that lower-income people are a valid control group for higher-income people and that changes in the incomes of the two groups would be identical had there been no change in taxes.[26] But, "if non-tax-related trends in income inequality, however, were driving up the incomes of the rich relative to other groups over this time period, the estimates would clearly be biased upward."[27] He goes on to note that

a large literature in labor economics has noted that, for reasons unrelated to taxation, income inequality was rising throughout the 1980s. If this pattern extended to the top of the income distribution, this would mean that the NTR experiments examining tax cuts at the top of the distribution suffer from potentially serious upward bias, since taxes decreased for the same people whose relative incomes were trending upward.[28]

These factors could include such developments as skill-based technical change, expansion of trade, the decline of unions, and the emergence of "winner-take-all markets."[29] As a result, the cash compensation of the rich has grown relative to the moderately rich, creating the spurious correlation between tax cuts and the income growth of the wealthy.[30]

When studies control for this factor, it turns out that tax cuts don't stimulate more work and in some cases lead to less. In perhaps the most comprehensive study, Goolsbee analyzed changes in tax rates going back to the 1920s and found mixed evidence for the supply-side hypothesis. The Coolidge tax cuts of the 1920s raised the before-tax incomes of the rich, but not by much. But the increases in the top rate in the 1930s also raised the before-tax incomes of the rich faster than any other group.[31] The tax increases of the 1950s had a modest negative effect on the income of the wealthy (about fifteen cents for every dollar of tax raised). The Kennedy tax cut also led to a slight decline in the income of the wealthy.[32] In a study of the effect of changes in tax rates from 1970 to 1994 on corporate salaries, a pretty good indicator of the effects of tax cuts on the wealthy, Goolsbee found that the highest-paid CEOs who enjoyed the biggest tax cuts in the 1970s actually saw the smallest increases in income.[33] To sum up his findings, changes in tax rates in the past century have had no consistent effect on the incomes of the wealthy.

There is another reason to suspect that changes in tax rates have little effect on work effort. If Americans were especially responsive to tax rates, you would expect to see incomes clustering around points where there is a significant shift in marginal rates. In other words, once a person earned enough to move them into a higher tax bracket, they would be less likely to earn more. But Saez finds no evidence of any such clustering.[34]

A more accurate measure of the effects of taxes on work is to look at their effect on pretax income. This avoids the problem of taxpayers substituting taxable income for nontaxable income or vice versa. Yet, even when economists use this method, they find little or no effects of taxes on income. Saez finds that when this definition of income is used, "only the reported incomes of taxpayers within the top 1 percent of the income distribution appear to be responsive to changes in tax rates over the 1960–2000 period. Even upper-middle income taxpayers (within the top decile, but below the top 1 percent), who experienced substantial changes in marginal tax rates, show no evidence of response to taxation, either in the short-run or the long-run."[35] In fact, when looking at the changes in tax rates in the bottom 99 percent of tax units between 1981 to 2000, Saez found a negative (although not statistically significant) relationship.[36] In other words, lower tax rates were associated with less income, not more, as supply-siders would predict.

Moreover, there is considerable evidence that the only time tax cuts had any effect on income was in the 1980s. Goolsbee found that "the behavioral responses, however, at least in these historical periods, are substantially smaller than claimed in the recent literature for the 1980s. Although that work emphasizes the potential importance of behavioral responses to marginal tax rates, the results in this paper suggest that the evidence on which those conclusions are based—evidence from the 1980s—is atypical in the historical experience."[37] Saez also found similar results that top earners only responded to the tax cuts during the Reagan years, not the prior Kennedy cuts. Likewise, Joel Slemrod, an economist at the University of Michigan and former senior economist for tax policy in President Reagan's Council of Economic Advisers, found that for the period 1950 to 1985, the increases in the share of income going to higher-income Americans can be largely explained by nontax factors. However, the 1986 tax cut may have had some impact on the growth in income of the wealthy.

In response to these studies, supply-siders will argue that even if most tax cuts didn't boost work effort, at least the Reagan tax cuts did. However, upon closer examination, even that assertion does not appear to hold up. Saez finds that the increase in income of the wealthiest taxpayers after the 1980s tax cuts was in large part because they shifted income out of higher-taxed corporations to lower-taxed partnerships and subchapter S corporations, legal entities taxed at the individual level. When corporate rates are lower than the top personal rate, as they were until the mid-1980s, there is no motivation for taxpayers to shift income this way. But after top individual rates fell to 28 percent in 1988, 6 percentage points lower than the corporate rate, wealthy individuals had strong motivations to reclassify income so that it flowed to them, not their companies. This kind of income shifting is in fact much more responsive to changes in taxes than changes in behavior like work and savings. As a result, Saez notes that "the surge in business income reported on individual returns in the 1980s cannot be interpreted as a supply-side success because most of these individual income gains came either at the expense of taxable corporate income or could have been obtained from the closing of tax shelters."[38] Slemrod confirms this, finding that "the tax cuts of the 1980s have generated a surge in business income taxed at the individual level."[39] He finds that a one-point increase in the tax differential between corporate and individual rates raised reported personal labor income by 3.2 percent and lowered the reported corporate rates of return by 0.147 percent.[40] This shifting of income between corporate form and individuals is perhaps why the Kennedy tax cuts didn't boost the income of those in the highest tax brackets: at that time, individual rates were higher than corporate rates.

Perhaps surprisingly, Larry Lindsey found similar results. In his book on the Reagan tax cuts, Lindsey studied the effects of the tax cuts on the taxes paid by the rich.[41] He found that *all* the increase in tax revenues from the tax cuts on the wealthiest Americans was from tax shifting, what Lindsey calls the pecuniary effect.[42] In fact, he found that lower taxes don't cause higher-income people to work more, arguing that "there is no reason to suspect factor supply as either the sole or even the dominant way that changes in tax rates affect tax revenues."[43] He goes on to admit that "changes in portfolio behavior and the form of compensation employees receive may be of more consequence."[44] So what he is really saying is that when top tax rates go down, employers and their high-priced employees switch back to taxable compensation and reduce nontaxable fringe benefits, offsetting some of the tax loss, but not spurring more work.

Even if tax cuts do not encourage work, one might hope that the kind of tax shifting that they do encourage will enhance economic growth by making the economy more efficient. Unfortunately for the supply-side case, this also does not appear to be true. Larry Lindsey admits as much, stating, "Unlike supply-side effects, [pecuniary effects] . . . have neither clear nor direct impacts on the size of the economy."[45] Likewise, it would be one thing if growing inequality made the economy more productive, but there is no evidence of this. But the increase in salaries of the top 1 percent since the 1970s has been accompanied by almost no growth for the bottom 99 percent of salary earners.

If the lower taxes of the Reagan era were supposed to stimulate work, then the tax increases of 1993 should have reduced work and incomes, at least according to supply-siders. One of the first economists to test the effects of the 1993 tax increases was Martin Feldstein. Feldstein found, consistent with supply-side doctrine, that higher earners indeed saw a reduction in taxable income from 1992 to 1993. Conservative organs like the *Wall Street Journal* touted the study as proof that the supply-siders were right and that Clintonomics was leading us down the road to ruin. But several subsequent studies, which the *Wall Street Journal* failed to report, found that this effect was simply the result of taxpayers shifting income back from the higher tax year of 1993 to the lower tax year of 1992. For example, 1993 January bonus payments could have been paid a month earlier, when they would have been taxed at the lower rates. Going the other way, individuals could have postponed charitable contributions from December to January. Indeed, this seems to have been the case. A New York State survey shows that two-thirds of Wall Street year-end bonuses were paid in December 1992, well above the one-third usually paid before the end of the year.[46] A Treasury Department study found that $20 billion of income was shifted back from 1993 to 1992. In fact, most of the income that Feldstein and Feenberg argued was destroyed by a

reduction in labor supply was instead realized a year earlier.[47] CBO economists Sammartino and Weiner found that 100 percent of the decline in the
share of income to this top group in 1993 was recouped by 1995. Moreover,
the share of total taxable income going to the top 1 percent of taxpayers even
went up from 1989 to 1995, at a time when their top rate increased from 28
percent to 39 percent. They note that "the average income for the highest-
income group grew significantly more (eight percent) between 1989 and 1995
than for the rest of the population of taxpayers (fairly flat change)."[48] A 2001
CBO study found the same results: "The income of households facing the
higher rates [from the 1990 and 1993 tax increases] rose much more rapidly
over the decade than did overall income."[49] Indeed, from 1989 to 1998, the
average after-tax income of the top 1 percent of tax filers went up by 40 percent, increasing by $171,000 per taxpayer in real dollars.[50] In short, the high-
est earners responded in just exactly the opposite way from that predicted by
supply-siders.

Saez also found that in spite of the increase in tax rates on the top 1 percent
of taxpayers from around 32 percent to 39.6 percent in 1993, their incomes
soared. He attributes much of the increase in wage income for the top 1 percent to the surge in stock options that increasingly replaced standard wage
compensation. Indeed, the share of options as income more than doubled
from 5.1 percent in 1970 to 12.6 percent in 2000.

Finally, while most studies have used income (pretax or after-tax) as a
proxy for work, a few studies have looked directly at work hours. Brookings
economists Barry Bosworth and Gary Burtless concluded that the reductions
in marginal tax rates in the 1980s led to a modest increase in labor supply,
with men between the ages of twenty-five and sixty-four working 5.2 percent
more hours than would have been predicted on the basis of past trends,
women working 5.8 percent more, and married women working 8.8 percent
more. However, they caution against drawing too firm a conclusion because
their models showed that lower-income men increased their labor supply by
the largest amount even though their tax rates either didn't change or
increased slightly.[51]

In their study that measures work hours, Moffit and Wilhem found, "The
evidence in these data is that hours of work are, as found in much of the
previous work, inelastic for prime-age males in the United States."[52] In other
words, with regard to the supply-side assertion that tax cuts boost more work,
they find that "there is essentially no evidence of any such response" to tax
cuts. In fact, looking at male heads of households, Moffit and Wilhem found
that their annual work hours have shown a gradual decline since the 1960s,
when rates were much higher. Professionals and managers averaged around
2,300 hours a year in 1967 when the top income tax rate was 70 percent, but

2,225 by 1997 when the top rate had declined to 39.6. Moreover, work hours for professionals and mangers increased after the 1993 tax increase, again exactly the opposite of what supply-side economics predicted.[53]

With scholarly research drawing a dry hole when it comes to findings that tax cuts in America boost work, supply-siders have started to look overseas for evidence favorable to the supply-side hypothesis. For example, conservative economist Edward Prescott looked at differences in European and American work hours, arguing, "Americans now work 50 percent more than do the Germans, French, and Italians. This was not the case in the early 1970s, when the Western Europeans worked more than Americans."[54] He claims that "the marginal tax rate accounts for the predominance of differences at points in time and the large change in relative labor supply over time." There are, however, two problems with this conclusion. First, other careful studies disagree. Three Harvard economists found that tax rates were not the driving factor in the difference in work hours between Europe and the United States. Rather, "the vast empirical labor supply literature suggests that tax rates can explain only a small amount of the differences in hours between the U.S. and Europe. . . . We argue that European labor market regulations, advocated by unions in declining European industries who argued 'work less, work all' explain the bulk of the difference between the U.S. and Europe. These policies do not seem to have increased employment, but they may have had a more society-wide influence on leisure patterns because of a social multiplier where the returns to leisure increase as more people are taking longer vacations."[55]

Second, supply-siders claim that high taxes curb not only work but also savings and productivity. Yet, while Europeans have higher taxes and lower work, they also have higher savings rates. Moreover, Prescott shows that over this particular period, European and Japanese productivity either stayed the same relative to the United States or increased.[56] Supply-siders can't have it both ways, claiming that lower taxes in the United States boost both work and savings, since the high-tax Europeans save more than us but work less.

In sum, as Slemrod notes, "Nearly all research concludes that male work hours respond hardly at all to change in after-tax wages and therefore to marginal tax rates. Some evidence suggests that decisions to work, especially by females, may be responsive to changes in taxes but these responses do not contribute enough to total labor supply to alter the conclusion that, overall, labor supply is not greatly affected by taxes."[57] Likewise, after reviewing the NTR literature, Goolsbee concludes, "An extensive literature in labor economics has shown that there is very little impact of changes in tax rates on labor supply for most people, particularly for prime-age working men."[58] A broad review of the NTR literature conducted by the Organisation for Economic Co-operation and Development (OECD) finds that lower taxes are associated with more work for married women who work part time. However, the work hours of full-time professional women are largely insensitive to tax rates. For men and for single women working full time, lower taxes are associated with slightly *less* work.[59] Moreover, the OECD found that with respect to the United States, higher taxes were associated with slightly higher work hours, just the opposite of what supply-siders would predict.[60] Moreover, the most recent research on married women finds that while lower taxes might have led to more work in the 1980s, today married women behave like men in terms of their view of their careers, and now, if anything, lower taxes lead to less work effort. In short, more than a decade of careful research has generally concluded that the effects on work of lower taxes are at best minimal and probably nonexistent or even negative. This is largely because, unlike the decision about whether to buy a hybrid car or one with a gasoline engine, where a tax incentive can make a big difference, the decision about how much to work is pretty much independent of taxes, especially at the tax rates of the 1990s.

LIMITATIONS OF MORE WORK AS AN
ECONOMIC STRATEGY

A core tenet of supply-side economics is that tax cuts grow the economy by inducing people to work more. But if supply-siders want to get Americans to work more, there's actually a straightforward, budget-neutral way to get there. The president could unveil a plan that would guarantee to grow the economy 20 percent in one year by proclaiming, "My fellow Americans, our great country can be even greater and even wealthier. So I am submitting legislation to Congress replacing the forty-hour workweek with a forty-eight-hour workweek. Yes, I know it will be a bit harder, especially for you workers with families, but look at the bright side: you'll earn more money!"

While a forty-eight-hour workweek would lead to a bigger economy, it wouldn't necessarily be a better one, for people would have less time to spend on other important activities. Yet, like the factory foreman who wants to get more hours out of his workers, supply-siders don't see it this way. Lindsey worries that higher taxes will reduce overtime, stating, "At the lower end of the economic scale, even middle-class taxpayers will discover the advantages of leisure when their overtime pay is taxed at 40 and 50 percent."[61] I hate to break it to Lindsey, but most working Americans, especially those with families, have already discovered the value of leisure; in their harried world of working more and more, spending more time getting to and from work, caring for their children and increasingly their own parents, and still finding time to participate in community and church activities, Americans have little leisure, and what little they have, they value intensely.

This leads to a final key problem with the NTR studies. While supply-siders assign to each additional hour of work the market value of wages earned, they assign a value of zero to each additional hour of nonwork a worker gains or loses. While workers may not value an extra hour of nonwork at the same rate that they value an extra hour of work, they do value it. This is in fact one of the major problems with the supply-siders' strategy of "get rich by working even more." Americans don't show an inclination to want to work even more. Even Lindsey grudgingly admits that "most people prefer more leisure to a long work week."[62]

Moreover, working more has significant societal costs. Longer work hours are associated with reduced health and higher levels of stress. They reduce the likelihood that people will participate in continuing education and boost their skills. They are associated with less civic engagement. As Harvard sociologist Robert Putnam found, longer work hours reduce people's involvement in civic activities, like the PTA, the local neighborhood association, and organized religion.[63] Yet a cornerstone of Bush's agenda of compassionate conservatism—which he appears to have thrown overboard soon after he was elected in 2000—was to encourage Americans to volunteer more so that they, rather than government, could help solve pressing social problems. Yet, if tax cuts are supposed to boost work, where do supply-siders think Americans are going to find the time to volunteer?

Perhaps most importantly, longer hours make maintaining healthy families and raising children even harder. More work reduces the amount of time parents spend with their kids, helping them with their homework, talking to them over dinner, or just plain spending time playing with them. Indeed, a growing body of research shows that too much work by both parents can have detrimental effects on children's well-being, particularly children aged zero to three.[64] Yet most parents would like to work less and spend more time with their children. One study found that 72 percent of parents would rather stay home and raise their children than work if money were not an issue.[65]

As a result, a progressive growth strategy should not be focused on getting Americans to work even longer and harder, but rather on boosting productivity so that American workers can produce and earn more without having to work more. In short, the focus should not be on boosting the quantity of labor but the quality of it, by helping workers boost skills and use more technologically advanced tools that boost productivity. Productivity is what matters, and working more doesn't raise productivity. In fact, it's likely to reduce productivity, since workers will be more tired and less focused.

So, if the Bush tax cuts had no effect on work effort, what about their effect on savings and investment, which supply-siders are quick to tout? It's to this question that we now turn.

NOTES

1. Ronald Reagan, *An American Life* (New York: Simon & Schuster, 1990), 231.

2. Lawrence Lindsey, *The Growth Experiment: How the New Tax Policy Is Transforming the U.S. Economy* (New York: Basic Books, 1990), 235.

3. Andrew Mellon, *Taxation: The People's Business* (New York: Macmillan, 1924).

4. Lindsey, *The Growth Experiment*, 80.

5. Even supply-siders sometimes get confused and claim that tax cuts lead to less, not more, work. For example, in 1997, House Speaker Newt Gingrich argued that tax cuts would mean "less time at work and more free time, so you can be a better volunteer, a better parent, more active in your community, and more involved in charitable activities." Cited in Jack Shafer, "Two-Headed Newt," *Slate*, 25 June 1997, http://slate.msn.com/id/1000029/ (accessed 29 November 2005).

6. Greg Mankiw, "Ax Taxes for Xers!" *Fortune*, 16 March 1998, www.economics.harvard.edu/faculty/mankiw/columns/mar98.html (accessed 24 January 2006).

7. Lindsey, *The Growth Experiment*, 67.

8. Supply-siders could make the claim that even if workers are in particular jobs that don't give them choice in work hours, they could switch jobs to find employers that would let them work less/more in response to higher/lower tax rates. But unless workers want to switch to part-time employment or self-employment, most employers have the same work hour/wage and salary policies.

9. One study of work hours in Australia found that the hypothesis that best explained the increase in work hours was the "consumerism" hypothesis that posed that workers increased work hours in order to consume more as new products and services were introduced. In this case, tax cuts would serve to limit work hour expansion since workers could consume more without working more. They also found support for the "ideal worker norm" hypothesis, which hypothesized that workers worked more because that was the new norm. Robert Drago, David Black, and Mark Wooden, "The Existence and Persistence of Long Work Hours" (Bonn, Germany: Institute for the Study of Labor, August 2005).

10. Christopher D. Carroll, "Why Do the Rich Save So Much?" In *Does Atlas Shrug?* ed. Joel B. Slemrod (Cambridge, MA: Harvard University Press, 2000), 478.

11. Christopher D. Carroll, "Why Do the Rich Save So Much?" 478.

12. Dora Costa, "The Wage and the Length of the Work Day: From the 1890s to 1991," *Journal of Labor Economics* 18, no. 1 (January 2000): 156–81.

13. Congressional Budget Office, "Effective Marginal Tax Rates on Labor Income" (Washington, DC: Congressional Budget Office, November 2005), 21.

14. These rates are not compounded.

15. Lindsey, *The Growth Experiment*, 180.

16. Randall Mariger, "Labor Supply and the Tax Reform Act of 1986: Evidence from Panel Data" (Washington, DC: Board of Governors of the Federal Reserve System, June 1994).

17. Peter R. Orszag, "Marginal Tax Rate Reductions and the Economy: What Would Be the Long-Term Effects of the Bush Tax Cut?" (Washington, DC: Center on Budget and Policy Priorities, 16 March 2001), www.cbpp.org/3-15-01tax.htm (accessed 21 November 2005).

18. Kyoo-il Kim and José Carlos Rodríguez-Pueblita, "Are Married Women Secondary Workers? The Evolution of Married Women's Labor Supply in the U.S. from 1983 to 2000" (Washington, DC: Congressional Budget Office, December 2005); and B. T Heim, "The Incredible Shrinking Elasticities: Married Female Labor Supply, 1979–2003" (working paper, Duke University, 2004), cited by Kim and Rodríguez-Pueblita.

19. Kim and Rodríguez-Pueblita, "Are Married Women Secondary Workers?"

20. Lindsey, *The Growth Experiment*, 23.

21. In fact, higher marginal tax rates lead to more charitable giving. Gerald E. Auten, Charles T. Clotfelter, and Richard L. Schmalbeck, "Taxes and Philanthropy among the Wealthy," in *Does Atlas Shrug?* ed. Joel B. Slemrod (Cambridge, MA: Harvard University Press, 2000).

22. Congressional Budget Office.

23. Austan Goolsbee, "Evidence on the High-Income Laffer Curve from Six Decades of Tax Reform," *Brookings Papers on Economic Activity*, Fall 1999, 2.

24. Daniel R. Feenberg and James M. Poterba, "Income Inequality and the Incomes of Very High Income Taxpayers: Evidence from Tax Returns" (working paper, National Bureau of Economic Research, Cambridge, MA, 1993).

25. Frank Sammartino and David Weiner, "Recent Evidence on Taxpayers' Response to the Rate Increases of the 1990s," *National Tax Journal* 50 (3 September 1997): 683–705.

26. Austan Goolsbee, "It's Not about the Money: Why Natural Experiments Don't Work on the Rich," in *Does Atlas Shrug?* ed. Joel B. Slemrod (Cambridge, MA: Harvard University Press, 2000), 42.

27. Goolsbee, "Evidence on the High-Income Laffer Curve," 9.

28. Goolsbee, "Evidence on the High-Income Laffer Curve," 14.

29. Robert H. Frank and Philip J. Cook, *The Winner-Take-All Society* (New York: Free Press, 1995).

30. Goolsbee, "It's Not about the Money," 142.

31. Goolsbee, "Evidence on the High-Income Laffer Curve," 28.

32. Goolsbee, "Evidence on the High-Income Laffer Curve," 30.

33. Goolsbee, "Evidence on the High-Income Laffer Curve," 37.

34. Emmanuel Saez, "Do Taxpayers Bunch at Kink Points?" University of California at Berkeley and National Bureau of Economic Research, 13 June 2000, http://emlab .berkeley.edu/users/saez/bunch.pdf (accessed 25 November 2005).

35. Emmanuel Saez, "Reported Incomes and Marginal Tax Rates, 1960–2000," in *Tax Policy and the Economy*, ed. James M. Poterba, 117–71 (Cambridge, MA: National Bureau of Economic Research, 2004), 120.

36. Saez, "Reported Incomes and Marginal Tax Rates," 139.

37. Goolsbee, "Evidence on the High-Income Laffer Curve," 31.

38. Saez, "Reported Incomes and Marginal Tax Rates," 160.

39. Joel Slemrod and Jon Bakija, *Taxing Ourselves: A Citizen's Guide to the Debate over Taxes* (Cambridge, MA: MIT Press, 2004), 160.

40. Slemrod and Bakija, *Taxing Ourselves*, 274.

41. Lindsey, *The Growth Experiment*.

42. Lindsey, *The Growth Experiment*.

43. Lindsey, *The Growth Experiment*, 86.

44. Lindsey, *The Growth Experiment*, 7.

45. Lindsey, *The Growth Experiment*, 61.

46. Peter Passel, "Do Tax Cuts Raise Revenue? The Supply Side War Continues," *New York Times*, 16 November 1995, D2.

47. Nouriel Roubini, "Supply Side Economics: Do Tax Rate Cuts Increase Growth and Revenues and Reduce Budget Deficits? Or Is It Voodoo Economics All Over Again?" http://pages.stern.nyu.edu/~nroubini/SUPPLY.HTM (accessed 25 November 2005).

48. Sammartino and Weiner, "Recent Evidence on Taxpayers' Response to the Rate Increases of the 1990s," 692.

49. Congressional Budget Office, "Budget Options" (Washington, DC: CBO, February 2001), 376.

50. Peter R. Orszag, "Marginal Tax Rate Reductions and the Economy: What Would Be the Long-Term Effects of the Bush Tax Cut?" (Washington, DC: Center on Budget and Policy Priorities, March 2001), 7.

51. Barry Bosworth and Gary Burtless, "Effects of Tax Reform on Labor Supply, Investment and Savings," *Journal of Economic Perspective* 6, no. 1 (Winter 1992): 3–25, 12.

52. Robert A. Moffitt and Mark O. Wilhelm, "Taxation and the Labor Supply Decisions of the Affluent," in *Does Atlas Shrug?* ed. Joel Slemrod (Cambridge, MA: Harvard University Press, 2000), 217.

53. Moffitt and Wilhelm, "Taxation and the Labor Supply Decisions," 202.

54. Edward C. Prescott, "Why Do Americans Work So Much More Than Europeans?" *Federal Reserve Bank of Minneapolis Quarterly Review* 28, no. 1 (July 2004): 2–13.

55. Alberto Alesina, Edward Glaeser, and Bruce Sacerdote, "Work and Leisure in the U.S. and Europe: Why So Different?" (Cambridge: Harvard University, 2005).

56. Edward C. Prescott, "Why Do Americans Work So Much More Than Europeans?" 3.

57. Slemrod and Bakija, *Taxing Ourselves*, 125.

58. Goolsbee, "Evidence on the High-Income Laffer Curve," 1.

59. Willi Leibfritz, John Thornton, and Alexandra Bibbee, "Taxation and Economic Performance" (Paris: Organisation for Economic Co-operation and Development, 1997), 40.

60. Leibfritz, Thornton, and Bibbee, "Taxation and Economic Performance," 39.

61. Lindsey, *The Growth Experiment*, 19.

62. Lindsey, *The Growth Experiment*, 181.

63. Robert D. Putnam, *Bowling Alone: The Collapse and Revival of American Community* (New York: Simon & Schuster, 2000).

64. Stanley I. Greenspan, "Child Care Research: A Clinical Perspective," *Child Development* 74 (2003): 1064.

65. "America's Toughest Job: A View of Contemporary Parenthood at the Beginning of the 21st Century" (survey conducted by Penn, Schoen and Berland, and the Luntz Research Companies for the I Am Your Child Foundation and *Parents* magazine, 2000).

Chapter Six

Do Lower Taxes Boost Savings and Investment?

Save a little money each month and at the end of the year you'll be surprised at how little you have.

—Ernest Haskins

Even if tax cuts don't boost work, supply-siders argue that at least they boost savings, which in turn boost investment and productivity. As Arthur Laffer notes in respect to tax cuts and savings, "Tax something, and you get less of it. Tax something less, and you get more of it."[1] Greg Mankiw agrees: "It is a good rule of thumb that when you tax an activity, you get less of it. If we stopped taxing estates, estate building would be more attractive, and that would be good for everyone in the economy."[2] But do tax cuts boost savings? As we will see, they do not appear to.

SUPPLY-SIDE SAVINGS PROPOSALS

The best way to boost savings, supply-siders argue, is to cut taxes on individuals, particularly on high earners and on savings and investment. This belief provides the rationale for virtually all of the Bush administration's tax-cutting proposals. Since the wealthy save more of their income than the average American, supply-siders focus on cutting top marginal rates, believing that if the rich pay less in taxes they will save more. But since lower-income people save less, one could make an equally compelling argument that since the rich are already saving a lot, boosting incentives (like the expansion of tax-free savings accounts and making it so that workers are more likely to enroll in 401(k) plans) for low- and moderate-income workers to save more is a more effective strategy.

The ultimate reduction in marginal rates is the flat tax, a perennial favorite

---

Why Don't Tax Cuts Boost Savings?

1. Lower taxes could actually lead people to save less since they would now have greater lifetime after-tax income.
2. Most people's savings decisions are not sensitive to tax rates.
3. Since the 1980s, the top marginal tax rate is already low and has little negative effect on savings.
4. Any possible induced savings are more than offset by increased government dissavings (increased national debt).

---

of supply-siders. Former House Republican leader Dick Armey championed a flat 17 percent tax during the 1990s. Steve Forbes made it a centerpiece of his quixotic Republican presidential primary campaign in 1996, and with his 2005 book, *The Flat Tax Revolution*, he is again promoting the wonders of the flat tax.[3] Forbes promises that a flat tax would make the economy $2 trillion bigger in ten years, much of it because of the increase in savings that it would spark.

Not only should we dramatically lower the top rates by instituting a much lower flat tax, but supply-siders argue that we should eliminate all taxes on all capital income (e.g., income from dividends, interest, and capital gains).[4] James Pinkerton, former policy adviser in the first Bush administration, argues that Republicans should make Americans a "big offer on taxation to create a system that no longer taxes capital formation at all."[5] The Bush administration used the same rationale to sell its efforts to cut taxes on dividends and capital gains. Greg Mankiw argued that "there is a significant academic literature suggesting that high tax rates on capital income distort saving decisions and impede economic growth. After all, if we don't tax income until it is spent, supply-siders believe that people will respond by spending less and saving more. This view provided the basis for President Bush's proposal to reduce the tax on dividends and capital gains."[6] This argument that cutting taxes boosts savings also underlay the logic behind President Bush's proposal to partially privatize Social Security and create tax-free personal savings accounts. Indeed, President Bush justifies these proposals on these grounds, arguing, "One of the reason's I'm so strong about personal savings accounts and Social Security is help for capital accumulation."[7] With private accounts, instead of giving money to the government—which, supply-siders say, usually wastes it—individuals would be required to save the money, thus boosting private savings, which they believe increases capital investment. (But this ignores that while private savings would go up, public savings would go down, since the money would not be flowing into the Social Security Trust Fund.) Boosting savings is also behind supply-siders' efforts to repeal the estate tax—what they have derisively labeled the "death tax"— for they believe that people are motivated to work harder if they can leave a larger inheritance to their children. Therefore, taxing inheritances (which currently only affects around the richest 1 percent of estates), they argue, reduces people's willingness to save.[8]

So fervent is their belief that tax cuts boost savings that some supply-siders even advocate that the government go into debt to finance tax cuts. Jude Wanniski tells us that,

> The phenomenon is accepted when it is seen in the microeconomic world of the private firm. The bond market assesses a corporation's bond floatation by examining the uses to which the funds will be deployed. If it believes the issue will produce a positive return on investment, the interest rate on the bond will be favorable, and the corporation's other debt may even trade up in the secondary market. There is no reason why government bond finance should not be treated the same way, especially when the bonds are being issued explicitly to finance tax cuts.[9]

Never mind that going into debt to finance tax cuts defeats the entire purpose of the cuts—to boost savings—so fervent is the belief in the powers of tax cuts that more are always better.

This dogged desire to boost private saving is why supply-siders object to government expenditures such as health insurance, aid for housing, unemployment insurance, workforce training, Social Security, and other social supports that help Americans cope with risk and insecurity. According to supply-siders, not only do these programs divert money from savings and investment, but they lead Americans to save less. It's why the Heritage Foundation's Daniel Mitchell argues, "Saving is important to help provide capital for new investment, yet the incentive to save has been undermined by government programs that subsidize retirement, housing, and education."[10] It's why Larry Lindsey can profess, "As a rule however, the traditional motives for saving have been blunted by government programs to care for the aged and disabled, to finance college, and to cushion unemployment. People may be saving less in part because they have less fear of hard times."[11]

Lindsey believes that if Americans were subject to even more risk and uncertainty than they face in today's dynamic, global economy—if they worked without a safety net—they would save more. In the perennial holiday classic *It's a Wonderful Life*, there is a moving scene where Mr. Potter, the old factory-era bank president, argues for shutting down George Bailey's Building and Loan because it was providing loans for people to buy houses before they had saved enough to buy them outright. Sounding like a Depression-era Larry Lindsey, Potter asked, "And what does that get us? A discontented, lazy rabble instead of a thrifty working class. And all because a few starry-eyed dreamers stir them up and fill their heads with a lot of impossible ideas?" To which Jimmy Stewart's character George Bailey replies, "Just remember this, Mr. Potter, that this rabble you're talking about, they do most of the working and paying and living and dying in this community. Well, is it too much to have them work and pay and live and die in a couple of decent rooms and a bath?" In his passionate oration to the Building and Loan's board, who were thinking of supporting Potter, Bailey pleaded, "You're all businessmen here. Doesn't it make them better citizens? Doesn't it make them better customers?" To which Lindsey/Potter would likely reply, "But if they get a roof over their head and are more secure in their retirement, they will save less!"

THE LOGIC OF SUPPLY-SIDE
PROPOSALS TO BOOST SAVINGS

While there is certainly a careful chain of logic behind the supply-siders' argument, upon close examination it does not stand up to scrutiny. First, tax-payers' decisions to save are not all that sensitive to tax rates. Just as most people's decisions to work are not that sensitive to marginal tax rates, neither are their decisions to save. If tax rates change, individuals still will need to save and invest money. In fact, Larry Lindsey admits as much, stating that "the income tax base is less sensitive to rate changes than many other taxes."[12] Moreover, just as there is an income effect to tax cuts with respect to their effect on work, there is an income effect with respect to savings. If a person's taxes are cut, they may actually save less because they have greater lifetime after-tax income and therefore need to save less.

Some supply-siders will acknowledge that across-the-board income tax cuts may not boost savings. However, they maintain that cutting taxes on savings, specifically, would. One proposal to do this was President Bush's proposed Personal Savings Accounts (PSA), savings accounts that are exempt from taxes when the money is withdrawn, not when it is deposited. In fact, PSAs are likely to do little to stimulate savings among middle-income tax-payers since they are unlikely to be able to afford to set aside extra savings without an immediate tax benefit. Indeed, the accounts could actually reduce savings since the administration proposed abolishing IRAs that provide a tax deduction at the time the money is deposited.[13] In this regard, boosting taxes could actually increase savings because it makes the tax benefit of investing in IRAs more generous. University of British Columbia economist Kevin Milligan found that, with respect to Canadian-style IRA plans, a 10 percentage point increase in the marginal tax rate boosts the probability of participating in the plan by 8 percent.[14]

If eliminating taxes on saving doesn't boost saving and investment, will cutting taxes on capital gains, dividends, and estates? Greg Mankiw argues, "Any increase in the tax burden on capital income is likely to reduce the amount of capital available to be taxed."[15] He makes the same argument with respect to the estate tax, arguing that "the estate tax makes estate building less attractive and probably reduces the size of bequests."[16]

But just like cutting income taxes may lead people to work less, cutting estate taxes may reduce saving and work as it leads heirs to retire early and stop working since they now have more after-tax income and need to work less. Indeed, Treasury Department economist David Joulfaian found this to be the case.[17] Likewise, it's not clear that taxes on dividends hurt growth. If individuals have to pay taxes on their dividend income, companies are more likely to keep the earnings and invest them internally. If policy makers are concerned about double taxation (dividends are now taxed at the corporate and individual levels), they could cut dividend taxes on the corporate side, so savings would flow to higher corporate investment and/or lower prices, instead of all to shareholders, as happens when dividend taxes are cut for individuals.

There is another more fundamental reason why tax cuts don't boost saving. Tax cuts reduce government revenues, reducing national savings, since government gets less revenue and will run a budget deficit. So most tax cuts designed to boost savings simply rob Peter (the government) to pay Paul (wealthy individuals), leading to no net increase in national saving. Another limitation of the tax cuts as an instrument of boosting saving is that people don't save all of their tax cut. Even high-income households save only about 60 percent of tax cuts, with moderate- and lower-income households saving even less. The resulting increases in national debt offsets increased private savings. Mark Zandi found that while eliminating the dividend tax can help reduce distortions, "the economic benefits, however, are significantly offset by the higher actual and anticipated future budget deficits that result. . . . Indeed, the economic drag of higher interest rates ultimately outweighs the economic benefits of eliminating or scaling back dividend taxation."[18]

In response to this contention, supply-siders make two arguments. First, they claim that if people know that the government is running a budget deficit, they will anticipate higher taxes in the future and will boost saving now to account for this. While economists may think this far ahead, average people certainly don't.

Second, supply-siders argue that the only thing keeping the tax cuts from boosting savings is government's failure to cut spending. Paul Craig Roberts argues that "the conventional view, which stressed the interest rate as the important factor in the cost of capital, suffered from the misconception that higher government revenues from increased taxation can spur capital investment by lowering deficits and interest rates or by creating budget surpluses and retiring debt. Because taxation reduces investment and economic activity, the only certain way to reduce 'crowding out' is to cut government expenditure."[19] The only problem with this line of reasoning is that while Republicans promise to trim spending as they cut taxes, they have done nothing of the sort, becoming instead the party of "tax cut and spend." In the debates with Jimmy Carter, Ronald Reagan told voters that "there is enough extravagance and fat in government. . . . We have a program for general reduction in government spending based on these theories."[20] He went on to promise that his economic plan could permit extra spending on defense, cut taxes, and provide for a balanced budget by 1983, if not before. Suffice to say that spending and the budget deficit expanded during his term, in part because Republicans raised spending on "their" programs (e.g., defense), while Democrats raised it on "theirs" (e.g., education), and both raised it on entitlements (like Social Security).

In the last five years with a Republican president and a Republican-controlled Congress, inflation-adjusted federal spending has increased 24 percent compared to just 10 percent for the entire eight years of the Clinton administration.[21] Republicans may try to cut spending on "Democratic programs" like housing, social services, and workforce training, but they boost it on "their" programs, like defense, farm subsidies and other corporate entitlements, and pork-barrel projects to buy votes back home. The reality is that the best way to boost national saving is to run federal budget surpluses to pay down the huge national debt. Yet conservatives will argue that government will waste any increased revenues, and therefore it's better to cut taxes so that at least some of the money is saved. Yet, as evidenced by the budget surpluses of the late 1990s, government can save, especially if there are strict pay-as-you-go budget rules in place.

There is one final problem with these supply-side proposals to reduce taxes on saving and investment: they distort the market, something supply-siders oppose. Glenn Hubbard warns that "if capital is exempt from tax, high-income people will seek out tax shelters to make wages look like capital (as they already do with capital gains). Self-employed people and small businesses will have an incentive to incorporate, pay the owner a low wage, and accumulate large untaxed profits."[22] But it gets worse. In relatively technical language, Hubbard points out that models arguing the benefits of eliminating taxes on financial capital

> ignore human capital—that is, investments people make in themselves to build skills that will pay future returns through higher wages. Larry Jones, Rodolfo Manuelli, and Peter Rossi showed that if it is optimal to exempt the returns on physical capital, then it is also optimal to exempt the returns on human capital. Indeed, the logical extension . . . is that wages should also be exempt from tax. So in this economic utopia, nothing would be taxed![23]

In other words, eliminating taxes on capital, a supply-siders' dream, violates a core principle of supply-side economics: tax neutrality.

EVIDENCE FROM THE REAL WORLD

While the logic behind the claim that lower taxes boost saving is tenuous at best, real-world experience provides even less support. Let's start with the supply-siders' claim that high saving rates lead to higher rates of growth.

Supply-siders argue that nations with higher rates of saving will have the highest rates of growth. But let's look at a few comparisons. While American households saved around 1 to 2 percent of GDP from 1996 to 2001, Japanese and German household saved around 10 percent. Yet their economies grew considerably more slowly than ours.

The evidence that tax cuts stimulate saving is equally weak. In the late 1920s, federal taxes were less than 4 percent of GDP, and the savings rate was about 15 percent. Since the 1950s, the savings rate has actually been slightly higher (around 17 percent of GDP), even though federal taxes were much higher (around 19 percent of GDP). From 1973 to 1980, when the top marginal income tax rate was 70 percent, private saving (the amount of saving by individuals and companies) averaged 7.8 percent of GDP. After the Reagan tax cuts, it dropped to just 4.8 percent of GDP. But the effect on national saving (private saving plus government saving) was even worse. As the Reagan budget deficit exploded, national saving fell from 7.7 percent of net national product in the 1970s to around 2 to 3 percent at the end of the 1980s.[24] This is not to say that the top tax rate shouldn't have been cut from 70 percent, but it is to say that cutting the tax rates to 28 percent didn't boost national savings.

In the face of this evidence, some supply-siders claimed that the decline in saving had nothing to do with tax cuts and instead resulted from baby boomers entering the early years of their careers, when they saved little. Thus, they predicted that saving rates would go up once boomers got closer to retirement and their peak saving years. Alas, personal saving rates have continued their downward slide. And, with the boomers' impending retirement, when they will be spending more than they are earning, their saving is likely to fall even further.

After Bill Clinton pushed through modest increases in the top marginal rate in 1992, the net national saving rate (the sum of personal, business, and government net savings/borrowing) increased 87 percent (see figure 6.1). After George W. Bush pushed through big tax cuts, most of which went to the wealthy, net saving proceeded to fall 80 percent to just 1.2 percent of GDP, the lowest level since the Department of Commerce started keeping track in 1948. Between 1981 and 2002, in direct contrast to supply-side doctrine, lower top-income tax rates have been strongly and positively correlated with a lower national savings rate.

In the last decade, most of the fruits of a growing economy have gone to the top earners. The top one-tenth of 1 percent of earners earned as much of the gain in wage and salary income between 1997 and 2001 as the bottom 50 percent combined, and only the richest 10 percent of earners enjoyed a growth rate of real wage and salary income equal to or above the average rate of economy-wide productivity growth.[25] While this is not the kind of economy that produces widespread prosperity, supply-side theory would predict that it's the kind of economy that produces high saving rates, since the wealthy are supposed to save more of their income. In fact, not only did the rich get more pretax income than average Americans, but they got even more after-tax income after the Bush tax cuts, and still, not only did national saving decline, but so too did personal saving, falling 25 percent to just 1.3 percent of GDP, also the lowest level since 1948. In fact, net personal savings amounted to just $7.4 billion in 2005, down from $139 billion in the first

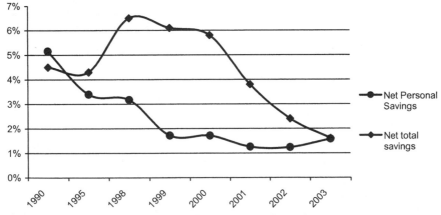

Figure 6.1   Net Personal and National Savings as a Share of GDP

Source: President's Council of Economic Advisors, *2005 Economic Report of the President* (Washington, DC: U.S. Government Printing Office, 2005).

quarter of Bush's first term. Moreover, the latest data releases suggest negative saving for 2005 for the first time since 1932–1933.

The result has been that not only did private saving go down, but because the federal budget deficit exploded, net national saving fell. As a result, the United States now must engage in massive borrowing from overseas, which has three pernicious effects.[26] First, by raising the global demand for dollars, overseas borrowing keeps the value of the dollar significantly higher than it otherwise would be. This in turn makes it more difficult for U.S.-based companies to compete internationally, since the price of imports is lower and the price of exports higher. The higher dollar amount is a factor contributing to companies moving jobs offshore and to companies like Ford and GM engaging in massive layoffs and plant closings. It also is a major factor contributing to America's record trade deficit. Second, federal borrowing runs up a growing debt that will eventually have to be paid off, most likely by the next generation. This will inevitably mean either higher taxes or lower government spending or some combination of the two. In either case, the next generation will be paying twice: once for much of our baby boomer's retirement income, and again for paying off this generation's profligate national debt.

Third, large budget deficits put upward pressure on interest rates, although to listen to supply-siders, they do nothing of the sort. Indeed, now that Republicans are in charge and are running up the budget deficit like drunken sailors, supply-siders have put on a full-court press to debunk the idea that budget deficits have any effect, arguing in the words of Vice President Dick Cheney, "Reagan proved deficits don't matter." (Perhaps they all received the same talking points that admonished them to just say there is *no evidence* that deficits lead to higher interest rates.) Conservative economist Robert Barro: "Federal budget deficits grew in the late 1980s, but there is no evidence that they raised interest rates or lowered investment."[27] White House budget director Mitch Daniels: "Well, the idea that there is some connection between deficits and interest rates is an article of faith for some people, but I say 'faith' because there's just no evidence, zero. And at least at the levels that we are now experiencing, historically very moderate—and as we see it, declining deficits—one would not expect an impact."[28] Heritage Foundation economist Daniel Mitchell: "Economists have failed to find a meaningful link between deficits and interest rates."[29] Former CEA chief Greg Mankiw:

> The government is once again confused to be at the center of good economic performance. A recent manifestation of this orientation has been the focus on accumulating government budget surpluses as the key, at times to the exclusion, of good economic performance. Despite essentially no evidence that surpluses are related to long-term interest rates—a finding that would stand in defiance of the increasing integration of world capital markets—proponents of this view argue that increasing the budget surplus is the key to faster growth.[30]

No evidence? There is indeed compelling scholarly evidence. It's the same evidence that led Larry Lindsey to admit (albeit in 1990, before he worked for Bush and had to toe the party line) that "high rates of government borrowing are a long-term problem."[31] It's the same evidence cited by Glenn Hubbard in the 2001 edition of his leading college economics textbook, when he wrote that large budget deficits of the 1980s led to higher interest rates and harmed growth, while the surpluses of the 1990s reduced interest rates and helped growth.[32] It's the same evidence that Greg Mankiw was calling on when he stated that "the expansionary effects of tax cuts will be offset to some degree by the effects of budget deficits that arise from lower revenues. Deficits can raise interest rates and crowd out of investment."[33] It's the same evidence that the Bush Council of Economic Advisers used when they found that a persistent $100 billion increase in the budget deficit (which is equal to approximately 1 percent of GDP) would raise long-term interest rates by 0.3 percentage points.[34]

In 2002, Orszag and Gale summarized the academic literature examining the relationship between deficits and interest rates and found that while the budget deficit in any particular year might not have a big effect, expectations of long-term budget deficits had significant effects on interest rates.[36] A more recent study by Thomas Laudbach, an economist at the Federal Reserve Bank, confirmed this finding.[35] Likewise, in reviewing the scholarly literature, Joel Slemrod concludes that "a persistent increase in the annual budget deficit of 1 percent of GDP causes real interest rates to rise about a quarter of a percentage point."[37]

Because tax cuts do little to boost personal savings yet do a lot to boost national debt, they lead to higher interest rates and relatively less investment. This is why a host of econometric studies find that supply-side tax cuts would actually hurt growth. It's why Federal Reserve Bank of New York economists found that government borrowing to finance the deficits in the 1980s caused net national savings to shrink from 7 percent of GNP in the 1970s to 3.5 percent in the 1980s, resulting in a drop in net national investment from 7.1 percent to 5.2 percent, leading to a 2.5 to 3.5 percent smaller economy. It's why economists Isabel Sawhill and Alice Rivlin found that the increase in the national debt of $5.3 trillion in the next decade would result in the economy's being about 1 percent smaller in 2014 than it would be otherwise.[38] It's why the Congressional Budget Office concluded that the supply-side effects (as opposed to the short-term Keynesian effects of putting more money into the hands of consumers) of the 2003 Bush tax cuts would actually end up reducing private investment by more than 4 percent over the next five years because interest rates would go up.[39] This analysis—essentially the final nail in the coffin of supply-side economic doctrine—is all the more striking since it employed a dynamic scoring method, long pressed for by Bush's economic advisers, including Douglas Holtz-Eakin, former chief economist of President Bush's Council of Economic Advisers, who headed the CBO. (Dynamic scoring means assessing the budgetary impact of a policy proposal by considering the effects of the proposal on growth and tax revenue.)

This is not to say that short-term, temporary tax cuts, particularly cutting the lower marginal rates, would not boost growth during an economic slowdown. In fact, President Bush was right to push for tax cuts in 2001, but they should have been temporary and not focused principally on top rates. Moreover, it's not that supply-siders are completely wrong when it comes to taxes and investment. Cutting taxes on capital income (e.g., income from interest, dividends, or capital gains) could have some modest positive effects on saving assuming that the lost tax revenues are offset through cuts in government spending. However, after conducting a thorough review of the research, OECD concluded that, "on balance, it appears that taxing capital income reduces savings, but not by very much. For example, results from one recent panel study of 21 OECD countries estimated that the elimination of the average capital tax rate of 40 percent (as it exists in some countries) would raise private saving by about 0.5 percent of GDP."[40] This may sound like a lot, but in fact it would lead to an increase in private saving in 2004 by just 3.3 percentage points. However, since the tax cuts would likely lead to an increase in the national debt, the effect on *national* saving would likely be negative.

As a result, the best policy to boost national saving is paying down the national debt. This is why an OECD study on taxation and growth concluded, "Given the empirical uncertainties regarding private saving, the most effective policy to raise national saving is likely to be through measures aimed at raising public saving."[41] Alan Greenspan agrees, stating that the best way to boost total saving is by fiscal discipline.[42] Even Glenn Hubbard admits that paying down the national debt is a surer way to boost saving. In recent testimony to Congress, Hubbard noted,

> Rather than radical tax reform, a surer path to economic growth is to reduce the deficit, which would increase national saving directly (by reducing public dissaving). Tax reform would be an ideal opportunity to address the deficit. Even revenue-neutral tax reform spells tax increases on many Americans. The losers from tax reform may be more willing to shoulder the greater burden if they knew that their children would pay lower taxes and enjoy a healthier economy as a result. And the best way to reduce the deficit would be to close the loopholes that allow businesses and high-income individuals to avoid their fair share of tax.[43]

While Hubbard did not sing that tune while in the White House, he deserves credit for his objectivity once he returned to academia.

Not deterred by these findings, many supply-siders will claim that any increases in public savings when the government runs a surplus are automatically offset by a decline in private savings. The theory, known as "Ricardian equivalence" after the eighteenth-century economist David Ricardo, holds that increases in public saving are canceled out by decreases in private saving as people pay more taxes and anticipate lower taxes in the future. In fact, a recent study by OECD of sixteen developed nations found some support for the theory. Between 1970 and 2002, an improvement in public finances was offset by a decline in savings of about two-thirds in the long term.[44] However, while true for most countries, it was not true for the United States. Here, the study found that a positive change in the budget had no statistically significant impact on private savings.

Even though it's clear that tax cuts have not produced an increase in savings, and in fact have led to a reduction in net national saving, supply-siders claim that the Reagan tax cuts at least produced a rebound in investment. Larry Lindsey claims, "The Reagan boom was distinguished by an especially rapid growth in business investment."[45] Again, the data paint a very different picture. As figure 6.2 shows, as a share of GDP, private investment fell throughout the Reagan and first Bush administrations, but increased during the Clinton administrations, before falling during the current Bush administration. In other words, investment went up when taxes were raised and went down when taxes were cut. Indeed, after a decade featuring two major tax changes, many economists now doubt that changes in individual tax rates

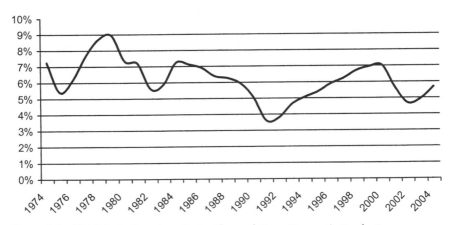

Figure 6.2 Net Private Investment as a Share of Gross Domestic Product

Source: Bureau of Economic Analysis, U.S. Department of Commerce.

have much effect on investment or saving. An analysis by two Federal Reserve Bank economists found that the Reagan tax cuts produced no net increase in private investment. In fact, net nonresidential investment actually declined from 3.5 percent of GNP in the 1970s to 3.0 percent in the 1980s.[46] Economist Alan Auerbach concluded that the 1986 tax cuts played a relatively unimportant role in explaining the level of investment in equipment and structures. Tax cuts not only have not produced faster growth, but they didn't even produce more capital. Moreover, the tax increases of the 1990s were followed by an investment rebound.

In fact, most careful studies of the relationship between taxes and saving find none. OECD concluded, "To date, the balance of this evidence suggests that the tax reforms had little overall impact on private savings, and some evidence to suggest that their impact on national savings may have been negative because of tax revenue losses and an associated decline in public saving."[47] In reviewing studies on the relationship between taxing and saving for the National Bureau of Economics Research, Douglas Bernheim finds that most of the estimates of the sensitivity (elasticity) of saving to taxes are around zero.[48] In other words, changes in personal tax rates play no role in determining savings rates. Bernheim goes on to note, "As an economist, one cannot review the voluminous literature on taxation and saving without being somewhat humbled by the enormous difficulty of learning anything useful about even the most basic empirical questions."[49] Tax policy expert Joel Slemrod agrees, stating, "If empirical evidence showed a strong positive relationship between savings and its after-tax rate of return, the economic costs of our income tax and the economic benefits of switching to consumption tax could be quite large. However, the available evidence does not readily reveal any such relationship."[50] He goes on to conclude that a "large number of studies . . . come to the conclusion that savings is not very responsive to incentives. . . . Given the state of the evidence, any claim that reducing or eliminating the tax on the return to saving would lead to large increases in saving must be viewed with skepticism."[51]

Supply-siders (and mainstream neoclassical economists) place such importance on savings because they see it as a means to boost investment. But at the end of the day, they do not have a very convincing explanation of what drives investment. They simply assume that increasing the supply of savings will increase the demand for it (e.g., investment). In contrast, Keynesian theory holds that efforts to increase savings have little or no effect on investment. In fact, Keynesian theorists argue that the causation is the other way. It's increased investment that leads to more income, which in turn produces more savings. Likewise, growth economics holds that increased savings stem from increased innovation and productivity that not only generate a surplus that can be saved but also increase the demand for more capital investment.

TAX CUTS AND ENTREPRENEURSHIP

Given the compelling evidence that tax cuts don't boost savings and actually lead to a decline in national savings when budget deficits are figured in, supply-siders are not deterred, for they have yet another argument for tax cuts as economic growth policy: they boost entrepreneurship. Supply-side economist Brian Wesbury argues as follows:

> Tax cuts work by increasing the incentives for new investment, not by stimulating demand. In the early 1980s, despite large tax cuts, consumers were not banging down the doors of local retailers for fax machines, cell phones, PCs, or broadband Internet connections. It was only after some very smart entrepreneurs decided to risk a great deal of money, time and talent developing these new goods and services that they became so ubiquitous. By cutting taxes on income and capital gains in the early 1980s, Ronald Reagan encouraged these entrepreneurs to take the risks necessary to develop these new technologies. To paraphrase Say's Law: supply created its own demand.[52]

Greg Mankiw agrees, arguing that "lower individual tax rates help sole proprietorships, partnerships and S corporations. For these taxpayers, income flows through to their individual tax returns. All of these initiatives lower firms' costs of capital."[53] When President Bush was trying to drum up support for his tax cuts, he used this argument extensively, arguing,

> So we're moving forward with an agenda to ensure that America is entrepreneurial heaven, the place where people can realize their dreams. . . . The agenda starts with keeping taxes low and restraining the spending appetite of the federal government. Tax relief left more money in the pockets of the people, and that has been a vital part of the growth of our economy. Yet, tax relief is set to expire in the years ahead. We need certainty in the tax code. We need to say to our risk takers, here's the way the tax code is going to look in the years ahead, therefore I think it's important that we make the tax relief permanent.[54]

There is a host of problems with the claim that tax cuts boost entrepreneurship, which in turn boosts growth. First, in contrast to the politically pleasing rhetoric employed by both sides of the aisle, it's large and midsized corporations, not small individually-owned businesses, that account for the overwhelming share of business investment, research and development, new products and services, and productivity growth, and individual tax rates don't affect them. Second, supply-siders would have us believe that there are vast numbers of small businesses aided by individual tax cuts. Glenn Hubbard claims that, "according to the Treasury Department, more than 30 million individual returns listed small business income in 2000."[55] This sounds like a lot, until you realize that it includes anyone who picks up a few bucks on the side and lists it as Schedule C business income. This would include me, as I got a modest advance from my publisher for agreeing to write this book, even though I was employed full time. It would also include President Bush, who reported $84 of Schedule C income on his 2001 taxes that he earned from his part ownership in an oil and gas company. But to call either George Bush or me a small-business person is stretching it, to say the least. Even Hubbard admits as much, noting, "Schedule C status does not necessarily mesh well with a definition of business ownership centered on studying fixed investment decisions."[56] The reality is that only one-tenth of all net income on 1998 returns with incomes greater than $100,000 was from farms and unincorporated businesses.[57]

Third, if individual tax rates matter so much, why did the rate at which new establishments were created go up after the Clinton tax increases and down after the Bush tax cuts? According to the Bureau of Labor Statistics, there were an estimated 1.17 million new establishments created in 1992. After Clinton raised taxes, that number went up to 1.29 million in 1995 and to 1.42 million in 1999. Yet after the Bush tax cuts, the number went down to 1.34 in 2003.[58] In fact, there is a strong positive (0.77) correlation between lower tax rates and less self-employment. Even during the vaunted 1980s when the Reagan tax cuts were supposed to have driven self-employment, the rate of Americans who were self-employed declined marginally. Correlation does not imply causation, but it does make it harder to assert that the modestly higher tax rates hurt entrepreneurship.

Finally, supply-siders talk about unleashing the energy of Americans by allowing them to reap the rewards of their ventures. Let's look at the logic behind this statement. *Unleash* assumes that Americans are being held back and that if they could only be unshackled, great things would happen. Well, let's unshackle Marc Andreessen, creator of Mosaic, the first graphical Web browser, which led to the formation of the company Netscape. If he were unshackled, he might not have attended graduate school at the University of Illinois' computer science department, since there would be less government support for the university and less support for student loans. And there may have been no Internet to need applications like Mosaic, since it was developed with government support. But personal tax rates would at least be low. Would that mean that Marc would be motivated to go out to Silicon Valley and start Netscape? Does anyone really believe that Andreessen would not have created Mosaic and moved to Silicon Valley if he had faced a 45 percent instead of 39.6 percent top tax rate?

The best way to help entrepreneurs and small-business persons is not to give them tax cuts while running up the national debt. It's to help them grow their businesses, and the best way to do that is to ensure that the economy grows, something that tax cuts on individuals don't lead to.

CONCLUSION

The Bush administration's mechanistic view of growth—pour more money in at one end through tax cuts and wait for growth to come out the other end—may have made sense in 1906, the era to which present-day conservatives look for inspiration. Then our emerging industrial economy needed to accumulate large amounts of capital to finance huge factories, and it did so by tapping the capital of wealthy tycoons. When an inventor needed capital to finance a new company or an entrepreneur wanted to expand a company, they were likely to go hat in hand to a top-hatted tycoon like J. P. Morgan. If J. P.'s taxes went up, he'd have less money to invest in Thomas Edison's electrical system or Andrew Carnegie's steel mill. This is why leading tax policy expert Thomas S. Adams advised in 1924 that cutting taxes on the wealthy was justified on the basis of giving "back to certain lines of business whose normal supply of credit comes from wealthy individuals, their normal and natural investment market."[59]

However, this 1906 approach to economic policy is woefully out of step in a 2006 economy where knowledge and competition drive growth and create opportunities for investment, where the cost of capital is much more important than who possesses it, and where capital markets are broad and global. With global capital flows and the proliferation of innovative financing instruments such as huge pension funds, mutual funds, and venture capital pools, America has the world's most innovative and liquid capital markets. To use one measurement of available capital, the ratio of what economists call M3 (the broadest definition of money, including bank deposits, money market deposits, and long-term deposits) to GDP rose from 60 percent in 1960 to 81 percent today, while bank credit increased from 37 percent to 56 percent. There's five times as much venture capital under management than there was in 1995. Though dropping recently because of slow global growth, foreign direct investment totaled over $95 billion in 2003, up from $45 billion in 1995. The market value of the Wilshire 5000, the broadest index for the U.S. equity market, increased from 35 percent of GDP in 1982 to 75 percent in

March 2002. And the cost of capital, as measured by interest rates, is at very low levels.

Today it is not limited financial capital that puts the brakes on growth; it's limited intellectual capital. To turn a phrase, there's plenty of capital chasing too few good ideas. In other words, while entrepreneurs with good ideas and good business acumen can usually find capital, capital cannot always find good ideas and innovations to invest in. This is not to say that changes in the corporate tax code cannot be a useful tool to stimulate investment by companies, but tax cuts on individuals is a roundabout and not very effective way of getting there. As OECD noted in an international study of taxation and investment, because savings flows are global, "as a practical matter, a tax policy aimed at raising investment would more usefully focus on reducing taxes on investment directly, rather than on subsidizing savings."[60] Rather than showering the wealthy with tax cuts, an effective growth strategy would provide companies with incentives to invest in research and development, workforce training, and capital equipment (including software). These kinds of steps, coupled with the right kinds of direct public investments, promise to be much more effective, less costly, and more progressive than shoveling tax cuts at the rich in hopes that they will save some of them and that some of those saved tax cuts will in turn find their way to companies investing in America.

NOTES

1. Larry Kudlow, "Cheney the Supply Sider," *National Review Online*, 24 July 2000.

2. N. Gregory Mankiw, "The Estate Tax Is One Death Penalty Too Many," *Forbes*, 4 September 2000, http://post.economics.harvard.edu/faculty/mankiw/columns/sept00.html (25 November 2005).

3. Steve Forbes, *Flat Tax Revolution: Using a Postcard to Abolish the IRS* (Washington, DC: Regnery Publishing, 2005).

4. For example, IPI argues that "All saving must receive the sort of tax treatment currently afforded pensions, various types of IRAs, 401(k), Keogh, SEP, and other saving-deferred plans currently in the tax code." Lawrence A. Hunter and Stephen J. Entin, "A Framework for Tax Reform" (Dallas, TX: Institute for Policy Innovation, 2005), 4.

5. James P. Pinkerton, *What Comes Next: The End of Big Government—and the New Paradigm Ahead* (New York: Hyperion, 1995), 262.

6. N. Gregory Mankiw, "Professor Mankiw Interview Questions, The Marshall Society Interview," 2004–2005, http://post.economics.harvard.edu/faculty/mankiw/columns/marshall.pdf (23 November 2005).

7. Cited in Daniel Altman, *Neoconomy* (New York: Public Affairs, 2004), 40.

8. CBO estimates that just 2 percent of estates have to file the tax, and only half of those are liable for any estate taxes. Congressional Budget Office, "Effects of the Federal Estate Tax on Farms and Small Business" (Washington DC: CBO, July 2005).

9. Jude Wanniski, "Fall 2003 SSU Lesson #5 The Laffer Curve," www.wanniski .com/PrintPage.asp?TextID = 2965 (22 November 2005).

10. Daniel J. Mitchell, "The Impact of Government Spending on Economic Growth" (Washington, DC: The Heritage Foundation, 15 March 2005).

11. Lindsey, *The Growth Experiment*, 196–97.

12. Lindsey, *The Growth Experiment*, 19.

13. Douglass B. Bernheim, "Taxation and Saving," in *Handbook of Public Economics* edited by A. J. Auerbach and M. Feldstein (North Holland: Elsevier Science Publishers, 2002), 46.

14. Kevin Milligan, "Tax-Preferred Savings Accounts and Marginal Tax Rates: Evidence on RRSP Participation," University of Toronto, Department of Economics, 8 May 2001.

15. N. Gregory Mankiw, "Remarks at the National Bureau of Economic Research Tax Policy and the Economy Meeting," Washington, DC: National Press Club, 4 November 2003, www.whitehouse.gov/cea/NPressClub20031104.html (23 November 2005).

16. N. Gregory Mankiw, "Remarks at the National Bureau of Economic Research."

17. U.S. Department of the Treasury, Office of Tax Analysis, "The Federal Estate and Gift Tax: Description, Profile of Taxpayers, and Economic Consequences" (Washington, DC: OTA, 1998).

18. Mark Zandi, "Statement before the Subcommittee on Economic Policy Senate Banking, Housing and Urban Affairs Committee," 22 May 2003, p. 5, http://banking .senate.gov/_files/zandi.pdf (26 November 2005).

19. Roberts, "My Time with Supply-Side Economics."

20. Ronald Reagan, Second Presidential Debate, 28 October 1980, www.pbs.org/news hour/debatingourdestiny/80debates/cart1.html (12 February 2006).

21. Office of Management and Budget, Budget of the United States Government: Fiscal Year 2006" (Washington, DC: OMB, 2005)

22. R. Glenn Hubbard, "Tax Code Revision," 7.

23. R. Glenn Hubbard, "Tax Code Revision," 7.

24. Barry Bosworth and Gary Burtless, "Effects of Tax Reform on Labor Supply, Investment and Savings," *Journal Of Economic Perspectives* 6 no. 1 (Winter 1992): 3–25, 15.

25. Ian Dew-Becker and Robert J. Gordon, "Where Did the Productivity Growth Go? Inflation Dynamics and the Distribution of Income," paper presented at the 81st meeting of the Brookings Panel on Economic Activity, Washington, DC, 8–9 September 2005, 76.

26. Foreign investors bought 81 percent of new treasury debt from March 2001 through September 2005. Gene Sperling and Christian Weller, "State of the Economy" (Washington, DC: Center for American Progress, 2006).

27. Robert Barro, "Bush's Tax Cuts: Reaganomics Redux," *Business Week*, 20 January 2003.

28. Mitch Daniels, "Press Briefing on the Budget by OMB Director Mitch Daniels," 3 February 2003, www.whitehouse.gov/omb/speeches/daniels_04budget.html (26 November 2005).

29. Daniel J. Mitchell, "Supplement to 'The Impact of Government Spending on Economic Growth'" (Washington, DC: The Heritage Foundation, March 15, 2005,)

30. R. Glenn Hubbard, "A Framework for Economic Policy."

31. Lindsey, *The Growth Experiment*, 11.

32. R. Glenn Hubbard, *Money: The Financial System and the Economy* (4th ed.) (Reading, MA: Addison-Wesley, 2001), 653.

33. N. Gregory Mankiw, "Remarks at the Annual Meeting of the National Association of Business Economists," Atlanta, Georgia, 15 September 2003, http://post.economics.harvard.edu/faculty/mankiw/columns/nabe.pdf (22 November 2005).

34. Slemrod and Bakija, *Taxing Ourselves*, 108.

35. Thomas Laubach, "New Evidence on the Interest Rate Effects of Budget Deficits and the Debt," Federal Reserve Working Paper (Washington, DC. Board of Governors of the Federal Reserve System, May 2003).

36. William G. Gale and Peter R. Orszag, "Budget Deficits, National Saving, and Interest Rates," *Brookings Papers on Economic Activity*, Fall 2004, 101–87.

37. Slemrod and Bakija, *Taxing Ourselves*, 107.

38. Isabel Sawhill and Alice Rivlin, "Restoring Fiscal Sanity: How to Balance the Budget" (Washington: Brookings Institution, 2004), 9.

39. Congressional Budget Office, "An Analysis of the President's Budgetary Proposals For Fiscal Year 2004" (Washington, DC: CBO March 2003).

40. Leibfritz, Thornton, and Bibbee, "Taxation and Economic Performance," 8.

41. Leibfritz, Thornton, and Bibbee, "Taxation and Economic Performance," 32.

42. "The Economics of Savings: The Shift Away from Thrift," *The Economist*, 7 April 2005.

43. R. Glenn Hubbard, "Tax Code Revision," Testimony to Committee on House Ways and Means Committee, 8 June 2005, 8.

44. "The Economics of Savings," *The Economist*.

45. Lindsey, *The Growth Experiment*.

46. M. A. Akhtar and Ethan S. Harris, "The Supply Side Consequences of U.S. Fiscal Policy in the 1980s" (New York: Federal Reserve Bank of New York, 1991).

47. Leibfritz, Thornton, and Bibbee, "Taxation and Economic Performance," 111.

48. Douglas B. Bernheim, "Taxation and Saving," in *Handbook of Public Economics* edited by A. J. Auerbach and M. Feldstein, (North Holland: Elsevier Science Publishers, 2002), 47.

49. Douglas B. Bernheim, "Taxation and Saving."

50. Slemrod and Bakija, *Taxing Ourselves*, 129.

51. Slemrod and Bakija, *Taxing Ourselves*, 130.

52. Wesbury, "Taking the Voodoo Out of Tax Cuts."

53. N. Gregory Mankiw, "Remarks of Dr. N. Gregory Mankiw. Chairman Council of Economic Advisers at the Annual Meeting of the National Association of Business Economists."

54. George W. Bush, President Outlines Economic Growth Agenda (White House Office of the Press Secretary, 26 October 2005).

55. Hubbard, "Testimony before the Special Committee on Aging."

56. R. Glenn Hubbard, "Commentary on Chapter 13," in *Does Atlas Shrug* edited by Joel B. Slemrod (Cambridge, MA: Harvard University Press, 2000), 457.

57. Martin A. Sullivan, "Do Economists Matter," *Tax Notes*, 15 January 2001, 278.

57. Clearly the 2001 recession did contribute to the decline in entrepreneurship. U.S. Department of Labor, Bureau of Labor Statistics, "Business Employment Dynamics."

58. Thomas S. Adams, quoted in Andrew Mellon, *Taxation: The People's Business*, 87.

60. Leibfritz, Thornton, and Bibbee, "Taxation and Economic Performance," 24.

Chapter Seven

Do Lower Taxes Lead to Higher Tax Revenues?

Blessed are the young for they shall inherit the national debt.

—Herbert Hoover

Perhaps the most widely known and most controversial claim made by many supply-siders is that cutting taxes boosts government revenue. As economist David Henderson states, "The term 'supply-sider' has come to mean someone who believes that an x percent cut in tax rates will—through its effect on the incentive to work, to save and invest, and to avoid and evade taxes—lead to much less than an x percent cut, and perhaps even to an increase, in tax revenues."[1] This notion of a free tax-cut lunch was made famous in the late 1970s by Arthur Laffer, whose Laffer curve predicted that above a certain rate, an increase in taxes would produce no revenue because people would work and invest less.

At one level, Laffer is right. If the government taxed income from work

---

Why Don't Tax Cuts Boost Revenues?

1. Since tax cuts on individuals don't boost work, savings, or investment they don't lead to faster economic growth or more revenues.
2. Since the 1980s, the top marginal tax rate is already low and is significantly below the point on the "Laffer curve" where reductions in tax rates boost revenues.
3. While tax cuts may produce some income shifting out of tax-exempt activities, producing some offsetting tax revenues, they are nowhere near enough to make up for the revenue loss.

and investment at 100 percent, there would be little work or investment and little revenue.[2] On the other hand, if it levied no taxes, there would be no revenue. But this simplistic formulation doesn't tell us anything useful. What we really need to know is where on the curve do increased taxes lead to lower revenues? Does reducing the top rate from 39.6 percent to 35 percent bring in more or less tax revenues?

The Laffer curve can't provide an answer to that question. But research can, and it's pretty clear that unless rates are much higher than their levels of the last two decades, lower taxes—surprise, surprise—will lead to lower government revenues. As Joel Slemrod notes, with respect to the evidence that tax cuts do not produce more revenues, "all but the most ardent supply-siders now concede this point."[3]

Not only do many concede it, but many supply-siders now claim that either they never said that tax cuts would pay for themselves, or if they did, it was a mistake. Conservative economist Stephen Moore maintains that "never did President Reagan nor any of his economic advisers predict that the tax-rate cuts would increase tax revenues. They merely predicted that the revenue losses from the tax cuts would be lower than anticipated."[4] Former Reagan administration economist William Niskanen agrees, stating, "Supply side economics . . . does not conclude that a general reduction in tax rates would increase tax revenues, nor did any government economist or budget projection by the Reagan administration ever make this claim."[5]

While many supply-siders will grant that some radical Lafferites claimed that tax cuts would pay for themselves, they dismiss them as charlatans who made it harder for "conventional" supply-siders to make the case for tax cuts. Martin Feldstein tells us that "the loose talk of the supply-side extremists gave fundamentally good policies a bad name and led to quantitative mistakes that not only contributed to subsequent budget deficits but that also made it more difficult to modify policy when those deficits became apparent."[6] William Niskanen also tries to disassociate himself from those pesky Lafferites, claiming that "supply-siders predicted their tax cuts would pay for themselves. This was nonsense from day one, because the credible evidence overwhelmingly indicates that revenue feedbacks from tax cuts is 35 cents per dollar, at most. Are we really gullible enough to accept a free dinner while still suffering the indigestion from our 'free' lunch?"[7] Given that the Bush administration actually consistently tells Americans that the tax cuts will *reduce* the budget deficit, supply-siders must think the answer is yes. It's quite common for the president to make statements like, "To continue reducing the deficit we need to keep the taxes low,"[8] and "There's a mind-set in Washington that says, you cut the taxes, we're going to have less money to spend. Well, the growth, the economic vitality that has been set off by the tax cuts has been good for our treasury."[9]

Not only does the Bush administration promote more tax cuts by claiming they are needed to *reduce* budget deficits, but the record shows that supply-side economists and conservative elected officials have been singing the same song for over eighty years. In arguing for cutting the top marginal tax rate in 1924, Coolidge Treasury Secretary Andrew Mellon argued that "high rates of taxation do not necessarily mean large revenue to the Government, and that more revenue may often be obtained by lower rates."[10] Sixty years later, Reagan-era officials repeated the same refrain. Former Reagan administration official Paul Craig Roberts admits that, "during the campaign Reagan said he would balance the budget. It was a traditional Republican theme and one that the Lafferite version of supply-side economics made too easy."[11] The *Wall Street Journal* editorial page dismissed the Congressional Budget Office's budget projections, which showed correctly that the Reagan tax cuts would lead to growing budget deficits, by stating, "If you think any of these estimates can tell you what the deficit will be in 1984, lie down until you get over it."[12] Supply-side champion Jude Wanniski agreed, stating that "interest rates declined as the Reagan tax cuts took effect and the deficits swelled. That combination led me to predict that as the lower tax rates would steadily increase the rate of economic growth over several fiscal years, the budget deficits would turn to surpluses."[13]

Ronald Reagan himself sold his tax cuts using the Laffer curve. Reagan was fond of quoting fourteenth-century Arab historian Ibn Khaldûn, who said, "It should be known that at the beginning of a dynasty, taxation yields a large revenue from small assessments. At the end of the dynasty, taxation yields a small revenue from large assessments."[14] In proposing his 1981 tax cuts, he proclaimed,

> The economic recovery package that I've outlined to you over the past weeks is, I deeply believe, the only answer that we have left. Reducing the growth of spending, cutting marginal tax rates, providing relief from overregulation, and following a non-inflationary and predictable monetary policy are interwoven measures which will ensure that we have addressed each of the severe dislocations which threaten our economic future. These policies will make our economy stronger, and the stronger economy will balance the budget which we're committed to do by 1984.[15]

He went on to argue that rescinding or stalling his tax cuts "might well stall recovery further, suppressing tax revenues and ensuring permanently high budget deficits."[16] In other words, *not* cutting taxes would lead to less revenue. Perhaps this is why he quipped, "I am not worried about the deficit. It is big enough to take care of itself." As *Business Week* states, "Reagan and his supply-side advisors believed that big tax cuts would pay for themselves by generating higher tax revenues through greater economic growth. It never happened."[17] In fact, the budget was in deficit every year of the Reagan and first Bush administrations.

Supply-siders' advocacy of "revenue-raising" tax cuts was so pervasive that supply-sider Greg Mankiw complained that, "in the past, however, some supply-siders pushed their arguments to ridiculous extremes—claiming, for instance, that tax cuts would generate so much growth that they would be self-financing. The experience of the Reagan years put this theory to rest."[18] In his best-selling macroeconomics textbook, Mankiw concludes, with respect to the Reagan years, "People on fad diets put their health at risk but rarely achieve the permanent weight loss they desire. Similarly, when politicians rely on the advice of charlatans and cranks, they rarely get the desirable results they anticipate. After Reagan's election, Congress passed the cut in tax rates that Reagan advocated, but the tax cut did not cause tax revenues to rise."[19] Still, Mankiw can't bring himself to completely reject Lafferism, stating, "I don't believe that the revenue feedback is enough to fully pay for a tax cut in most cases, but it is likely to make a meaningful offset."[20] In other words, tax cuts may not make money for government, but they don't lose much either.

How do supply-siders think tax cuts were supposed to produce revenues? Was it through more work, savings, and investment? Not exactly. As Lindsey admits, "There is no reason to suspect factor supply as either the sole or even the dominant way that changes in tax rates affect tax revenues."[21] Rather, "Changes in portfolio behavior and the form of compensation employees receive may be of more consequence." In other words, tax cuts don't boost work or savings, but they do lead people to rearrange their income so that they pay a bit more taxes than they would otherwise. As we saw in chapter 6, lower taxes do induce taxpayers, especially higher-income ones, to rearrange their finances. This kind of tax reshuffling is why Lindsey argued that the Reagan tax cuts on the wealthy brought in more money than they lost, while tax cuts for the upper-middle class "just about broke even," and tax cuts for everyone else were money losers.[22]

But wait a minute. Even if cutting taxes encourages some high earners to give a bit less to charity, switch a bit less income to stock options, and invest in fewer tax-free government bonds, that's not much of an effect. This kind of income shifting has no effect on economic growth. And while it may produce some offsetting tax revenues, they are nowhere near enough to make up for the revenue loss. It's comparable to saying "we will cut taxes and get no economic growth, but at least we'll only lose 75 cents on the dollar." But actually it's even worse than that. If tax cuts don't lead to a one-for-one loss of revenue because taxpayers do not deduct as much income from their taxes, it still means that taxpayers are giving less to charity, are investing less in low-income housing, are buying fewer municipal bonds, and are generally making fewer socially desirable investments.

Perhaps it's possible to chalk up supply-siders' belief in the Laffer curve during the 1980s as youthful enthusiasm. The effects on the budget of the 1980s tax cuts experiment were not yet fully upon them. However, the many supply-siders who have kept the Laffer curve flame burning bright long since have no such excuse. Larry Lindsey admits that some supply-siders "maintained that the right tax cut would substantially pay for itself."[23] And he's one of them. His 1990 book, *The Growth Experiment*, sounds at times like Arthur Laffer wrote it, as when he states, "It therefore seems likely that the revenue maximizing top marginal tax rate for the personal income tax is below the 70 percent statutory rate which existed prior to 1982."[24] Perhaps a tax rate that high might reduce revenues, or certainly wouldn't raise as much as expected. In this sense, supply-siders are right. But the debate has never been about whether the Laffer curve is right or not. At some level, exorbitant tax rates would reduce revenue. But there is little evidence to claim that tax rates below 45 percent are in that range. Lindsey goes on to note that "tax increases would tend to slow the rate of economic growth not only for the treasury but for all Americans."[25] In other words, tax increases would reduce net tax revenue.

Bob Dole sold his 10 percent across-the-board tax cut proposal in 1996 in part on the claim that it would pay for itself. The same year, *Forbes* magazine praised a study claiming that if taxes had been dramatically lower since 1948, government would have generated even more revenues than it lost, "enough to fund all programs now enacted—and eliminate all deficits since 1949."[26] Five years later, the Heritage Foundation argued that tax cuts "will spur the economy, which in turn will lead to even more tax revenue."[27] That same year, Larry Kudlow predicted that because of the Bush tax cuts, "future budget surpluses will rise, not fall, paving the way for new tax reform and simplification opportunities."[28] Greg Mankiw argued that repealing the estate tax would actually raise more tax revenues than it lost.[29]

When considering the revenue effects of moving to a 17 percent flat tax, former GOP presidential candidate Pete du Pont argued that the results would be "very positive, because income tax rate reductions tend to raise income tax receipts."[30] A year later in 2002, Glenn Hubbard argued that "pro-growth tax policies that lower marginal tax rates and reduce the tax on productive risk-taking are good long-run policies to build budgetary resources over the long term."[31] He later contended that "the tax relief the President suggested in his January [2003] proposal does not significantly worsen the government's fiscal position."[32] Most recently, Stephen Moore argued that increases in tax revenues in 2005 over what were projected were "an eye-popping vindication of the Laffer Curve."[33] But this modest growth was simply a result of an economy emerging from a protracted anemic recovery. What has been vindicated is not the Laffer curve, but the fact that supply-siders still believe that lower taxes will not produce lower tax revenues.

The belief in the Laffer curve is perhaps why the Bush administration's budget predictions have been so notoriously overoptimistic. As Daniel Gross notes, in "February 2002 the administration projected that revenues for Fiscal 2003 . . . would be $2.048 trillion. Instead . . . they came in at $1.782 trillion—thirteen percent below the estimate. The next year the administration predicted that Fiscal 2004 revenues would grow from an estimated $1.836 trillion in Fiscal 2003 to $1.922 trillion in Fiscal 2004—up 4.6 percent. But the amount turned out to be only $1.88 trillion." As Gross notes, "Detect a pattern? (Something tells me this isn't what the administration had in mind when it promised to use dynamic scoring.)"[34]

If voters realized that budget deficits follow tax cuts like spring follows winter, they might not be so willing to support low taxes and the elected officials who push for them. This is what the *Wall Street Journal* was so worried about when they warned in 1981 that if people realize that the Laffer curve is bogus, "we will be back in the same old rut of trying to balance the budget three years hence by allowing inflation to raise taxes."[35] Indeed, supply-siders correctly fear that paying off the national debt will preclude further tax cuts (just as many liberal Keynesians worry that paying off the debt will preclude future spending increases). Conservative economist John Makin argues, "The biggest downside to simply paying off the [national] debt over the next decade arises from the need for taxes and tax rates to be higher than they would be if we aimed just to stabilize the debt-to-GDP ratio."[36] He goes on to pose the question, "Spending a trillion to lower tax rates. Is it more likely to benefit the economy than leaving tax rates at current levels in order to cut the federal debt by another trillion dollars?" Indeed, he calls proposals to pay down the national debt a "preposterous idea."

EVIDENCE FROM THE REAL WORLD

Anyone wanting to refute the Laffer curve has only to look at the experience of the last twenty-five years. After the Reagan tax cuts, the budget deficit exploded. After the Clinton tax increases and the bipartisan 1995 budget deal, the budget deficits turned into budget surpluses, enabling our nation to pay off some of the national debt accumulated over the prior couple of decades.

Now, after the Bush tax cuts, budget deficits are back with a vengeance. This is not to say that the Clinton taxes were the sole cause of the turnaround in the budget. Clearly the technology-led transformation of the economy starting in the mid-1990s provided a strong boost. But tax policy helped.

Because the 1980s budget deficits are such a repudiation of Lafferism, supply-siders take great pains to blame them on anything but tax cuts. Let's look at the facts. Because the federal government ran up huge deficits to finance World War II, the national debt peaked at 118 percent of GDP in 1946. As the economy grew and most Republican and Democratic administrations practiced fiscal discipline, by the last year of the Carter administration, public debt had fallen to 26.5 percent as a share of GDP. But as the Reagan administration added more debt than the prior thirty-nine administrations combined, the debt had swelled to 64 percent of GDP by the time Bill Clinton took office.[37]

Supply-siders do not dispute these numbers, but they claim that spending increases, rather than tax cuts, were the culprit. Larry Lindsey claims that "the Reagan tax cuts contributed only trivially to the booming deficits of the 1980s."[38] Paul Craig Roberts agrees, stating that "the 'Reagan deficits' occurred because inflation fell substantially below the budget assumptions, and therefore real spending rose above projections."[39] Reagan himself joined the fray, arguing in 1982 that "a propaganda campaign would have you believe these deficits are caused by our so-called massive tax cut and defense build up. . . . But there is simply no escaping the truth, current and projected deficits result from sharp increases in non-defense spending."[40] Most recently, Bush budget director Mitch Daniels defended the Bush tax cuts by trying to rewrite the 1980s budget history. He urged us to

> get the history right first. After the tax cuts of the '80s, like the tax cuts of the '60s, and like most other tax cuts, revenues in the next few years went up a lot. Revenues went up a lot. Now, there was a lot of other history going on in the '80s, and that involved the rebuilding of defenses, it involved a Congress which wanted to keep on spending on a number of other fronts. And also it involved, until those tax cuts took hold, a weak economy. And that's what gave you the deficits. So the answer is, if we take those steps—and the President has proposed yet again aggressive steps to grow the economy—that's our best chance of another unexpected surplus coming back.[41]

Let's turn to the OMB numbers. Under Reagan, federal tax revenues fell from 20.1 to 18.6 percent of GDP, a decline of 1.5 percentage points, and as figure 7.1 shows, income taxes declined even more. Because revenue was down and debt up, the share of the budget devoted to interest payments increased from 2.3 to 3.3 percent of GNP between 1981 and 1995. Moreover,

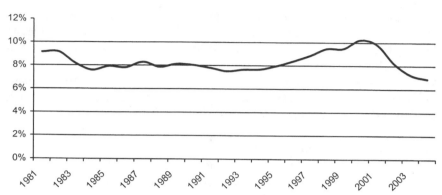

Figure 7.1   Income Taxes as a Share of GDP

Source: Office of Management and Budget, *Budget of the United States Government, FY 2007.*

to the extent that spending increased, it was spending that the Reagan administration wanted, not runaway spending pushed by Democrats. Defense
spending increased from 5.3 to 6.4 percent of GDP, while nondefense outlays
actually declined from 15.1 to 14.1 percent between FY 1980 and FY 1984.[42]

The role of growing interest payments due to tax cuts should not be underestimated. One problem with "starving the beast" by cutting taxes is that
interest payments to service the growing national debt go up. Journalist
Michael Kinsey calculated that if a dollar of tax cuts leads to a spending cut
of fifty cents (an optimistic assumption at best), within twenty years total
government spending would be back to where it was in year one and would
grow after that because of increased compounded interest payments.[43]

When Bill Clinton was elected, he inherited the results of the fiscal irresponsibility of the Reagan administration. But Clinton was able to bring
down the budget deficit by boosting taxes and working with Republicans in
Congress to hold the line on spending growth. As a result, the budget went
from a deficit $290 billion in 1992 to a surplus of $236 billion in 2000, while
the national debt fell. (See figures 7.2 and 7.3.) After the Clinton tax
increases, income taxes increased from 7.2 to 10.2 percent of GDP from 1993
to 2000. Even Greg Mankiw credits this commonsense approach, writing,
"It's important to understand how we got to this happy state. Clinton tries to
take credit by saying he's reduced the size of government. There is, surprisingly, some truth to the claim. Federal outlays as a percentage of GDP have
fallen from 21.5% in 1993 to 18.7% in 1999, the lowest level since 1974.
This fall of 2.8 points of GDP compares with a drop of only 1.0 point during
the eight years of the so-called Reagan revolution. Perhaps we've learned an
important lesson: A Democratic President with a Republican Congress may
be more fiscally conservative than the opposite combination."[44]

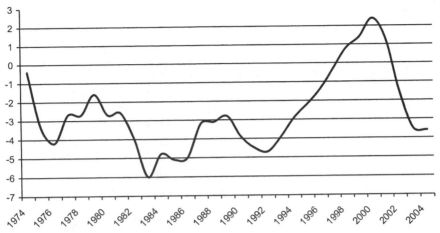

Figure 7.2   Federal Budget Deficits as a Share of GDP

Source: Office of Management and Budget.

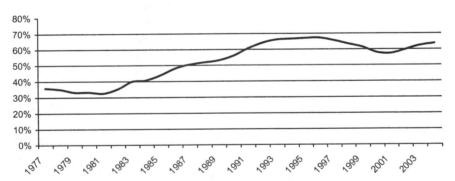

Figure 7.3   Federal Debt as a Share of GDP

Source: Office of Management and Budget.

Certainly this was a more fiscally responsible combination than the current arrangement of a Republican president and Congress. While President Bush inherited a $128 billion surplus in FY 2001, it quickly reversed to a $412 billion deficit in FY 2004. During the first four years of the administration, the Republican-controlled Congress increased the national debt limit by a stunning $3 trillion—a 50 percent increase in the cumulative debt from all of America's prior history. Through the first five years of the Bush administration, over $1.7 trillion has been added to the national debt. It now stands at $7.4 trillion, equal to $49,600 for every American worker, more than their average yearly income.

Taking a page out of the Reagan playbook, the Bush administration blames high spending for this most recent swelling of the debt. This time, they are partly right; high spending as well as large tax increases contributed to this unhappy situation that the nation finds itself in. While during the Clinton administration federal expenditures as a share of GDP fell from 21.8 percent in 1992 to 18.2 percent in 2000, they had increased to 19.5 percent in 2005. As the libertarian Reason Institute noted, Bush "is generous with the money of people who are in no position to object, either because they are too young or because they haven't been born yet."[45] Republican fiscal hawk Pete Peterson quips, "So-called conservatives are outpandering LBJ [Lyndon Johnson]. They must have it all: guns, butter, *and* tax cuts."[46]

One reason the deficit and debt have gotten out of control is that the Bush administration failed to work with the Republican-controlled Congress to extend the budget rules that were so effective during the Clinton administration in controlling spending and limiting tax cuts. Moreover, having never met a spending bill he didn't like, President Bush is the first president serving a full term since John Quincy Adams not to have vetoed a single piece of legislation. Reagan was only slightly better: federal spending grew faster during his administration than under any president since before World War II. In fact, the evidence shows that the so-called starve-the-beast strategy may actually be counterproductive, with lower taxes actually corresponding to higher spending. The libertarian Cato Institute recently concluded that, "controlling for the unemployment rate, federal spending [from 1981 to 2000] increased by about one-half percent of GDP for each one percentage point decline in the relative level of federal tax revenues."[47] Even though it's fashionable today in supply-side circles to claim that tax cuts don't raise more revenue than they cost, most supply-siders now declare that tax cuts don't yield a one-for-one loss of revenue. If so, then tax cuts really don't starve the beast as much as put it on an Atkins diet.

But even with increases, federal spending as a share of the economy is still below its average of the last four decades, in large part because of efforts during the 1990s to restrain the growth of spending.[48] The more serious problem has been on the revenue side. In 2004, federal revenues were just 16.2 percent of GDP, compared to an average of 18.3 percent from 1962 to 2001.[49] Non–Social Security revenues fell from 15.1 percent of GDP to a sixty-two-year low of just 11.3 percent.[50] Robert McIntyre, head of Citizens for Tax Justice, ranked non–Social Security tax receipts as a share of the economy since 1943: FYs 2003 and 2004 are tied for the lowest, FY 2002 ranks as third lowest, and FY 2005 will probably rank fifth lowest. And while economic difficulties have contributed somewhat to the slowdown in revenues, the lion's share of the drop-off stems from the Bush tax cuts. Income tax revenues plunged from 9.8 percent of GDP when Bush took office to 6.9 percent in 2004 and fell from $1,004 billion in 2000 to just $765 billion in 2004. Gale and Orszag estimate that the tax cuts in 2004 reduced revenues by $286 billion, or about 2.5 percent of GDP.[51] Even the administration's own Office of Management and Budget 2004 Mid-Session Review admits as much, calculating that tax cuts accounted for 57 percent of the budget deterioration.[52]

The Bush administration tries to defend their lack of fiscal discipline in three ways. First, they argue correctly that as a share of GDP, the debt is not at an all-time high. But that peak was reached when the United States had undertaken total mobilization to fight World War II, hardly an appropriate benchmark. A better one would be during the Clinton administration, when the average annual deficit was approximately 0.25 percent of GDP compared to 1.9 percent during the Bush administration.

Second, they claim that they plan to cut the deficit in half. But this is like a basketball team losing by thirty points and claiming that in the next game it will cut the gap to only fifteen and then declare victory. Moreover, even if they can accomplish that, it would be a dubious accomplishment, since they would still be piling on the debt. Even worse, it's unlikely that they will pull it off, for their deficit projections are based on rosy assumptions such as that the tax cuts will not be made permanent, that there will be no new tax cuts, and that domestic discretionary spending outside of homeland security will be cut by 12 percent below 2004, adjusted for inflation.[53]

Realistic budget projections paint a more disturbing picture. CBO was recently asked to study future budget projections assuming that Bush's tax cuts will be enacted and the prior tax cuts made permanent. It assumed a big slowdown on spending on Iraq, tight caps on domestic agency budgets, and new individual Social Security accounts. It predicted that the budget deficit will rise to $370 billion by 2009, the year the Bush White House predicts a deficit of $162 billion. Even worse, the deficit would hit $521 billion for 2015, just when baby boomers are retiring in droves.

It would be one thing if this increase in spending were going to investments in areas like research and development, education, or infrastructure. But a growing share goes to pay interest to the holders of federal bonds. Interest payments are projected to increase to $254 billion in 2008, costing the average working taxpayer almost $1,400 per year, almost as much as they pay for health care and prescription drugs combined.[54] In fact, under reasonable assumptions, the national debt, which hit a near-term low of 33 percent of GDP in 2001, is projected to grow from 38 percent of GDP in 2004 to 46 percent in 2013, and then to skyrocket to untenable levels (approaching 100 percent of GDP) as baby boomers retire en masse. Moreover, the long-term picture is worse, if that's possible.

Finally, they claim that they are trying to cut spending but that Democrats won't let them. It's true that many Democrats have opposed reining in spending, especially in needed areas like Social Security and Medicare. But so have some Republicans. Moreover, there are plenty of areas in the budget—such as agricultural price supports, expansion of NASA, defense spending, and Medicare—where the administration has taken the lead, or at least has done nothing to resist significant increases.

When confronted with this fiscal mess, the response of former Bush budget director Mitch Daniels was that the government fiscally is "in fine shape."[55] Tell that to my fourteen-year-old son who will one day have to pay off my share of the national debt with his higher taxes (or lower federal spending). By 2015, when he turns twenty-two and presumably graduates from college, his present will be an invoice from Uncle Sam for a staggering $82,000 (his share of the projected national debt of $13.7 billion).[56] As we ask our youth to shoulder the primary responsibility for fighting the war against terror by risking their lives as soldiers, is it right for us to avoid acting with fiscal responsibility toward them?

EVIDENCE REGARDING TAX CUTS AND REVENUES

If Lafferites look for comfort in scholarly studies, they will surely be disappointed. Most studies of the effect of tax cuts on government revenues support the commonsense notion that they reduce revenues. Most if not all of the studies touted by supply-siders that claim to refute this commonsense rely on faulty assumptions or use only certain years to make their point.

Perhaps the economist with the most at stake in sustaining Lafferism is Laffer himself. He begins his defense by claiming a Laffer effect from the Coolidge tax cuts of the 1920s. He shows that federal tax revenue went down 9.2 percent from 1920 to 1924, but went up 0.1 percent from 1924 to 1928 after top rates were cut.[57] But taxes were cut in 1921, when federal revenues were $5.6 billion. They proceeded to fall to $3.7 billion in 1925. They only gradually increased to $4.2 billion in 1930 as the economy grew. However, after the Depression—which, according to supply-side theory, was not supposed to happen, since taxes had been recently slashed to 25 percent and stayed at that level until 1931—tax revenues fell, and it was not until 1938 that they exceeded 1921 levels.[58]

Conservative economists Martin Feldstein and Daniel Feenberg used a similarly misleading selection of years when they found that the 1993 tax increases led high-income taxpayers to report 7.8 percent less taxable income in 1993 than otherwise would have been expected given the increased tax rates. They estimated that this decline caused the treasury to lose more than half the extra revenue that would have been collected had there been no compensating Laffer effect. Yet Sammartino and Weiner found that almost all of this tax revenue loss was due to one-year shifting of income back to 1992 and that when the period was extended out to 1995, there was no reduction in tax revenue.[59]

As further proof of the Laffer curve, supply-siders point to the fact that the 1986 Tax Reform Act (TRA) did not lead to a precipitous fall in revenues as might otherwise be expected after a cut in rates. But, besides cutting rates, the TRA also closed a significant number of tax loopholes, bringing in compensating revenues. As Goolsbee argues, using the TRA as a "natural experiment" is rife with difficulties, because the act "embodied many tax changes, not just marginal rate cuts."[60] Joel Slemrod notes,

> Although that work emphasizes the potential importance of behavioral responses to marginal tax rates, the results in this paper suggest that the evidence on which those conclusions are based—evidence from the 1980s—is atypical in the historical experience. . . . The notion that governments could raise more money by cutting rates is, indeed, a glorious idea. Unfortunately for all of us, the data from the historical record suggest that it is unlikely to be true at anything like today's marginal tax rates. It seems that, for now at least, we will just have to keep paying for our tax cuts the old-fashioned way.[61]

Slemrod notes that one reason most studies don't find evidence for the Laffer effect is that with top federal rates below 40 percent—presumably well below the peak of the Laffer curve—the notion that tax cuts can produce significant offsetting revenues is simply not relevant. Even Larry Lindsey admits that the positive revenue effects of cutting the top rate from 33 to 19 percent would be "very small compared to the positive effects of cutting the top rate from 70 to 50 or even from 50 to 33."[62] He goes on to admit that "the new tax rates after Reagan's first tax cuts, ranging from 38 to 50 percent seem to be generally below the revenue-maximizing rate."[63] But even this judgment from Lindsey doesn't stop supply-siders—including the nation's supply-sider in chief, George Bush—from continuing to try to sell tax cuts with the claim that they will lose little, if any, money for the treasury.

NEW REPUBLICANS AND BUDGET DEFICITS

Though the intellectual ties of modern-day Republicans to early twentieth-century Republicans are considerable, there is one major area of difference: their approach to fiscal responsibility. Republicans used to stand for fiscal discipline. Now they stand for tax cut discipline.

Emblematic of the former attitude of fiscal rectitude was William McKinley, who once said, "It has been our uniform practice to retire, not increase, our outstanding obligations, and this policy must again be resumed and vigorously enforced." Coolidge Treasury Secretary Andrew Mellon agreed, arguing that "the public debt must be paid in order to stop the tremendous interest charges which are paid each year out of taxes."[64] Now supply-side Republicans don't mind debt, but they hate taxes. Larry Lindsey asserts that "paying off the national debt should not be an end in itself." For supply-siders, cutting taxes is an end in itself, even if it means passing on an $8 trillion national debt to the next generation. Running deficits once in a while may be justifiable when the economy is in recession, but what's different today is that Republicans are willing to run deficits in good and bad times, leading to a rapidly expanding massive national debt. While some level of national debt may be justifiable, there seems to be no justification for a debt the size of the current one, which is projected to keep growing.

Should political ideology—a long-standing commitment to reduce taxes, eliminate the progressive tax, and minimize the role of government whether it makes sense or not—be masquerading as economic policy in the world's largest economy? Today's Republicans are "factory-era" Republicans when it comes to taxes (fewer and flatter taxes are better), but they are "mass-production corporate era" Republicans when it comes to spending (more spending on "their" programs is better). Not only do individual tax cuts not boost work or savings, but they lead to significant declines in government revenues and significant increases in government debt. On top of that, they lead to vastly increased inequality, as most of the tax cuts flow to the most well-off Americans. It is to this that we now turn.

NOTES

1. David R. Henderson, "Are We All Supply-siders Now?," *Contemporary Economic Policy* 7, no. 4 (1989): 116–28.

2. It's possible that some people work out of other motives than pecuniary ones, such as altruism.

3. Joel Slemrod and Jon Bakija, *Taxing Ourselves: A Citizen's Guide to the Debate over Taxes* (Cambridge, MA: MIT Press, 2004), 151.

4. Stephen Moore, "Think Twice about Gregory Mankiw: This Harvard Economist Does Not Belong on the Bush Economic Team," *National Review Online*, 28 February 2003, www.nationalreview.com/moore/moore022803b.asp (accessed 25 November 2005).

5. William Niskanen, *Reaganomics: An Insider's Account of the Policies and the People* (New York: Oxford University Press, 1988).

6. Martin Feldstein, "Supply Side Economics: Old Truths and New Claims" (working paper 1792, National Bureau of Economic Research, Cambridge, MA, January 1986), 5.

7. William A. Niskanen and Stephen Moore, "Supply Tax Cuts and the Truth about the Reagan Economic Record," Cato Policy Analysis no. 261 (Washington, DC: Cato Institute, 22 October 1996).

8. George W. Bush, "President Outlines Economic Growth Agenda," White House Office of the Press Secretary, 26 October 2005.

9. George W. Bush, "President Discusses Strong and Growing Economy," Chicago, 6 January 2006, www.whitehouse.gov/news/releases/2006/01/20060106-7.html (accessed 31 January 2006).

10. Andrew Mellon, *Taxation: The People's Business* (New York: Macmillan, 1924), 16.

11. Paul Craig Roberts, *The Supply-Side Revolution: An Insider's Account of Policy-making in Washington* (Cambridge, MA: Harvard University Press, 1984), 90.

12. Quoted in Roberts, *The Supply-Side Revolution*, 128.

13. Jude Wanniski, "Fall 2003 SSU Lesson #5 The Laffer Curve," www.wanniski .com/PrintPage.asp?TextID = 2965 (accessed 22 November 2005).

14. 'Abd-ar-Rahmân Abû Zayd ibn Khaldûn, *The Muqaddimah: An Introduction to History*, trans. Franz Rosenthal, ed. N. J. Dawood (Princeton, NJ: Princeton University Press, 1967), 23.

15. Ronald Reagan, "Economic Recovery Program" (speech delivered 28 April 1981), www.townhall.com/documents/recovery.html (accessed 22 November 2005).

16. Roberts, *The Supply-Side Revolution*, 230.

17. *Business Week*, "The Real Economic Legacy of Ronald Reagan: There's Much More to It Than Tax Cuts and Small Government," 21 June 2004, 154.

18. Gregory Mankiw, "Remarks at the Annual Meeting of the National Association of Business Economists," Atlanta, GA, 15 September 2003, http://post.economics.harvard .edu/faculty/mankiw/columns/nabe.pdf (accessed 22 November 2005).

19 Mankiw omitted these offending passages in his latest edition of *Macroeconomics* after George W. Bush was elected president. Nevertheless, unappreciative hardcore Laffer-ites opposed his nomination as head of the CEA. For example, Stephen Moore campaigned against Mankiw's being appointed to the CEA under Bush, stating, "This (CEA chair) is a pivotal position in the White House. It is imperative that President Bush put a strong and persuasive advocate of supply-side economic policies in this top job—someone to help sell the financial benefits of the current tax-cut plan and pursue even bolder pro-growth policies down the road." Stephen Moore, "Think Twice about Gregory Mankiw: This Harvard Economist Does Not Belong on the Bush Economic Team," *National Review Online*, 28 February 2003, www.nationalreview.com/moore/moore022803b.asp (accessed 25 November 2005).

20. Mankiw, "Remarks at the Annual Meeting of the National Association of Business Economists."

21. Lindsey, *The Growth Experiment*, 7.

22. Lindsey, *The Growth Experiment*, 10.

23. Lindsey, *The Growth Experiment*, 8.

24. Lindsey, *The Growth Experiment*, 35.

25. Lindsey, *The Growth Experiment*, 179.

26. Peter Brimelow, "It's the Taxes Stupid," *Forbes* 157, no. 3 (12 February 1996): 461.

27. Peter B. Sperry, "Growing Surplus, Shrinking Debt: The Compelling Case for Tax Cuts Now" (Washington, DC: Heritage Foundation, 7 February 2001), 6.

28. Larry Kudlow, "Looking Up, Down the Road," *National Review Online*, 29 May 2001, www.nationalreview.com/kudlow/kudlow052901.shtml (accessed 24 November 2005).

29. Gregory N. Mankiw, "Remarks at the National Bureau of Economic Research Tax Policy and the Economy Meeting" (Washington, DC: National Press Club, 4 November 2003), www.whitehouse.gov/cea/NPressClub20031104.html (accessed 23 November 2005).

30. Pete du Pont, "Flattery Will Get You Everywhere: On Tax Reform, Steve Forbes Has the Right Idea," *Wall Street Journal*, Wednesday, 31 August 2005, www.opinion journal.com/columnists/pdupont/?id = 110007183 (accessed 26 November 2005).

31. R. Glenn Hubbard, "Economic Outlook and Economic Policy" (remarks at the Macroeconomic Advisers Conference, Washington, DC, 19 September 2002, http://www 0.gsb.columbia.edu/faculty/ghubbard/speeches/9.19.02.pdf (accessed 26 November 2005).

32. R. Glenn Hubbard, "Testimony before the Special Committee on Aging," United States Senate, 4 February 2003, 14, http://aging.senate.gov/public/_files/hr92gh.pdf (accessed 21 November 2005).

33. Stephen Moore, "Real Tax Cuts Have Curves the Economy Booms, and Arthur Laffer Has the Last Laugh," *Wall Street Journal*, 19 June 2005, www.opinionjournal.com/ extra/?id = 110006842 (accessed November 2005).

34. Daniel Gross, "Field of Dreams," *Slate*, 2 February 2004, www.slate.com/id/ 2094801 (accessed 25 November 2005).

35. *Wall Street Journal*, "John Maynard Domenici," 16 April 1981.

36. John Makin, "The Mythical Benefits of Debt Reduction," Washington, DC: American Enterprise Institute, 2000, 1.

37. The national debt refers to the total amount of money the government owes bondholders. The budget deficit refers to the gap between government revenues and expenditures in any particular year. A deficit in one year makes the national debt larger.

38. Lindsey, *The Growth Experiment*, 12.

39. Paul Craig Roberts, "My Time with Supply-Side Economics," *Independent Review* 7, no. 3 (Winter 2003): 393–97, www.vdare.com/roberts/supply_side.htm (accessed 21 November 2005).

40. Roberts, *The Supply-Side Revolution*, 296.

41. Mitch Daniels, "Press Briefing on the Budget by OMB Director Mitch Daniels," 3 February 2003, www.whitehouse.gov/omb/speeches/daniels_04budget.html (accessed 26 November 2005).

42. Martin Feldstein, "Supply Side Economics: Old Truths and New Claims" (working paper 1792, National Bureau of Economic Research, Cambridge, MA, January 1986).

43. Michael Kinsey, "A Beast of an Idea: Can Big Deficits Starve the Government Down to Size? Not in This Universe," *Time*, 12 January 2004, 84.

44. N. Gregory Mankiw, "Candidates Need Clues, Not Tax Plans," *Fortune*, 20 March 2000, http://post.economics.harvard.edu/faculty/mankiw/columns/mar00.html (accessed 22 November 2005).

45. Jacob Sullum, "A Flood of Red Ink: The Fiscal Fallout from Hurricane Katrina,"

Reason Online, 23 September 2005, www.reason.com/sullum/092305.shtml (accessed 25 November 2005).

46. Peterson finds it especially galling that Bush tax cuts amount to "a tax cut for us, but a tax increase on our children." Peter G. Peterson, *Running on Empty: How the Democratic and Republican Parties Are Bankrupting Our Future and What Americans Can Do About It* (New York: Farrar, Straus & Giroux, 2004).

47. William A. Niskanen, "'Starving the Beast' Will Not Work," *Cato Handbook on Policy*, 6th ed. (Washington, DC: Cato Institute, 2005), 114.

48. David Kamin, Richard Kogan, and Robert Greenstein, "Deficits and the Mid-Session Review: The Administration's Efforts to Make Harmful Deficits Appear Benign" (Washington, DC: Center for Budget and Policy Priorities, 1 October 2004), 2.

49. Kamin, Kogan, and Greenstein, "Deficits and the Mid-Session Review," 11.

50. Robert S. McIntyre, "Down Is Up (Or So Some Say)," *American Prospect*, August 2005, 9.

51. Gale and Orszag, "Tax Policy in the Bush Administration: Revenue and Budget Effects," *Tax Notes* 105, no. 1 (2004): 105–18.

52. Kamin, Kogan, and Greenstein, "Deficits and the Mid-Session Review," 2.

53. Isaac Shapiro and David Kamin, "Concentrating on the Wrong Target" (Washington, DC: Center for Budget and Policy Priorities, 5 March 2003).

54. Data on consumer expenditures from U.S. Bureau of Labor Statistics, www.bls.gov/cex/csxann01.pdf.

55. OMB director Mitch Daniels, quoted in Mike Allen, "A Deficit, Yes, But Few Regrets," *Washington Post*, 9 June 2003.

56. While foreign debt is not necessarily owed by individuals, it will eventually have to be paid back by running consistent and large trade surpluses, and this will only happen when the value of the dollar declines, which in turn will act as a tax on Americans, raising the prices of goods and services they consume.

57. Arthur B. Laffer, "The Laffer Curve: Past, Present, and Future," *Laffer Associates*, 6 January 2004.

58. Thomas J. Hailstones, *A Guide to Supply-Side Economics* (Reston, VA: Reston Publishing Company, 1981).

59. Frank Sammartino and David Weiner, "Recent Evidence on Taxpayers' Response to the Rate Increases of the 1990s," *National Tax Journal* 50 (3 September 1997): 683–705.

60. Austan Goolsbee, "Evidence on the High-Income Laffer Curve from Six Decades of Tax Reform," *Brookings Papers on Economic Activity* 1 (Fall 1999): 14.

61. Joel B. Slemrod, "The Economics of Taxing the Rich," in *Does Atlas Shrug?* ed. Joel Slemrod (Cambridge, MA: Harvard University Press, 2000), 37.

62. Lindsey, *The Growth Experiment*, 231.

63. Lindsey, *The Growth Experiment*, 90.

64. Mellon, *The People's Business*, 44.

Chapter Eight

Do Lower Taxes Affect Income Inequality?

An imbalance between rich and poor is the oldest and most fatal ailment of all republics.

—Plutarch

Besides asserting that supply-side tax cuts don't reduce tax revenues, many supply-siders claim that supply-side tax cuts are not unfairly tilted toward the wealthy and don't increase income inequality. The answer to Larry Lindsey's question in the title of the chapter "Did the Rich Get Richer?" is that "there is no more than a tiny kernel of truth" to the claim.[1] When they do acknowledge that the rich benefit most, even by only a tiny bit, it's usually with the caveat that middle- and lower-income Americans benefited even more. Lindsey argued that Bush's tax cuts provide "middle and working-class families with desperately needed tax relief."[2] Governor Bush made the same contention during the 2000 presidential campaign when he argued that most of his proposed tax cuts would go to low- and middle-income Americans, and now more recently that "American families all across this country have benefited from the tax cuts on dividends and capital gains."[3] Amazingly, he now goes on the stump making it sound as if Congress only wanted to cut taxes on certain people (implying that it was on the rich) and that he, Bush the populist, fought to make sure we cut taxes on everyone: "And so I went to Congress and said, look, we've got problems; let's be aggressive about how we address it; let's cut the taxes on everybody. I remember the debate, they said only some people should have tax cuts. So we lowered rates for everybody. If you all have tax relief, everybody who pays taxes ought to get relief; you ought not to try to play favorites with who gets it and who doesn't get it."[4] In other words, it would be unfair to all those millionaires not to have their taxes cut too.

It's true that most of the Bush tax cuts did not go to the richest families. But that's because they account for only a small share of households. The

---

Why Do Supply-Side Tax Cuts Boost Inequality?

1. High income earners receive a much larger tax cut than low and moderate-income earners, both in percentage terms and absolute amount.
2. Supply-side tax cuts also focus on cuts in taxes on capital income (e.g., interest, dividends, and capital gains) which accrue much more to higher-income earners.
3. While the highest earners are paying more in taxes than they did twenty years ago, it's because they are earning so much more. As a share of total taxes paid, highest earning Americans now pay less than they did twenty-five years ago.

---

fact is that one-third of the Bush tax cuts go to the highest 1 percent of taxpayers, with 43 percent going to the highest 5 percent of taxpayers.[5] Even in terms of percentage cuts, the wealthy got cuts almost three times bigger than the middle class.[6] In 2004, households making more than $1 million received an average federal income tax cut of $123,592, while those in the middle 20 percent of the income range received an average cut of just $647.[7] The 2003 dividend tax cuts were even more regressive, with 40 percent of the benefits going to the top 0.5 percent of taxpayers, who would see annual tax savings of around $26,000.[8] If the administration really wanted to help low- and middle-income Americans, why not cut the lowest one or two rates and not the top rates? Their claim is that it's cuts on top rates that have the biggest effect on work and savings, but as we saw in chapters 5 and 6, that's simply not true.

These unfairly tilted tax cuts have not only failed to generate faster economic growth (especially compared to other tax cuts that were temporary and focused more on low- and moderate-income taxpayers who were more likely to spend them), but they have exacerbated fast-growing income inequality, bestowing considerable bounty on wealthy Americans whose incomes had already surged over the last quarter century. According to the Congressional Budget Office, the average after-tax income of the top 1 percent of the population increased 139 percent from 1979 to 2001, rising from $294,300 to $703,100 (adjusted for inflation), while households making up the middle one-fifth of households enjoyed just a 17 percent increase, and the poorest one-fifth of households saw increases of just 8 percent. Take one example:

Radio shock jock Howard Stern will get paid $500 million in cash over five years for agreeing to sign with satellite radio broadcaster Sirius. Not only does Stern get $500 million, but the Bush tax cuts will save Stern an estimated $23 million in taxes. But of course if Stern didn't get those tax cuts he might have chosen not to go back to work after losing his job on over-the-air radio broadcasting. In short, the Bush tax cuts have poured gasoline on this flame of growing inequality. At this rate, gilded-age inequities will soon be back.

SUPPLY-SIDE ECONOMICS AND PROGRESSIVE TAXES

The animosity toward progressive taxes has a long history in classical economics and conservative circles. Many classical economists viewed progressive taxes as akin to theft. In *The Wealth of Nations*, Adam Smith wrote what was essentially a defense of a flat tax:

> The subjects of every state ought to contribute towards the support of the government, as nearly as possible, in proportion to their respective abilities; that is, in proportion to the revenue which they respectively enjoy under the protection of the state. The expence of government to the individuals of a great nation is like the expence of management to the joint tenants of a great estate, who are all obliged to contribute in proportion to their respective interests in the estate.[9]

A hundred and twenty-five years later, conservative Republicans bitterly opposed Woodrow Wilson's efforts to institute a progressive national income tax, and when they regained power in the 1920s, they proceeded to lower the top rates on the wealthy. However, after a decade of the New Deal and higher top rates, most conservatives resigned themselves to the inevitability of progressive taxes. But as conservatives rediscovered their classical economics roots in the 1970s, they also rediscovered their animus toward progressive taxation. Progressive taxation became not just unfair and theft, but a burden on growth.

To make their case for flatter taxes, conservatives developed a host of arguments. Conservative scholar Robert Nozick argued that as long as individuals earn income in ways that are just, the resulting distribution of income should be inviolate. Greg Mankiw argued that ascertaining what is fair is quite difficult: "Fairness, unlike simplicity, is an elusive concept, which is as much in the realm of political philosophy as economics."[10] Others argue that the current system isn't even progressive, claiming, incorrectly, that the rich take advantage of loopholes to not pay more taxes. Former House Republican

leader Dick Armey would have us believe that "even by its very own definition of fairness, progressive tax rates are a complete fraud."[11] Yet just a few
pages later, Armey complains that the wealthy pay too much in taxes: "Even
with their deductions and breaks and tax shelters, the wealthiest 5 percent of
American taxpayers pay about 20 percent of all federal tax revenues."

Supply-siders' arguments against progressive taxation are often simplicity
itself. The conservative Institute for Policy Innovation argues, "It is improper
to tax some income at a higher rate than other income, either through gradua-
ted tax rates or by imposing multiple layers of tax on some types of income
but not on other types of income."[12] President Bush believes that "no one
should pay more than a third of the money they earn in federal income taxes,
so we lowered the top rate to 33 percent."[13] Why is it improper? Because it
just is.

What's at the heart of supply-sider's opposition to progressive taxes?
Some argue that it's simply an ideological ruse to justify rewarding the
wealthy party faithful. David Stockman, head of Reagan's Office of Management and Budget, was famously quoted as saying in reference to the Reagan
tax cut legislation, "Kemp-Roth was always a Trojan horse to bring down the
top rate. . . . The original argument was that the top bracket was too high, and
that's having the most devastating effect on the economy. Then, the general
argument was that, in order to make this palatable as a political matter, you
had to bring down all the brackets."[14] Stockman went on to confess that "it's
kind of hard to sell 'trickle down,' so the supply-side formula was the only
way to get a tax policy that was really 'trickle down.' Supply-side is 'trickle-
down' theory."[15] More recently, conservative commentator Larry Kudlow
said the same thing about the Bush tax cuts: "The world has become a bit
safer for rich people and for those non-rich who through innovative ideas and
hard work will get to keep more of what they earn in order to become rich."[16]
But while this deep empathy for the wealthy may play some role, a more
fundamental reason for supply-siders' support of flatter taxes is that they
believe that progressive taxes are just simply unfair. In pushing for his flat
tax proposal, Dick Armey tells us that "the progressive tax did not rid us of
robber barons, but merely gave America a new set of robber barons. To pil-
lage wealth and trample peoples rights, from 1916 onward you first had to
get elected to Congress."[17]

For supply-siders, fairness means that a high-income person should pay the
same tax rate as a moderate-income person. However, because most Americans believe that a high-income person should pay a higher tax rate than a
moderate-income person, supply-siders are usually not explicit about their
support of flat taxes. But every once in a while their views leak out, as they
did when the *Wall Street Journal* editorial board recently referred to nontax-

paying low-income Americans as the "lucky duckies." They may be lucky not to have to pay taxes, but I doubt many would consider themselves lucky for having low incomes in the first place.

Finally, in response to the claim that supply-side tax cuts are unfair, some supply-siders will claim that it is impossible to structure tax cuts without benefiting the wealthy. Yet that's not quite true. For example, payroll taxes could be cut, which are currently paid on only the first $94,200. Even income taxes could be cut more fairly than was the case with the Bush tax cuts. For example, the lowest tax rate (now 10 percent) could be cut. While this would cut the taxes of the wealthy, it would also cut the taxes of the poor by almost as much and would be certainly more progressive than cutting the top marginal rate, which only the wealthiest earners face. Of course supply-siders will argue that cutting the top marginal rate gets more bang for the buck in terms of work and savings.

TRENDS IN INCOME DISTRIBUTION

This debate about the role of the tax code in income distribution is particularly critical in an era when income inequality has gone up to dangerous levels. To determine changes in income inequality, economists compare changes in the ratios of deciles of earners. For example, the 90-50 ratio refers to the average income of the richest 10 percent of Americans compared to the average income of the average household, the 50th percent quintile. The 90-10 ratio compares the richest 10 percent to the poorest 10 percent.

Using this method, we can see significantly worsening trends. The 50-10 gap began to grow significantly in the late 1970s, but since the early 1990s has grown only slowly. In contrast, the gap between the wealthiest and the rest of Americans (the 90-50 and 90-10 ratios) has continued unabashed (see figure 8.1).[18] Because growth was both slow and unevenly shared from 1979 to 1997, real after-tax income declined for the lowest 20 percent of households, increased just 5 percent for the middle quintile, and skyrocketed more than 250 percent for the top 1 percent of earners.[19] The earnings of the top 0.01 percent of taxpayers went from fifty times more than the average taxpayer's income in 1970 to 250 times by 1998. The average compensation of highly compensated CEOs went from around $5.5 million in 1970 to almost $40 million in 1999 (adjusted for inflation).[20] Those lucky enough to be in the small elite group—whether it is CEOs, entertainers like Howard Stern, sports figures, attorneys, or doctors—have been able to increasingly live "lifestyles of the rich and famous."

This "winner-take-most" phenomenon has meant that the share of wage

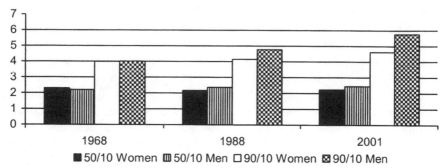

Figure 8.1   U.S. Income Ratios 1968–2001

Source: U.S. Census Bureau, Historical Income Inequality Tables.

and salary income going to the top 10 percent, 5 percent, and 1 percent of taxpayers has not been higher since before the Great Depression.[21] In contrast, for at least half the population, twenty years of economic growth have produced few gains, in part because over one-third of the total increase in GDP went to the richest 1 percent of wage earners. Were the top 5 percent of earners getting the same share of national income as they did in 1978, the average worker today would enjoy earnings of $6,100 more per year.

While most Americans are troubled by skyrocketing levels of inequality, some supply-siders look favorably on them, since for them more inequality provides greater rewards to spur hard work and entrepreneurial spirit. Heritage Foundation economist Tim Kane maintains, "In this income data I see a snapshot of a very innovative society. . . . Lower taxes and lower marginal tax rates are leading to more growth."[22]

Other supply-siders say essentially, "So what if inequality has gotten worse." Bruce Bartlett argues that, "as long as people think they have a chance of getting to the top, they just don't care how rich the rich are."[23] Michael Cox and Alvin Alm argue that "annual snapshots of the income distribution might deserve attention if we lived in a caste society, with rigid class lines determining who gets what share of the national income—but we don't live in a caste society."[24] They cite University of Michigan panel data showing movement across income classes over people's lifetimes. For example, only 5 percent of individuals in the lowest income quintile in 1975 were there in 1991. So even if inequality has gone up, we'll all be rich some time.

There are problems with their rosy analysis. A considerable portion of the movement of individuals from low wages to higher wages over the course of their lifetime occurs as students or workers in their first jobs gain higher wage work as they get older. For example, Tom Ryan, the CEO of CVS pharmacy, was probably one of those, as he started his career with CVS as a store pharmacist. And while this kind of movement is certainly positive, it's not the same as movement of large numbers of people who are born to poor families moving up to be become higher-income earners. In fact, while there is some movement across income classes, it's not all that fluid. Of the 20 percent of individuals in the top income quintile in 1975, by 1991 fully 86 percent either remained in it or had dropped to the fourth highest.

Other supply-siders simply deny growing inequality, arguing that because average household incomes have gone up, everything is fine. For example, *Wall Street Journal* editors Stephen Moore and Lincoln Anderson argue that "the vast majority of families have experienced a rapid growth in their income and wealth."[25] But much of this increase in household income has been a result of a significant increase in two-earner households. When it comes to actual wage levels, the picture has been much less Pollyannaish. Over the last twenty-five years, wage levels have actually grown more slowly than the rate of productivity growth for all but the top 10 percent of wage earners.[26]

Finally, supply-siders try to deflect concerns by claiming that while inequality might be unpleasant, it's inevitable. Cox and Alm argue, "America isn't an egalitarian society. It wasn't designed to be."[27] But we are not limited to just two choices: a hypothetical communist society with perfectly equal distribution and a laissez-faire capitalist society with whatever distribution happens to be in effect. Of course there are and should be inequalities; higher earnings reward the acquisition of high skills and hard work. The real question is whether the inequalities should be as extreme as they are today. Given the virtual stagnation of incomes for the bottom half of Americans in the last twenty-five years, the answer is clearly no.

DID SUPPLY-SIDE TAX CUTS REALLY LEAD THE RICH TO PAY MORE IN TAXES?

Given the unfairness of the Bush tax cuts, supply-siders have worked hard to obscure the distributional impact. Greg Mankiw argues, "Even more difficult is evaluating who bears the burden of the tax system, or equivalently, who wins and loses from any tax cut. Most discussion of distributional burdens is fundamentally flawed."[28] The discussion may be flawed, but the data are not.

Supply-siders approvingly point to the fact that the rich pay a larger share of total personal income taxes than they did a quarter century ago. Lindsey notes, "The Reagan tax cut, often denounced as a huge favor to the rich, actually reaped a larger share of tax revenue from the rich and upper-middle-class

taxpayers than the old tax code had and substantially reduced the relative contribution of middle-income taxpayers."[29] The Republican-controlled congressional Joint Economic Committee agrees, noting that

> in 1981 the top one percent paid 17.6 percent of all personal income taxes, but by
> 1988 their share had jumped to 27.5 percent, a ten percentage point increase. The
> share of the income tax burden paid by the top ten percent of taxpayers increased
> from 48.0 percent in 1981 to 57.2 percent in 1988. Meanwhile, the share of income
> taxes paid by the bottom 50 percent of taxpayers dropped from 7.5 percent in 1981
> to 5.7 percent in 1988.[30]

As a result, Greg Mankiw tells us that Bush's "tax policy to date has made
the system more progressive. According to estimates from the Congressional
Budget Office, Americans with the highest 20 percent of incomes are
expected to pay 64.6 percent of all federal taxes in 2004, up from 64.0 percent
without the tax cuts. Each of the bottom three quintiles is paying a lower
share of federal taxes as a result of the Administration's tax relief."[31]

These data do not lie. But what supply-siders don't mention is that the
reason higher-income Americans pay more in taxes is that their incomes went
up so much faster than everyone else's. And had their taxes not been cut
significantly, their tax payments would have increased even more, dramatically reducing the national debt. According to the IRS, the adjusted gross
income for the largest four hundred tax returns increased from $17.4 billion
in 1990 to $52.8 billion in 2000 (in constant 1990 dollars). As a result, their
share of national income more than doubled, from 0.52 percent to 1.09 percent. IRS economists show that the share of income accounted for in the top
1 percent of the income distribution climbed steadily from 9.6 percent in
1979 to 16.5 percent in 1996. Moreover, people in the top 1-to-10 percent
class saw their share of national income grow from 23.5 percent to 26 percent. In contrast, every other group saw declines in their share of national
income. As a result, by 1996 the top 1 percent of earners earned more than
the bottom 50 percent, up from about half in 1979.[32] And as we saw in chapter
5, this wasn't because they were working any harder. The economy grew
faster with more widely shared prosperity in the postwar era when their tax
rates were much higher.

A more accurate measure of the tax burden on income groups is the ratio
between adjusted gross income and taxes paid. As figure 8.2 shows, the top
1 percent and 5 percent of earners actually pay a lower share of taxes relative
to their share of national income today than they did thirty years ago. So, not
only are the wealthy receiving a much larger share of national income, but
they face lower effective tax rates. As Petska and Studler show, the effective
tax rate on the top 1 percent of earners fell from 34 percent in 1979 to 26

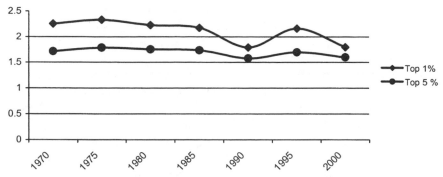

Figure 8.2   Ratio of National Share of Adjusted Gross Income to National Share of Income Taxes for Top 1 and 5 Percent of Earners

Source: President's Council of Economic Advisors, *Tax Notes 30th Anniversary, Remarks* (Washington, DC: U.S. Government Printing Office, 2002).

percent in 1996, and it's even lower after the Bush tax cuts.[33] An OECD report confirms these trends, stating,

> Lower-income families (one-half median income) gained little from the reforms [in the 1980s] in terms of the effective tax rates: their average combined income tax and social security tax burden was actually higher than at the start of the decade and their marginal combined tax burden only slightly lower. . . . [F]or middle-income families, the increase in social security taxes broadly offset the cut in average income taxes; the average tax rate was slightly higher at the end of the period than the beginning, but the marginal tax declined markedly after both reforms and by about 17 per cent over the period as a whole. . . . [T]he largest reduction in tax burden was received by high-income families; for a family on twice the median income the average tax rate fell slightly over the period as a whole and the marginal tax rate declined by about 35 per cent.[34]

Duke University economist Kirk White finds that the dramatic decline in the top tax rates in the 1986 Tax Reform Act was responsible for almost all of the increase in after-tax income inequality during the late 1980s.[35]

It's not just liberals and centrists who argue that the Bush tax cuts exacerbated income inequality; some supply-siders admit that they have as well. In recent congressional testimony, Glenn Hubbard stated, "Nonetheless, by cutting top individual income tax rates, phasing out the estate tax, cutting the corporate income tax, and expanding opportunities for tax-free saving, the 2001–2004 tax cuts on balance made the tax system less progressive. Measured as a share of income, the top tenth of one percent of taxpayers—that's one in one thousand—got tax cuts 18 times as large as the bottom fifth got."[36] He goes on to note, "Households in every income class benefited from the tax cuts, but that view is misleading. Since none of the tax cuts were offset by tax increases or spending cuts elsewhere, it is impossible to say who the winners and losers are. If the resulting budget deficits lead to cuts in programs mostly benefiting middle- and lower-income households, then they and their children will be the big losers."[37]

But Hubbard is not turning in his supply-side credentials yet, since according to him even if taxes are unfair in one year, they balance out over time. Hubbard tells us that, "even at the highest incomes, where the top 1 percent of filers pay more than one-third of individual income taxes, four times as many individuals benefit [from tax cuts] over 10 years than in a single year."[38] Cutting the taxes of the top 4 percent of Americans may be better than cutting only the top 1 percent's, but not by much.

Moving to a flat tax, the supply-side promised land, would make matters even worse. According to a secret Treasury Department memo reported in former Treasury Secretary Paul O'Neill's recent book, a flat tax would be more regressive, raising taxes on middle-class families. The memo noted that "it is very difficult to make the Flat Tax as progressive as the current tax system. Even with the EITC and personal exemptions, the Flat Tax would reduce the tax burden of those at the top of the income scale. Because capital income is concentrated among high income families, eliminating tax on income from new capital will disproportionately benefit them."[39] (To be fair, not all flat tax proposals would exempt capital income.) Tax expert Joel Slemrod agrees, finding that

> moving to a 17.2 percent single-rate flat tax would mean that the taxes for a family with two kids who have average deductions, dividend income, and capital income for their income class would lead to tax increases on all families making less than around $135,000 in 2003 dollars. Earners above this level would see their tax payments go down, by about 9 percentage points for a household earning $400,000.[40]

So what if the wealthy are getting a growing share of both the pretax and the after-tax pie. Supply-siders argue that this is good for America because the wealthy do good things with their money, like donate to charity. It's true that many high-income people donate a substantial share of their wealth to worthy causes, although, surprisingly, as a group they donate only a slightly larger share of their income than do lower-income households. However, over the past quarter century, the share of the wealthy's income going to charitable causes has actually declined. In 1979, the top 1 percent of taxpayers gave 4.13 percent of their income to charity, but just 3.51 percent by 1994. While it's true that charitable donations from the wealthy increased as a share of national income (from 0.25 percent to 0.30 percent), this was because their total incomes went up so much faster than the rest of taxpayers' incomes.[41] Why have the wealthy given less as a share of income? The answer is lower taxes, which make it less advantageous to give. So supply-side tax cuts not only reduce government revenues, they also lead to lower charitable contributions.

Tax cuts not only make after-tax incomes more inequitable, but they may also make pretax income more unequal. As Saez notes, "It is plausible to think that the drastic reduction in top marginal rates, which started in the 1960s, opened the possibility of the dramatic increase in top wages that started in the 1970s and accelerated in the 1980s and 1990s."[42] Nonmarket and institutional changes—changes that are hard to quantify and put into models—appear to have played important roles in explaining wage inequality. In the last two decades, changing social norms have increasingly legitimized more unequal incomes. When Michael Douglas's character Gordon Gecko proclaimed in the 1980s movie *Wall Street* that "greed is good," he was reflecting a changed social ethos that much larger and growing distributions of income were now acceptable, even desirable (even though he did go to jail at the end of the movie). The high marginal taxes before the 1980s served as an economic and social brake on high salaries, since it was expensive for companies to reward top executives who would "lose" most of it to the government. Since then, tax cuts on high earners only encouraged corporations to pay more to top earners, since they faced lower rates. Tax cuts on the rich essentially sent a message to society that said the old bargain is off: now the norm is to "get as much as you can."

IS MORE INEQUALITY A SPUR TO GROWTH?

Even if supply-siders admit that income inequality has gone up and that tax cuts have made it even worse, many believe that higher inequality boosts growth by motivating people to work hard and take risks. Kevin Hassett of the American Enterprise Institute (AEI) asserts that, "in developed nations . . . economies have tended to do better when inequality is higher."[43] As a result, Hassett warns that efforts to redistribute incomes may "undermine economic growth and create an authoritarian government that opposes our freedoms."[44] So now we have to worry about progressive taxes because they are the first step on the slippery slope to totalitarianism?

Yet this link between higher inequality and faster growth is tenuous at best.[45] If more inequality led to more growth, why did the economy grow faster in the 1950s and 1960s when income inequality was lower, and slower in the 1980s and early 1990s when it was higher? Economists Don Correy and Andre Glyn note that the postwar growth experience of most countries was faster in the beginning, when inequality was lower, than later.[46] Why did the economy grow in the 1990s after Bill Clinton boosted the top marginal income tax, hereby counteracting growing income inequality?

Moreover, in contrast to Hassett's assertion, the vast majority of scholarly studies find that higher inequality is not associated with higher growth. In a cross-country comparison, Alesina and Rodrik found that higher levels of income inequality were associated with lower levels of subsequent growth in per capita income.[47] Moreover, in contrast to supply-side assertions about inequality and savings, Schmidt-Hebbel and Serven found no evidence of a statistically significant link between income inequality and national savings rates.[48] As an OECD study summarizes,

> Both Persson and Tabellini (1994) and Benabou (1996) observe that there is little empirical relation between the scale of transfer payments and growth. The view that redistribution enhances growth receives support from Birdsall, Ross and Sabot (1995) who find that in East Asia low inequality of income (before taxes) increases economic growth and attribute the low inequality of income to the redistributive role of public-financed education.[49]

As Slemrod points out, "There is considerable agreement in the scholarly literature that higher levels of inequality—which according to supply-siders should boost growth—is correlated with lower subsequent growth."[50]

It's not clear why high inequality is associated with lower growth. One theory is that high inequality could damage social capital, the glue that lets people cooperate to create a dynamic and collaborative economy. Knack and Keefer found an association between a nation's economic development and a positive response to the question, "Generally speaking, would you say that most people could be trusted?"[51] If high inequality hurts trust, growth would suffer. Another reason could be that increased inequality can mean a smaller mass market, as economies split into markets for luxury goods and services on the one hand and low-end goods and services with fewer middle-market opportunities on the other. Companies would have a harder time taking advantage of economies of scale that would result from large middle-class markets. Another theory holds that below a certain income level, the poor lack the resources to fully develop their talents and resources. Still another possible explanation is that a highly unequal society can mean that a minority has succeeded in creating a society that prevents "outsiders" from competing against the established oligarchy.

WHAT'S WRONG WITH MORE EQUAL INCOME DISTRIBUTION?

Given that the preponderance of evidence suggests that less inequality has either no effect on growth or even a positive effect, it's worth asking why we should not make greater use of the tax code as a tool for more income equality. While growing the economy is the single most important task for economic policy, a fairer distribution of that growth is also essential.

Conservative economist Herbert Stein makes a compelling point that even if redistribution were to reduce growth slightly, it may take a long time for those getting the redistribution to have done better off by growth. He asks us to consider a situation where the lowest 20 percent of the population get 4 percent of income, and then a spending program enables them to earn 5 percent but slows down economic growth. If the rate of growth declines from 2.5 percent per year to 2.4 percent, it would take 228 years for the lowest 20 percent to be as well off from the higher growth and less redistribution than they would from lower growth and more distribution.[52]

While Stein admits that distribution matters, most supply-siders argue that all that matters is growth. On this score, it's worth comparing Germany and the United States. During the last half of the 1980s and the first half of the 1990s, *average* income went up 15.5 percent in the United States and just 10.4 percent in Germany. Looking at growth in *median* hourly income (the income at which half the earners are above and half are below) reveals a different story: U.S. median hourly income actually went down 2 percent, while German median income went up 14.7 percent. In other words, Germany saw less growth, but because it was spread widely among the lower and middle earners instead of going to a small number at the top as in America, many more people benefited.

There is another compelling reason why policies that move society more in the direction of equity are important. One of the basic rationales behind a progressive tax system is the fact that the marginal value of an extra dollar is less for someone with a million of dollars than it is for someone with only $20,000. Think of it this way: the rich spend money on things that often have relatively low value to them. Is Ted Turner's twenty-third house more valuable to him, or is someone's first house more valuable? In contrast, moving from a small cramped apartment to a single-family home is quite valuable to the low- or moderate-income person who moves. In this sense, more equal distribution of income maximizes economic utility in society.

Not only can progressive taxes make society as a whole better off, but they can actually make everyone better off. Cornell economist Robert Frank notes that individuals value not just money but status and that their choice of more work or more leisure is not just based on an income-versus-leisure trade-off. It's also based on people's perception of a status trade-off. If a person chooses more leisure, his consumption ranking goes down. He is less able to buy that Armani suit or that Lexus car. In contrast, if he works more, he moves up in the consumption ranking (being able to afford the Armani suit and Lexus) and basks in the social glow of being seen as wealthier. Thus Frank argues, "In the end, consumers end up selling more than the socially optimal quantity of leisure [by working more]. Thus, suppose consumers could agree collectively to ignore the effect of selling leisure on their consumption rank." In this case, more progressive taxes, far from introducing a distortion as supply-siders assert, actually mitigate an existing distortion. And hence "progressive taxation may enhance efficiency rather than reduce it."[53] In response to those neoclassical economists who might argue that worrying about whether an Armani suit gives you more status is irrational, Frank sites a study by David Neumark and Andrew Postlewaite, who tried to determine if an individual's choice of jobs and careers depended on the incomes of important reference group members. To measure this, they compared sisters. They found that if sister B's husband earns more than sister A's husband, sister A is 16 to 25 percent more likely to work outside the home. In other words, their labor-supply decision is partially dependent on the income of their sister's family because they are competing with them for the status that income brings. As Richard Layard once put it, "In a poor society a man proves to his wife he loves her by giving her a rose, but in a rich society he must give her a dozen roses."[54] As Frank notes, "If relative consumption is important, it follows logically that this condition cannot be satisfied, because each person's consumption imposes negative externalities on others."[55] By reducing the pressure to "keep up with the Joneses," more progressive taxes, not necessarily higher taxes, can make almost everyone's life better.

CONCLUSION

We are at a critical juncture in our nation's history. We can continue to follow the supply-side path that is impelling the economy toward more inequality, or we can choose a path that works to reduce inequalities, brings all Americans together, and gets more growth to boot. In 1992, business management guru Peter Drucker observed "There is a danger that the post-capitalist society will become a class society unless service workers attain both income and dignity."[56] He was referring to the trend, which has only grown since he wrote that, of a declining group of middle-wage production and service jobs with a concomitant rise of high-wage knowledge jobs (e.g., software engineers, marketing executives, doctors) and low-wage, lower-skilled jobs (e.g., janitors, health care aids, retail clerks, and restaurant workers). That danger is becoming more and more real every year.

The core of the American dream, of owning a home and of doing better than your parents, was always more than just some individuals doing better;

it was a dream about all Americans moving up. If we don't address growing inequality, then indeed the American dream will wither.

NOTES

1. Lawrence Lindsey, *The Growth Experiment: How the New Tax Policy Is Transforming the U.S. Economy* (New York: Basic Books, 1990), 14.

2. Lindsey, *The Growth Experiment*, 81.

3. During the third election debate, October 2000. Also George W. Bush, "President Discusses Strong and Growing Economy," Chicago, 6 January 2006, www.whitehouse.gov/news/releases/2006/01/20060106-7.html (accessed 31 January 2006).

4. George W. Bush, "President Highlights Importance of Small Business in Economic Growth," 19 January 2006, www.whitehouse.gov/news/releases/2006/01/20060119-2.html (accessed 20 January 2006).

5. Tax Policy Center, www.taxpolicycenter.org.

6. According to the CBO, under the Bush tax plan, in percentage-point terms, the lowest income quintile will see a decline of 1.5 percentage points to 5.8, the next lowest a 1.4 percentage-point cut to 12.4, the next a 1.2 cut to 15.9, and the next a 1.1 cut to 20.1. The top 10 percent see a 1.8 cut to 27.9, the top 5 percent a 2.1 cut to 29, and the top 1 percent a 3.1 cut to 30.4.

7. Center for American Progress, "A Fair and Simple Tax System for Our Future: A Progressive Approach to Tax Reform," Washington, DC: January 2005, 5.

8. Brian Roach, "Read My Lips: More Tax Cuts—The Distributional Impacts of Repealing Dividend Taxation" (working paper 03-01, Global Development and Environment Institute, Tufts University, February 2003).

9. Adam Smith, *The Wealth of Nations* (New York: Penguin Classics, 2000), bk. 5, ch. 2, v. 2.25.

10. Gregory N. Mankiw, "The Economic Agenda," International Tax Policy Forum, (Washington, DC: American Enterprise Institute, 2 December 2004), 2, http://post.economics.harvard.edu/faculty/mankiw/columns/AEIspeech.pdf (accessed 22 November 2005).

11. Richard Armey, *The Flat Tax* (New York: Ballantine Books, 1996), 31.

12. Lawrence A. Hunter and Stephen J. Entin, "A Framework for Tax Reform" (Dallas: Institute for Policy Innovation, 14 January 2005), 4.

13. Cited in Larry Kudlow, "W. Holds His Ground," *National Review Online*, 28 February 2001, www.nationalreview.com/kudlow/kudlow022801.shtml (accessed 25 November 2005).

14. William Greider, "The Education of David Stockman," *Atlantic Monthly*, December 1981, 46–47.

15. Quoted in David Greider, "The Education of David Stockman," *The Atlantic Monthly*, December 1981, 46–47.

16. Larry Kudlow, "Looking Up, Down the Road," *National Review Online*, 29 May 2001, www.nationalreview.com/kudlow/kudlow052901.shtml (accessed 24 November 2005).

17. Armey, *The Flat Tax*, 41.

18. David H. Autor, Lawrence F. Katz, and Melissa S. Kearney, "Trends in U.S. Wage Inequality: Re-Assessing the Revisionists" (working paper 11627, National Bureau of Economic Research, Cambridge, MA, September 2000), 63.

19. Congressional Budget Office, "Effective Tax Rates, 1979–1997" (Washington, DC: Congressional Business Office, October 2001).

20. According to *Business Week*, the average CEO of a major corporation made 42 times the average hourly worker's pay in 1980, 85 times in 1990, and a staggering 531 times in 2000. www.aflcio.org/corporateamerica/paywatch/ceou/ceou_compare.cfm.

21. Thomas Piketty and Emmanuel Saez, "Income Inequality in the United States, 1913–1998," *Quarterly Journal of Economics* 118, no. 1 (February 2003): 1–39.

22. David Cay Johnston, "The Richest Are Leaving Even the Rich Far Behind," *New York Times*, 5 June 2005.

23. Bruce Bartlett, *Reaganomics: Supply Side Economics in Action* (Westport, CT: Arlington House Publishers, 1981).

24. Michael W. Cox and Richard Alm, *Myths of Rich and Poor: Why We're Better Off Than We Think* (New York: Basic Books, 1999), 72.

25. Stephen Moore and Lincoln Anderson, "Great American Dream Machine," *Wall Street Journal*, 21 December 2005, A18.

26. Ian Dew-Becker and Robert J. Gordon, "Where Did the Productivity Growth Go? Inflation Dynamics and the Distribution of Income" (paper presented at the 81st meeting of the Brookings Panel on Economic Activity, Washington, DC, 8–9 September 2005), 76.

27. Cox and Alm, *Myths of Rich and Poor*, 87.

28. Gregory N. Mankiw, "Remarks at the Annual Meeting of the National Association of Business Economists," Atlanta, GA, 15 September 2003, http://post.economics.harvard.edu/faculty/mankiw/columns/nabe.pdf (accessed 25 November 2005).

29. Lindsey, *The Growth Experiment*, 11.

30. Joint Economic Committee, "The Reagan Tax Cuts: Lessons for Tax Reform" (Washington, DC: U.S. Congress, April 1996), www.house.gov/jec/fiscal/tx-grwth/reagtxct/reagtxct.htm (accessed 23 November 2005).

31. Mankiw, "The Economic Agenda," 2.

32. Tom Petska and Mike Studler, "Income, Taxes, and Progressivity: An Examination of Recent Trends in the Distribution of Individual Income and Taxes" (Washington, DC: Internal Revenue Service, Statistics of Income Division).

33. Petska and Studler, "Income, Taxes, and Progressivity."

34. Willi Leibfritz, John Thornton, and Alexandra Bibbee, "Taxation and Economic Performance" (Paris: Organisation for Economic Co-Operation and Development, 1997), 108.

35. Kirk White, "Marginal Tax Rates and the Tax Reform Act of 1986: The Long-Run Effect on U.S. Wealth Distribution" (working paper, Duke University, Department of Economics, 15 November 2001).

36. R. Glenn Hubbard, "Tax Code Revision" (testimony to the House Ways and Means Committee, 8 June 2005), http://www0.gsb.columbia.edu/faculty/ghubbard /speeches/6.8.05.pdf (accessed 21 November 2005).

37. Hubbard, "Tax Code Revision."

38. R. Glenn Hubbard, "Measure Tax-Cut 'Fairness' over a Lifetime," *Wall Street Journal*, 8 January 2003.

39. Ron Suskind, "The Price of Loyalty, the Bush Files: Economy, Fundamental Tax Reform; the Bush Plan," http://thepriceofloyalty.ronsuskind.com/thebushfiles/archives/000093.html (accessed 26 November 2005).

40. Joel Slemrod and Jon Bakija, *Taxing Ourselves: A Citizen's Guide to the Debate over Taxes* (Cambridge, MA: Harvard University Press, 2004), 191.

41. Gerald E. Auten, Charles T. Clotfelter, and Richard L. Schmalbeck, "Taxes and Philanthropy among the Wealthy," in *Does Atlas Shrug?* ed. Joel B. Slemrod (Cambridge, MA: Harvard University Press, 2000), 410.

42. Emmanuel Saez, "Reported Incomes and Marginal Tax Rates, 1960–2000: Evidence and Policy Implications," in *Tax Policy and the Economy*, ed. James M. Poterba, 117–71 (Cambridge, MA: National Bureau of Economic Research), 168.

43. Kevin Hassett, "Rich Man, Poor Man: How to Think about Income Inequality (Hint: It's Not as Bad as You Think)" (Washington, DC: American Enterprise Institute, May 2003), www.aei.org/news/newsID.17509,filter./news_detail.asp (accessed 25 November 2005).

44. Hassett, "Rich Man, Poor Man."

45. Persson and Tabellini have shown that inequality has had a negative relation to growth in the United States and in several European countries since at least the mid-nineteenth century. They found a similar correlation in a larger sample of countries since World War II. Torsten Persson and Guido Tabellini, "Is Inequality Harmful for Growth? Theory and Evidence," *American Economic Review* 84 (1994): 600–21.

46. Don Corry and Andrew Glyn, "The Macroeconomics of Equality, Stability and Growth," in *Paying for Inequality: The Economic Costs of Social Injustice*, ed. Andrew Glyn and David Miliband (London: Rivers Oran, 1994).

47. Alberto Alesina and Dani Rodrik, "Distribution Politics and Economic Growth," *Quarterly Journal of Economics* 109 (1994): 465–90.

48. Klaus Schmidt-Hebbel and Luis Serven, "Does Income Inequality Raise Aggregate Saving?" *Journal of Development Economics* 61 (April 2000): 417–46.

49. Leibfritz, Thornton, and Bibbee, "Taxation and Economic Performance," 16.

50. Joel B. Slemrod, "The Economics of Taxing the Rich," in *Does Atlas Shrug?* ed. Joel B. Slemrod (Cambridge, MA: Harvard University Press, 2000), 16.

51. S. Knack and P. Keefer, "Does Social Capital Have an Economic Payoff? A Cross-Country Investigation," *Quarterly Journal of Economics* 112, no. 4 (1997): 1252–88.

52. Herbert Stein, *What I Think: Essays on Economics, Politics, and Life* (Washington, DC: American Enterprise Institute Press, 1998), 22.

53. Robert H. Frank, "Progressive Taxation and the Incentive Problem," in *Does Atlas Shrug?* ed. Joel B. Slemrod (Cambridge, MA: Harvard University Press, 2000), 498.

54. Quoted in Robert H. Frank, "Frames of Reference and the Quality of Life," *American Economic Review* 79, no. 2 (1989): 80–85, 82.

55. Robert Frank, "Frames of Reference and the Quality of Life," 82.

56. Peter Drucker, *Post-Capitalist Society* (New York: Harper Business, 1993), 96.

Chapter Nine

Do Lower Taxes Lead to Higher Rates of Economic Growth?

Prosperity is necessarily the first theme of a political campaign.

—Woodrow Wilson

At the end of the day, when it comes to choosing between competing economic doctrines, the proof is in the pudding: does the implementation of a particular doctrine generate the fastest, most sustained, and most widely shared economic growth? Supply-siders say theirs wins this test. However, as we have seen, the two principal ways in which supply-side economics purports to generate growth—more work and more saving—fall down on both these measures. We saw that supply-side economics leads to large structural budget deficits, which raise interest rates, leading to slower growth. We also saw that supply-side policies exacerbate already growing income inequality. Therefore, it shouldn't be a huge surprise that the evidence for the claim that supply-side policies boost economic growth is equally weak. But that's obviously not what supply-siders argue.

SUPPLY-SIDE CLAIMS

If there is one claim that supply-siders will stake everything on, it's that their policies are the most effective at boosting growth. Indeed, they have long promised a veritable cornucopia of wealth if only policy makers would follow the supply-side path. In 1924, Treasury Secretary Andrew Mellon claimed that "a decrease of taxes causes an inspiration to trade and commerce which increases the prosperity of the country so that the revenues of the Government, even on a lower basis of tax, are increased."[1]

In the last two decades, supply-siders have resurrected Mellon's argument. AEI scholar John Makin promises that "a reduction in federal tax revenues

---

Why Don't Supply-Side Tax Cuts Boost Growth?

1. They do little to stimulate work and actually lead to lower national savings.
2. In the new knowledge economy, more capital—which supply-side economics tries to expand—accounts for a small share of growth. It's innovation that matters, and tax cuts on wealthy individuals do little or nothing to stimulate that.

---

by a gross amount of $1 trillion would add $3.44 trillion to total GDP available to the economy over the next decade. That is a return of 13.1 percent a year." Robert Barro asserts that "a cut in non-productive government spending and taxes by 1% of GDP raises growth by about 0.1% per year."[2] President Bush tells us that "the American economy grows when the American people are allowed to keep more of their own money so they can save and they can invest and they can spend as they see fit."[3]

This growth is portrayed as sitting there for the taking, but only if politicians are willing to make tough choices of cutting taxes and discard concerns with fairness and progressivity. As Lindsey argues, "The conflicts between raising revenue, encouraging the economy, and being fair are much less pronounced, but at the margin there are real conflicts that must be confronted and resolved."[4] By and large, supply-siders have succeeded in framing the debate this way as one of a tough choice. Given this trade-off between growth and more progressive taxes, supply-siders say it's important to make the tough choice and go for growth. Many liberal demand-siders will say that this is just too high a price to pay, for we cannot turn our backs on the most needy among us even if it means a bit faster economic growth. If this were the trade-off that policy makers were actually faced with, it would indeed be a tough choice. But Lindsey is wrong about the tough trade-off, at least in terms of a trade-off between growth and fairness when considering the kinds of fiscal and social policies in place during the 1990s. At best, the evidence is unclear that lower and/or flatter taxes boost growth. At worst (for the supply-side claim), it's clear that they have either no effect on growth or actually hurt growth. Indeed, economic theory does not predict a trade-off between higher levels of economic equity induced by government policies and growth, and economic evidence finds little or no evidence of the trade-off.

EVIDENCE FROM THE REAL WORLD

Perhaps the most damning rebuttal to supply-siders' claims that lower taxes, especially on high incomes and savings, boost growth is historical experience. As Gale and Orszag point out, from 1870 to 1912—the supply-siders' golden era—the United States had no income tax, and federal tax revenues were just 3 percent of GDP. In contrast, from 1947 to 1999, the highest income tax rate averaged 66 percent, the government collected estate taxes and corporate taxes, and federal tax revenues were at about 18 percent of GDP. If supply-side economics is right, growth in the earlier period should have been through the roof, with the latter period suffering virtual stagnation. In fact, growth rates of real GDP per capita were the same.[5]

Supply-side economics fares even worse when looking at growth since 1929. From 1929 to 1992, there was actually a strong positive correlation between taxes as a share of GDP and the change in real GDP per capita. As Federal Reserve Bank economists Wenli Li and Pierre-Daniel Sartre point out, "On the basis of these [neoclassical supply-side] models, the dramatic increase in income taxation which took place in the early 1940s would have been expected to contemporaneously decrease the U.S. per capita growth rate."[6] In classic economist understatement, they conclude, "This did not appear to be the case."

In response to these findings, supply-siders will argue that things are different in the last twenty-five years. They point to the 1980s, claiming that Reagan's supply-side policies led, in the words of former *Wall Street Journal* editor Robert Bartley, to "Seven Fat Years." Interpreting the 1980s as a period of untrammeled prosperity has become a cottage industry for supply-siders, for if it was in fact a boom, then supply-side economics appears vindicated. Larry Lindsey would have us believe that "the current economic expansion, which officials date from 1991, is better viewed as stretching back to 1982."[7] Why was growth supposedly so strong then? Easy, says Lindsey: "The prime force behind this recovery was a revolution in economic policy that was scorned by many orthodox economists."[8] Americans were willing to hold their nose and drink their supply-side medicine (or, in their case, guzzle their supply-side cola of tax cuts), and growth was the result. At least that's what supply-siders would have us believe.

But as Disraeli put it, there are three kinds of lies: lies, damn lies, and statistics. In this case, supply-siders make selective use of statistics to paint the very best interpretation of the Reagan years. In particular, they point to the fact that GDP grew almost 4 percent per year from 1983 to 1990—the "Seven Fat Years." John Makin tells us that "the 4.5 percent growth for 1982 to 1987 was a full percentage point above the average growth rate of 3.5 percent over the four decades since 1959."[9] Yet that account conveniently leaves out Reagan's first two years and his last. When his entire term from 1981 to 1989 is used as the measure, the picture isn't so good (GDP grew slightly slower than the 1970s, 3.4 percent vs. 3.6 percent). Moreover, productivity grew more slowly in the 1980s than in the 1970s (by about 10 percent). In short, the economic performance of the 1980s was not exceptional, and compared to the 1990s, it was downright disappointing.

If growth, particularly productivity growth, was not remarkable in the 1980s when taxes were cut, it was clearly remarkable in the 1990s when taxes were raised. For supply-siders, this is an unexpected, puzzling, and troubling development. How do they explain it? They don't. As Greg Mankiw wrote, "The unexpectedly strong economy of the 1990s remains a mystery."[10] It's especially a mystery if you believe that higher taxes on individuals must inevitably slow growth.

CROSS-NATIONAL COMPARISONS

Economists don't look just at growth over time to determine the relationship between economic policies and growth. They also compare growth across nations. While some early studies initially supported the supply-side hypothesis, suggesting that lower taxes were associated with faster growth, subsequent studies have established otherwise. In two studies widely touted by supply-siders, Barro and Plosser found a significant negative correlation between government spending and taxes and economic growth.[11]

However, these studies suffered from significant problems. First, it turns out that there is a strong positive correlation between the level of taxes and the initial level of income (taxes are generally lower in poorer countries). When growth economists William Easterly and Sergio Rebelo reexamined these studies and controlled for the initial level of income, they found that Barro and Plosser's results no longer held. Moreover, as OECD's comprehensive review of cross-country growth studies found, "If other determinants of growth (such as, for example, exports to GDP and domestic credit growth) are included in the analysis, the government distortions [taxes and spending] variable becomes insignificant."[12]

The Barro and Plosser studies suffered from a second problem. They did not allow for the fact that some forms of government investment (e.g., infrastructure, education, research) can boost growth. Instead, they just assumed that all spending hurts growth. However, as the OECD notes, "More and better public goods and services may also increase the productivity of private fixed and human capital and hence increase economic growth. . . . This suggests that the assessment of particular tax increases or tax cuts should take into account the type of spending to be financed or reduced by the measure."[13] When Federal Reserve Bank economists Li and Sartre did just that, they found that, "when government spending is allowed a productive role . . . the initial adverse effects of a tax increase on growth are small, and may even be reversed."[14]

When these and other factors that affect growth are incorporated, many studies actually find a *positive* relationship between higher taxes and faster growth. Tanzi and Zee found that the relative size of government is higher in rich countries.[15] This is consistent with the finding that, across countries, taxes and government expenditures as a share of GDP were *positively* correlated with per capita income growth between 1976 and 1997. Supply-siders might argue that these results are biased because they include lower-income developing nations that tend to spend less on government. However, the relationship is even stronger when just the richer OECD nations are considered.[16] As Li and Sartre find, "If anything, the link between per-capita growth rates and the relative size of public expenditures is *increasing*."[17]

In sum, most cross-country studies find either no relationship between tax levels and growth or a positive one. After reviewing the growth literature, Easterly and Rebelo conclude that "the evidence that tax rates matter for growth is disturbingly fragile."[18] Slemrod agrees, noting that "sophisticated statistical analysis of the relationship between economic growth and the level of taxation, which attempt to hold constant the impact of other determinants of growth to isolate the tax effect, have come to no consensus."[19] Li and Sartre find that "cross-country studies . . . have suggested that long-run growth is independent of fiscal policy. . . . Cross-country data suggest that economic growth does not change much or even increases with the share of tax revenue in GDP."[20] In other words, given all the studies conducted and all the models run, economists have failed to find compelling evidence that lower taxes lead to higher growth. But that doesn't stop supply-siders from repeating the mantra: cut taxes to boost growth.

WHY ARE LOWER TAXES NOT ASSOCIATED WITH HIGHER GROWTH?

Why does the supply-side narrative about taxes and growth turn out not to hold up to scrutiny? To understand why, it's important to revisit the supply-siders' account of how growth occurs. For them, growth results from a chain of steps. Working backward, accumulation of capital (e.g., higher amounts of capital equipment) drives growth; more savings in turn boosts capital accumulation; and tax cuts, especially on the rich and on savings, boost savings. Therefore, cut taxes on the rich, get more savings, get more capital investment, and get more growth. But not a single link on this chain of logic holds up to scrutiny. As chapter 6 demonstrated, tax cuts do not lead to increased savings, and more savings do not lead to more capital accumulation. But, more importantly, economists are increasingly coming to the realization that accumulation of capital itself is not the major driver of growth.

The insistence by supply-siders that capital accumulation drives growth is deeply grounded in neoclassical models of economic growth. Early studies of what was called "growth accounting" tried to allocate growth among various factors, such as supply of capital and labor, increased economies of scale, and other factors. These studies found that greater accumulation of these traditional inputs contributed surprisingly little to economic growth. Nobel economist Robert Solow described this fairly large residual—what was left over after accounting for capital and labor—as "technical advances," defined as any change in how we produce goods and services. This technical advance thereby increased an economy's growth potential above its limit based on rates of accumulating more capital and labor. As U.C. Berkeley economist Brad Delong notes, "Growth accounting studies in the tradition of Solow have found that capital deepening is responsible for only a small part of advances in labor productivity."[21] In spite of these findings, supply-siders and neoclassical economists have generally preferred to focus on capital, seeing the residual that described technical advances as, in the words of early growth accounting economist Moses Abramovitz, "the measure of our ignorance." Rather than trying to learn more, they simply focused on what they already knew: capital.

So why does capital play a much smaller role than supply-side economists would have us believe? Stanford economist Paul Romer, a leader in the "new growth economics," argues as follows:

> We now know that the classical suggestion that we can grow rich by accumulating more and more pieces of physical capital like fork lifts is simply wrong. The problem an economy faces (but that a family putting its savings in the bank can ignore) is what economists call "diminishing returns." In handling heavy objects, a fork lift is a very useful piece of equipment. When there were few fork lifts in the economy, the return on an investment in an additional fork lift was high. But as we increase the total number of fork lifts the value of each additional fork lift drops rapidly. Eventually, additional fork lifts would have no value and become a nuisance. The return on investment in an additional fork lift diminishes and eventually becomes negative. As a result, an economy cannot grow merely by accumulating more and more of the same kinds of capital goods.[22]

Within the last decade, a new field of growth accounting that includes innovation in the model has emerged. This "new growth theory" reformulates the traditional growth model so that knowledge and technology are not simply treated as something that just happens outside economic activity (exogenous). Rather, it seeks to explicitly understand and model how technological advance occurs, seeing it as a result of intentional activities by economic actors, including government. Many studies in this tradition have found that innovation, including technological change, is much more important to growth than is accumulation of capital.

One of the reasons for the rise of new growth theory was the growing recognition that the old economic models, created in an industrial era dominated by commodity goods production, could no longer adequately explain growth, especially in an economy powered by knowledge and innovation. New growth theory stresses the difference between "knowledge" and other forms of capital. Previously, knowledge was assumed to be a pure public good that moved freely from person to person and from firm to firm. New growth theory assumes that technology and knowledge vary in terms of the ability of more than one person to use it at the same time (rivalry) and the ability of someone to prevent others from using it (excludability). For example, a software program is a nonrival good that can be used by more than one person at a time, but it is excludable to the extent that intellectual property protections can prevent others from using the program without the permission of the owner of the software. The fact that knowledge can often be used by others means that the economic benefits cannot be captured solely by the innovator. Thus knowledge is neither a pure public nor a pure private good. New growth theory also recognizes the importance of the institutional context of technological innovation and that innovation is not something that comes about simply in reaction to impersonal price signals. It suggests that the development of new institutions to boost innovation will require both experimentation and evaluation of public policies as we attempt to find our way in this new era of knowledge-based economics.

Two leading growth economists, Robert Hall and Charles Jones, recently studied 127 nations to determine why some grew so much faster and were so much richer than others. To no one's surprise, they found that "output per worker in the five countries in 1998 with the highest levels of output per worker was 31.7 times higher than output per worker in the five lowest countries." However, what they found next would probably come as a surprise to supply-side economists who see more saving as the key: "Relatively little of this difference was due to physical and human capital."[23] (Human capital refers to the level of education of workers.) Instead, they found that wealth was determined not so much by how much capital (physical or human) a country had, but by how effectively it was used. How capital was used was 4.6 times more important in driving growth than how much capital a nation had. Another way to appreciate this is to note that of 127 nations, the United States ranks first in output per worker, thirteenth in productivity, but thirty-ninth in capital-output ratio.[24] As a result, Hall and Jones conclude that "differences in physical capital intensity and differences in educational attainment explain only a small fraction of the differences in output per worker."[25]

Other studies have come to similar conclusions. Klenow and Rodríguez decomposed the cross-country differences in income per worker into shares that could be attributed to physical capital, human capital, and total factor productivity (growth in total factor productivity represents output growth not accounted for by the growth in inputs like physical and human capital). They found that more than 90 percent of the variation in the growth of income per worker was a result of how effectively capital is used, with differences in the actual amount of human and financial capital accounting for just 9 percent.[26] Not all studies have found such a large share, but almost all find that innovation and how capital is used is the main driver, with the expansion of capital accounting for a much smaller share.[27]

Even these percentages may overstate the importance of capital. When new and more productive technologies are developed—for example, software that can recognize voice prompts—their development can actually lead organizations to invest even more money in capital equipment. Remember that supply-siders believe in a variant of Say's law—savings drives capital investment. Growth economics postulates that it's not savings that magically drives investment, but innovation. If the only tools you have aren't very good, you aren't likely to buy many more, no matter how high the savings rate or how low the interest rate is. In contrast, if new tools that can do amazing new things are available, organizations are likely to invest much more, even if interest rates are a bit higher. This is because high productivity makes investment more profitable. As a result, innovation and high productivity induce capital accumulation.[28] Innovation and rapid learning by firms induces more rapid accumulation of education and capital.[29] As firms innovate and shift to more technically advanced production, they draw in more capital and more skilled workers, which in turn lead people to save more and get more skills. In this case, it's not more capital that drives growth, but growth that drives more capital formation. A cross-country study by Blomström, Lipsey, and Zegan found this exact result, that growth of per capita income preceded capital accumulation.[30]

Before discussing what drives innovation, it's important to clarify the relationship between human capital (education) and physical capital (equipment) and growth. While growth economics makes clear that it is not changes in the amount of capital (e.g., more machines or more years of schooling) that are key to increased productivity, this is not to say that investment in equipment and education and skills is not important. Perhaps the best way to think about this is that it is not so much the quantity of capital (physical and human) that matters; it's the quality. It's not just the stock of capital but how often it is refreshed and replaced with newer and more productive machinery, equipment, and software.

One way to understand this is to consider a machinist. Which machinist would be better for the economy, one that obtained a college degree twenty years ago or one with a high school degree but who regularly takes courses to keep his skills at the cutting edge to match the pace of change in machining technology? I think the answer is clear: the latter machinist engaged in life-long learning would be more productive. While he might have less human capital than the one who got a college degree (at least in terms of how economists measure human capital), his human capital is better matched to the needs of the economy as it is being constantly refreshed. The same process is true for physical capital. Using Romer's example of forklifts, what would be better, an economy with 20 percent more forklifts or an economy where existing forklifts are replaced with new ones that are robotically controlled (assuming that these could be developed)? Assuming that the new ones cost 20 percent more, the capital-to-GDP ratio would be the same either way, but the economy would be significantly more productive with robotic forklifts (assuming that they are more than 20 percent more productive). In other words, while adding more forklifts will show diminishing returns (each additional one would be less productive than the prior one), better forklifts will not, at least in the short run (since each additional one would be more valuable than the one it replaced). Eventually, even better forklifts, or similar technology, would need to be developed. Likewise, while more years of education will show diminishing returns (would we really be that much more productive if every worker had a Ph.D.?), continued lifelong learning (either on the job or in school) to keep up to date with changing technologies and work environments shows fewer diminishing returns. So, in other words, it's not how many machines an economy has that is most important; it's how advanced the machines are and how well they are used, and that's where the importance of innovation comes in. Likewise, it's not just how many years of schooling the population has that is most important; it's how well matched their skills are to a constantly evolving production process. That is why policies to boost competition and technological innovation and to encourage continual reskilling of workers and continual adoption of new generations of equipment (including computers, software, and other information technology innovations) are so important.

There is one other reason why in the new network economy a predominant focus on expanding capital is misplaced. One could envision any number of scenarios where the amount of capital goes down but productivity goes up. For example, if consumers purchased all their music online to play in their Apple iPods, then music stores, distributors, and CD manufacturing plants would go out of business. The capital equipment needed to run a few robust music networks—like Apple iTunes for example—would be vastly less than the computers, trucks, cash registers, buildings, and machines needed to produce, distribute, and sell hundreds of millions of plastic CDs. So what would be better for the U.S. economy, more capital through savings, or ubiquitous digitization of the economy? Likewise, in the New Economy, new production systems like lean production (originally pioneered by Toyota) allow companies to more efficiently use existing capital and space to be more productive. So what would be better, if companies used more capital and conventional production systems or less capital and lean production systems? While these are not exclusive choices, the latter would be better because it would enable the same productivity with less capital.

So if the key to productivity growth is how human and physical capital are used and how new human and physical capital are developed, what determines these factors? Hall and Jones conclude that differences in productivity between countries "are fundamentally related to differences in *social infrastructure* across countries."[31] They define "social infrastructure" as the ability to efficiently and innovatively organize the capital and labor at hand to be more productive. One key component of social infrastructure is the ability to develop and widely adopt technological innovations. As Paul Romer states, "Ultimately, all increases in standards of living can be traced to discoveries of more valuable arrangements for the things in the earth's crust and atmosphere. . . . No amount of savings and investment, no policy of macroeconomic fine-tuning, no set of tax and spending incentives can generate sustained economic growth unless it is accompanied by the countless large and small discoveries that are required to create more value from a fixed set of natural resources."[32] One key driver of discoveries is investment in research and development. Charles Jones estimates that if the U.S. economy invested only the same amount on R&D as a share of GDP today that it did in 1950, productivity would be 17 to 32 percent lower.[33] He also finds that R&D accounts for around 1.38 percentage points of annual growth. At the end of the day, what matters is how many new innovations are developed and implemented, not how much money we saved.

Notwithstanding the fact that capital accumulation is much less important than technological innovation, supply-siders and neoclassical growth economists generally have, in the words of Helpman, continually "emphasized the accumulation of physical and human capital as major forces behind income growth."[34] More bluntly, *Business Week* chief economist Michael Mandel sees neoclassical economists as "capital fundamentalists who believe that savings and investment in physical capital and (sometimes) human capital are the only forces driving growth. [They] generally ignore or minimize the role of technology."[35] As a result, for the most part they "remain profoundly ambivalent or even hostile toward most areas of technology. . . . They grudgingly acknowledge the importance of technological change, but they don't understand it or trust it."[36] This is a large part of why supply-siders have no real explanation for what determines productivity growth in the real world. As Greg Mankiw admits, "The sources of strong productivity growth [in the 1990s] are hard to identify."[37] Believing that taxes are the most important determinant of productivity growth makes the sources even harder to identify.

Why do supply-siders (and neoclassical economists) generally ignore the most important factor driving growth—innovation—preferring instead to focus almost exclusively on savings and capital? There are several reasons. First, it's actually quite difficult to measure things like the skill levels of workers, adoption of new production systems, or the expansion of innovation. In contrast, it's easier to measure and put into mathematical models factors such as the value of equipment and the number of years of schooling, and even easier to measure things like saving and tax rates. Second, as Helpman argues, this focus on capital is also because "accumulation of these factors was thought to respond to economic incentives."[38] A bit like the drunk looking for his keys under the light when he dropped them over in the dark alley, supply-siders ignore innovation and focus on capital (including human capital) because they believe that capital responds to tax levels and that innovation is the "black box" over in the alley. As Helpman notes, neoclassical economists "treated technological change as an exogenous process" (meaning it was outside their models) and therefore "as one outside of the influence of economic incentives."[39] As a result, "they paid only rudimentary attention to technological change."

This may stem in part from neoclassical economists' unfamiliarity with technology, having, in Mandel's words, "learned supply and demand, not semiconductors, in school." Indeed, ever since the 1950s, when the economics profession became wedded to increasingly complex mathematical models focused predominantly on prices (inflation rates, stock prices, and savings rates), it has largely ignored technology and entrepreneurs. That's what other disciplines like history, business administration, planning, organizational psychology, and engineering studied, not economics. Perhaps this is why noted economist Kenneth Boulding is said to have quipped, "Mathematics brought rigor to economics. Unfortunately, it also brought mortis." As Columbia

University economist Richard Nelson notes, "The science of economics can be made precise only by shifting the study to an arena far simpler than that in which we are really interested. And this, many would argue, is exactly what has happened in much of economics. While the results may make for some nice economic theoretical arguments, they do little to illuminate real policy issues."[40] As Mandel notes, the result is that "economists know how to cut the budget deficit, but they don't understand how to encourage or influence technology."[41]

This point was reinforced for me when I sat next to a leading economist, who was noted for questioning the productivity rebound of the New Economy, at a luncheon in 2000 at a White House conference on the New Economy. He informed me that information technology could not have played a role in the current economic boom because the last two major IT innovations—the automatic teller machine and the Sabre airline reservation system—were put in place in the 1970s. When I asked him whether he thought new e-commerce applications such as the B-to-B Web exchange used by Covisint in the auto industry or Orbitz in the travel industry were important, he admitted that he had never heard of them. Having never visited an automobile assembly plant, a check processing facility of a bank, a telecommunications central office, or any other production facility, many neoclassical economists have little bottom-up understanding of the technology, work organization, and entrepreneurial activities that drive productivity and innovation in the twenty-first-century American economy. Because they don't understand technology but do understand finance and complex mathematical equations, they put all their eggs in the capital/savings basket.

Supply-side economists are particularly prone to this almost exclusive focus on capital. In part this is because their roots are in the classical economics paradigm that prevailed during the economy of the early twentieth century. In that world, accumulating large amounts of capital to invest in factories, railroads, and other capital projects was a key driver of growth. Economies that could save or attract money to invest grew rapidly. Economies that could not, did not. In the economy of the early twenty-first century, it's innovation that matters, and individual tax rates have little to do with it. Just think of all the changes in the economy of the last fifteen years; they are not because we got more capital to invest in even bigger steel mills or car factories. They are because we developed a wide array of new technologies (to name just a few: cell phones, the Internet, fast computer chips, genetic engineering, fiber optics, robotics, and the list goes on and on) and because many organizations (for profit, nonprofit, and government) adopted these technologies and restructured work, created new products and services, and reached out to new markets. While capital was needed for these products, it was neither the driver of them nor was it a commodity in short supply. Innovation was the driver.

FAITH-BASED ECONOMICS

At the end of the day, the great debate about how to best grow the economy will not be resolved by additional econometric studies or by even more complicated mathematical models, for the dirty little secret of economics is that for all its pretensions of being a science like physics, it is still an art in which the practitioners' political beliefs and personal inclinations play a key role in determining results and recommendations. As Joel Slemrod notes, "It is a troubling fact for the aspirations of economics to be a hard science that our values about equity end up being so correlated with our beliefs about what kind of fiscal, or tax, policy works best for the economy."[42] Larry Lindsey agrees, noting that "many people have a political stake in showing that the numbers support different positions."[43] He goes on to note that, "in part, the continuing argument is a product of philosophical disagreements about human nature and the role of government and cannot be fully resolved by economists no matter how sound their data."[44]

Indeed, supply-side economics is embraced by conservatives not because it is a demonstrably superior growth strategy. In fact, the evidence suggests that it is actually a deficient one to guide a twenty-first-century knowledge-based, global economy. Rather, supply-side economics has such a stranglehold on conservative economic thinking because it leads to policies that are consistent with their deeply held views of the proper role of government, markets, and individuals. At its heart, the motivation behind supply-side economics goes back to first principles, and for conservatives that principle is liberty. Progressive taxes are seen as a threat to individual liberty because they take from some individuals and give to others. Government spending and regulation is a threat to liberty because it tries to substitute collective judgment for individual judgment.

Ronald Reagan may have said it best when, in what became known in conservative circles as "the speech," he proclaimed in 1964,

> You and I are told increasingly that we have to choose between a left or right, but I would like to suggest that there is no such thing as a left or right. There is only an up or down—up to a man's age-old dream, the ultimate in individual freedom consistent with law and order—or down to the ant heap totalitarianism, and regardless of their sincerity, their humanitarian motives, those who would trade our freedom for security have embarked on this downward course.

More recently, in a speech to the conservative Heritage Foundation, Lawrence W. Reed, president of the equally conservative Mackinac Center for Public Policy, summed up the conservative view: "We want to limit government—ultimately—because we support freedom and the free society. . . . With regard to government, at the 'core' of our core principles are these unassailable truths: Government has nothing to give anybody except what it first takes from somebody, and a government that is big enough to give you everything you want is big enough to take away everything you've got."[45]

This fundamental belief in the primacy of liberty—in this case, the liberty to keep more of your income and do what you want as long as it doesn't directly impinge on another's life or property—is why conservatives continue their embrace of supply-side economics as a growth strategy despite evidence of its ineffectiveness. For, just as many on the left continue to put equality ahead of growth, many on the right put "freedom" ahead of growth. If the government could take actions to boost productivity but had to boost taxes to do it, many supply-siders would oppose such steps, even if they were presented with incontrovertible proof that an expansion of government would boost standards of living. Many would rather submit to a lower standard of living in order to enjoy a higher standard of freedom that smaller government supposedly permits. Frederick Hayek, the patron saint of economic conservatives, summed up this view, writing that he would be willing to accept the lower standard of living of the early 1900s over the higher standard of living of the 1940s, since the latter came with the growth of government. He said, "Personally, I should much prefer to have to put up with some such inefficiency than have organized monopoly control my ways of life."[46] In his 1996 acceptance speech for the Republican nomination for president, Bob Dole sounded like a modern-day Hayek, stating in reference to the prosperity of Clinton's first term:

> No one can deny the importance of material well-being. And in this regard it is time to recognize that we have surrendered too much of our economic liberty. I do not appreciate the value of economic liberty nearly as much for what it has done in keeping us fed as I do for what it has done in keeping us free. The freedom of the market is not merely the best guarantor of our prosperity, it is the chief guarantor of our rights. A government that seizes control of the economy for the good of the people, ends up seizing control of the people for the good of the economy. Our opponents portray the right to enjoy the fruits of one's own time and labor as a kind of selfishness against which they must fight for the good of the nation. But they are deeply mistaken, for when they gather to themselves the authority to take the earnings and direct the activities of the people, they are fighting not for our sake, but for the power to tell us what to do.[47]

For supply-siders, limited government and the low taxes that accompany it are ends in themselves. As the conservative Institute for Policy Innovation writes, "A fundamental purpose of democratic government is to protect life and property. One's income is a basic component of one's property. . . . The tax system should not be used as an instrument of wealth and income redistribution or social engineering."[48] The supply-side argument that lower taxes and small government boost growth provides reassuring support for these beliefs.

While supply-siders may value liberty more than a larger income, most Americans are a bit more pragmatic. As long as actions are within the bounds set by a democratic, market-based society, most Americans are willing and even eager to support what works, as long as it leads to higher growth and a better life for them and their children. That's what matters most to most people in terms of economy and society: a good quality of life, satisfying work, and a growing standard of living.

So what are the keys to growth? In some ways they are profoundly simple. William Easterly notes that prosperity "happens when government incentives induce technological adaptation, high quality investments in machines and high-quality schooling."[49] Nobel Prize winning economist Douglass North argues that "we must create incentives for people to invest in more efficient technology, increase their skills, and organize efficient markets."[50] Paul Romer states,

> The conservative save-more and liberal spend-more policy prescriptions miss the crux of the matter. Neither adjustments to monetary and fiscal policy, nor increases in the rate of savings and capital accumulation can by themselves generate persistent increases in standards of living. . . . The most important job for economic policy is to create an institutional environment that supports technological change.[51]

It is to that task that we now turn.

NOTES

1. Andrew Mellon, *Taxation: The People's Business* (New York: Macmillan, 1924).

2. Cited in Nouriel Roubini, "Supply Side Economics: Do Tax Rate Cuts Increase Growth and Revenues and Reduce Budget Deficits? Or Is It Voodoo Economics All Over Again?" http://pages.stern.nyu.edu/~nroubini/SUPPLY.HTM (accessed 25 November 2005).

3. George W. Bush, "President Discusses Strong and Growing Economy," Chicago, 6 January 2006, www.whitehouse.gov/news/releases/2006/01/20060106-7.html (31 January 2006).

4. Lawrence Lindsey, *The Growth Experiment: How the New Tax Policy Is Transforming the U.S. Economy* (New York: Basic Books, 1990), 161.

5. William Gale and Peter Orszag, "Bush Administration Tax Policy: Effects on Long Term Growth," *Tax Notes*, 18 October 2004, 420.

6. Wenli Li and Pierre-Daniel Sartre, "Growth Effects of Progressive Taxes" (working paper, Federal Reserve Bank of Richmond, November 2001), 2.

7. Lawrence B. Lindsey, "The Seventeen-Year Boom" (Washington, DC: American Enterprise Institute, 2000), 1.

8. Lindsey, *The Growth Experiment*, 4.

9. John Makin, "The Mythical Benefits of Debt Reduction" (Washington, DC: American Enterprise Institute, 2000), 2.

10. Greg Mankiw, "So Who Do We Thank for This Boom?" *Fortune*, 11 October 1999, http://post.economics.harvard.edu/faculty/mankiw/columns/oct99.html (accessed 25 November 2005).

11. Robert J. Barro, "Economic Growth in a Cross Section of Countries," *The Quarterly Journal of Economics* 106, no. 2 (May 1991): 407–43; Charles I. Plosser, "The Search for Growth," in *Policies for Long Run Economic Growth: A Symposium Sponsored by the Federal Reserve Bank of Kansas City* (1992): 57–86.

12. Willi Leibfritz, John Thornton, and Alexandra Bibbee, "Taxation and Economic Performance" (Paris: Organisation for Economic Co-Operation and Development, 1997), 18.

13. Leibfritz, Thornton, and Bibbee, "Taxation and Economic Performance," 15.

14. Li and Sartre, "Growth Effects of Progressive Taxes," 3.

15. V. Tanzi and H. Zee, "Tax Policy for Emerging Markets; Developing Countries," *National Tax Journal*, June 2000, 299–322.

16. Li and Sartre, "Growth Effects of Progressive Taxes," 27.

17. Li and Sartre, "Growth Effects of Progressive Taxes," 2.

18. William Easterly and Sergio Rebelo, "Fiscal Policy and Economic Growth," *Journal of Monetary Economics* 32 (1993): 417–58.

19. Joel Slemrod and Jon Bakija, *Taxing Ourselves: A Citizen's Guide to the Debate Over Taxes* (Cambridge, MA: MIT Press, 2004), 120.

20. Li and Sartre, "Growth Effects of Progressive Taxes," 2.

21. J. Bradford DeLong, "Productivity Growth and Investment in Equipment: A Very Long Run Look," *Growth and Equipment*, August 1995, 4, www.j-bradford-delong.net/pdf_files/JEH_Machinery.pdf (accessed 24 November 2005).

22. Paul M. Romer, "Beyond Classical and Keynesian Macroeconomic Policy," *Policy Options*, July–August 1994.

23. Robert E. Hall and Charles I. Jones, "Why Do Some Countries Produce So Much More Output Per Worker Than Others?" *Quarterly Journal of Economics*, February 1999, 85–116, 92.

24. Hall and Jones, "Why Do Some Countries Produce So Much More?" 109.

25. Hall and Jones, "Why Do Some Countries Produce So Much More?" 94.

26. Peter J. Klenow and Andrés Rodríguez, "The Neoclassical Revival in Growth Economics: Has It Gone Too Far?" *NBER Macroeconomics Journal* 12 (1997): 73–103.

27. William Easterly and Ross Levine, "It's Not Factor Accumulation: Stylized Facts and Growth Models," *World Bank Economic Review* 15 (2001): 177–219.

28. Elhanan Helpman, *The Mystery of Economic Growth* (Cambridge, MA: Belknap Press, 2004), 26.

29. See Richard R. Nelson, *Technology, Institutions, and Economic Growth* (Cambridge, MA: Harvard University Press, 2005).

30. Cited in Helpman, *The Mystery of Economic Growth*, 159, n8.

31. Hall and Jones, "Why Do Some Countries Produce So Much More?" 94.

32. Paul M. Romer, "Implementing a National Technology Strategy with Self-Organizing Industry Boards," *Brookings Papers on Economic Activity, Microeconomics* 2 (1993): 345–97, 345.

33. Charles I. Jones, "Sources of U.S. Economic Growth in a World of Ideas," *American Economic Review* 92, no. 1 (2002): 220–39.

34. Helpman, *The Mystery of Economic Growth*, 9.

35. Mandel, *Rational Exuberance*, 47.

36. Mandel, *Rational Exuberance*, xii.

37. Cited in Mandel, *Rational Exuberance*, 57.

38. Helpman, *The Mystery of Economic Growth*, 9.

39. Helpman, *The Mystery of Economic Growth*.

40. Nelson, *Technology, Institutions, and Economic Growth*, 191.

41. Mandel, *Rational Exuberance*, 62.

42. Joel Slemrod and Jon Bakija, *Taxing Ourselves: A Citizen's Guide to the Debate Over Taxes* (Cambridge, MA: MIT Press, 2004), 141.

43. Lindsey, *The Growth Experiment*.

44. Lindsey, *The Growth Experiment*, 12.

45. Lawrence W. Reed, "Why Limit Government?" (Washington, DC: Heritage Foundation, June 2004), 217, www.heartland.org/pdf/15354.pdf (accessed 22 November 2005).

46. Reed, "Why Limit Government?"

47. Bob Dole, Speech to the 1996 Republican National Convention.

48. Lawrence A. Hunter and Stephen J. Entin, "A Framework for Tax Reform" (Dallas: Institute for Policy Innovation, 14 January 2005), 5.

49. William Easterly, *The Elusive Quest for Growth: Economists' Adventures and Misadventures in the Tropics* (Cambridge, MA: MIT Press, 2002), 289.

50. Douglas C. North, "Poverty in the Midst of Plenty" (Stanford, CA: Hoover Institution, October 2000), www-hoover.stanford.edu/pubaffairs/we/current/north_1000.html (accessed 23 November 2005).

51. Paul M. Romer, "Beyond Classical and Keynesian Macroeconomic Policy," *Policy Options* (July–August 1994), 21.

Part Three

CRAFTING AN ALTERNATIVE

An objective and careful critique of supply-side economics is only the first step in helping to put in place the kind of economic doctrine and policies that will lead to robust and widely shared growth in the twenty-first century. But an objective appraisal and critique of supply-side economics is not enough. It's incumbent to propose an alternative. Currently there are three economic narratives that could serve as that alternative: (1) the liberal story of the importance of the Keynesian and redistributionist policy framework of the old economy; (2) the centrist neoclassical story that sees fiscal discipline and boosting savings (albeit by helping low- and moderate-income Americans save) as the key; and (3) the New Economy growth economics story that puts boosting innovation first.

While parts of the Keynesian framework developed in the old economy remain relevant, overall it is an inadequate guide to growing the New Economy. And while there are important insights contained in the centrist neoclassical story of fiscal discipline and progressive savings, at the end of the day it is not a sufficient growth strategy. A growth economics model that puts boosting innovation and productivity through public-private partnerships at the center is the key to growing the twenty-first-century economy.

Before discussing the growth economics alternative, it's worth first looking at the limitations of the first two doctrines.

Chapter Ten

Demand-Side Economics: An Alternative Blast from the Past

The difficulty lies, not in the new ideas, but in escaping the old ones, which ramify, for those brought up as most of us have been, into every corner of our minds.

—John Maynard Keynes

While the rise of supply-side economics as the Republican Party's de facto economic doctrine is understandable, what's harder to understand is the Democratic Party's inability to prevent the supply-side tide from inundating Washington. Democrats have failed in this task for at least three main reasons. First, they have used the wrong arguments in their fight against supply-side economics. Second, they have underestimated just how radical the Republican plan is, preferring to believe that the supply-side agenda is being driven by fringe actors rather then being a central part of Republican doctrine. And finally, while they were able to articulate a cogent and effective growth strategy in the 1990s—Clintonomics, with its combination of targeted public investments, fiscal discipline, and support for smart globalization—since then, Democrats have not been able to articulate a coherent growth strategy, instead all too often trying to preserve an old-economy, demand-side, populist economics framework.

IT'S TIME TO TAKE THE FIGHT TO
THE SUPPLY-SIDERS' HOME COURT

In successfully pushing through their supply-side agenda, President Bush and his Republican colleagues have been nothing if not nimble, using a variety of justifications to drive their tax cut agenda. But they always come back to one: tax cuts, especially on the wealthy, unleash capital, stimulate work, and drive growth. Without tax cuts, they argue, the economy will have higher unemployment, less investment and productivity, less innovation, and declining international competitiveness. In other words, without our agenda, they say, some pretty bad things will transpire.

It's not that Democrats have not tried to mount an intellectual assault against supply-side economics. However, their offensive has largely been conducted on equity grounds. Calling it "trickle-down economics"—where the rich get the lion's share of the benefits with a bit trickling down to average Americans—Democrats have complained that the preponderance of the Bush tax cuts go to the wealthy at the expense of "working families."

This kind of framing starts with liberal neoclassical economists agreeing with supply-siders that we must make a trade-off between fairness and growth, but maintaining that Democrats should choose fairness. Perhaps the leading proponent of this view is Alan Blinder, former head of Clinton's Council of Economic Advisers. In his 1987 book *Hard Heads, Soft Hearts*, Blinder argued that Republicans are hard headed and for growth while Democrats are soft hearted and for fairness. As a result, Blinder counsels that it's okay to give up a bit on growth and the hard heart if the result is to help the needy. He even cedes that "Republicans typically know their economics better than do Democrats."[1] Blinder goes on to argue that "the Democratic Party has shown more concern for the principle of equity while the Republican Party has paid more respect to the principle of efficiency."[2] And presumably this is okay, since he notes, "We need not summarily reject a substantial redistributive program just because it inflicts some minor harm to economic efficiency. . . . Policy changes that promoted equity (such as making the tax code more progressive or raising welfare benefits) would often harm efficiency."[3]

By framing the issue this way, Blinder and many liberal neoclassical economists end up tacitly agreeing with supply-siders, differing only by arguing that fairness is of such overriding importance that if it comes at the price of higher taxes and lower growth, then so be it. Another proponent of this view is Charles Schultze, Brookings Institution economist and former head of President Carter's Council of Economic Advisers. Schultze once quipped, "There is nothing wrong with supply-side economics that division by 10 couldn't cure."[4] While intended as a knock on supply-side economics, in fact it's a tacit endorsement. While conservative supply-siders can proudly proclaim that if taxes are cut the result is robust growth, liberal 10 percenters end up being able to only gripe, "If taxes are cut we get some growth, but a lot more inequity." Blinder succumbs to the same logic when he states that "the nugget of truth in supply-side economics—that lower tax rates improve incentives to work, to save, and to invest, is both valid and valuable."[5] He goes on to state that "at least in one respect, Reaganomic reasoning was sound: lower marginal rates do indeed enhance economic efficiency by reducing tax distortions."[6] And in true 10 percenter fashion, he agrees that "people are encouraged to do things the tax man favors, and to shun the things he penalizes—regardless of the underlying economic merits of these actions."[7] What Blinder blames supply-siders for is getting carried away with promising so much—an end to inflation, much higher growth, and no budget deficit. So his analysis can be boiled down to this: supply-side economics is okay as a growth strategy, but don't overpromise. But both the 100 percenters and the 10 percenters are "capital fundamentalists" who believe that capital, rather than innovation, is the key driver of the economy. As we saw in chapter 10, this neoclassical economics model of growth—liberal or conservative—fails to account for what really drives economic growth in today's economy.

It's not surprising, given the way the party's leading economists frame the issue, that most Democratic elected officials frame the issue the same way, aiming their ire not at the ineffectiveness of supply-side policies in producing growth, but at their distributional impacts. House Democratic leader Nancy Pelosi criticized the Bush tax cut plan as a "Trojan Horse to wheel in some tax breaks for the high end that they're so fond of."[8] Then Senate Democratic leader Tom Daschle agreed, arguing that the tax cuts would "almost exclusively go to help the wealthiest Americans."[9]

Given that Democrats frame the issue this way, it's not surprising that the media does as well. For example, the cover of the January 20, 2003, issue of *Business Week* proclaimed, "Class Warfare? Suppose Bush's tax plan works: It raises long-term growth, reduces unemployment, boosts workers' wages and eventually cuts a rising deficit to manageable levels. Good, right? Now suppose the rich get richer and income inequality gets worse. Time to vote: Favor the Bush plan [or] oppose the Bush plan."

While many supply-siders will deny that their tax cuts are unfair, they are delighted to have the debate framed this way. For they can simply respond that even if tax cuts give more to the wealthy, that's a small price to pay for faster growth (and tax cuts) that benefits everyone. When this is the choice, it's an easy verdict for many Americans: they'll take the tax cuts and growth. Besides, the average voter may reason, even if I am not in that top tax bracket now, I may get there one day. Most voters would rather not have to make this choice; they'd like their economic policy to "taste great" *and* be "less filling." In other words, they would like to be able to support an economic policy that promises "growth, fairly distributed." But when forced to choose between the Republicans' growth and the Democrats' fairness, many will elect for the former.

Thus, it's no accident that the only time a Democrat has won the White

House in the last twenty-five years was when he offered a message of private-sector growth, more fairly shared. When Democrats go back to their default position of criticizing Republican supply-side economics because it's unfair (coupled with populist corporate bashing), rather than because it's a flawed growth strategy, and then on top of this fail to articulate their own compelling growth strategy, Republicans win the debate hands down. However, as we saw in chapter 8, there is no inherent trade-off between fairness and growth, and as we will see in chapter 11, it is possible to design economic policies that produce both.

While most liberals attack supply-side policies on equity grounds, most centrists attack them on fiscal responsibility grounds, arguing that big tax cuts have led to deficits "as far as the eye can see." And indeed, while Dick Cheney can blithely slough off deficits by saying that "Reagan proved deficits don't matter," as we saw in chapter 6 the preponderance of economic studies clearly shows that they do. Centrists rightly argue that big budget deficits negate any increases in savings purportedly generated from the tax cuts, and that thereby they lead to higher interest rates, all else being equal. But while true, this line of attack, like the "trickle-down" critique, also fails to go to the heart of the supply-siders' argument.

If Democrats are so worried about the budget deficit, Republicans counter, why don't they join with us to cut spending? As Bush recently declared, "Unfortunately, we have too many politicians back in Washington who preach fiscal discipline while voting against spending cuts—and too many who think the only answer for runaway spending is to raise your taxes."[10] If Washington cuts spending, so the argument goes, then it's possible to get the growth benefits of the tax cuts (and the benefits to taxpayers of lower taxes) without the problems of the deficit—a real win-win. To which Democrats can only rejoin that government spending including unsustainable entitlement spending is needed to help solve social problems, including helping the needy. Once again they are forced to put redistribution ahead of growth, clearly not a winning proposition.

It is not that these Democratic arguments are not valid and important. In an economy where the highest-income earners have done much better over the last two decades than low- and moderate-income earners, it's the height of unfairness to push for tax cuts that predominately accrue to the top earners. And in an economy where the national debt is already north of $8 trillion and our nation is about to face huge costs associated with the impending retirement of the baby-boom generation, it is fiscal folly to push large permanent tax cuts. Yet, while both critiques are valid, both fail to go to the heart of the matter. If supply-side tax cuts on individuals actually are the best way to grow the economy, maybe more inequality and higher budget deficits are a price that just has to be paid. But they are not.

ARGUMENT BY INSULT

Surprisingly, given the success the Bush administration has had in putting their supply-side agenda into practice, Democrats have not launched a frontal assault on the supply-siders' claim that their doctrine constitutes an effective growth strategy. To some degree, this is because many Democratic pundits and thought leaders feel that there must be something morally or intellectually defective with these supply-siders, who after all must be some kind of cranks and "right-wing nut jobs" to actually believe all that supply-side drivel. After all, what else could explain their heresy and abandonment of the true path? As a result, the left-wing critique all too often descends into insults and mockery. It's as if they are convinced that name-calling and invective should be enough to convince voters of the bankruptcy of supply-side economics. Liberal economist Paul Krugman is a case in point, arguing that "supply-side economics, then, is like one of those African viruses that, however often it may be eradicated from the settled areas, is always out there in the bush, waiting for new victims."[11] In wondering why it cropped back up in Bob Dole's 1996 presidential campaign, Krugman speculated that it was because "it appeals to the prejudices of extremely rich men and it offers self-esteem to the intellectually insecure." He goes on to lament the lack of government funding for "true" economics research and complains that the supply-side doctrine has been promoted by institutions funded by "a handful of wealthy cranks" and employing economists who "are not exactly the best and brightest."

It's not just Krugman who succumbs to argument by slur; many liberal economists do. In *Hard Heads, Soft Hearts*, Alan Blinder cites not a single academic study critiquing supply-side economics, but he does provide a copious array of insults, including arguing that "the early years of Reaganomics marked instead the abandonment of the celebrated Republican hard head. Where we once got cool-headed rationality, shape-penciled calculations, and fiscal rectitude, we started to get wishful thinking, rosy scenarios, and unbounded deficits. Thus did Reaganomics offer up the worst of both worlds: a soft head and a hard heart."[12] It only gets worse as he tells us that "macroeconomic analysis will contribute to sounder economic policy only when those in authority learn to distinguish between sound advice and snake oil," putting supply-side economics in the latter category.[13] Not content with just this diatribe, Blinder goes on to carp, incorrectly as it were, that "had Jimmy Carter been reelected, what we now call supply-side economics would have gone down as a minor footnote in history—an intellectually negligible doctrine of no great interest."[14] He continues on, noting, in reference to the supply-side economics of the Reagan era, "Thus something between a gimmick and a slogan became the official policy of the greatest economic power in the world. P. T. Barnum would have been proud."[15] This kind of name-calling is supposed to constitute a refutation of supply-side economics? It would be one thing if it were reinforced with careful scholarly analysis of the supply-side claims, but it's not. It's like the conservative economists of the old economy who were so frustrated that the "snake oil" peddled by Keynes was accepted by leaders that all they could do was spout insults and diatribes. But as any high school debater can tell you, insults and diatribes don't win debates.

To be sure, there is much to disagree with concerning supply-side economics, and much of this book has shown the limitations of supply-side economics as a growth strategy. However, it's simply wrong to imply that most supply-side economists, including leading talented economists such as Glenn Hubbard, Larry Lindsey, and Greg Mankiw, are somehow not as intellectually gifted as liberal economists, or are intellectually insecure. These kinds of ad hominem attacks fail to take supply-side economics seriously as a well-thought-out, coherent, and powerful economic worldview.

IT'S OKAY: WE'RE NUMBER ONE

Another factor lulling many Democratic officials and pundits into complacency is that they believe that while their party may be less popular in the areas of national security and values, at least it leads on economics. After all, they say, it must be obvious to voters that Bush is for the rich and wants to dismantle Social Security, while Democrats are for the workers. At first glance, the polls seem to confirm this comforting interpretation. As Democratic polling expert Ruy Texiera notes, a recent poll

> found that voters preferred Democrats on a wide range of economic issues, many by hefty margins. These include: fighting for the middle and working middle class (+ 31); budget deficits (+ 20); dealing with rising health care costs (+ 17); keeping jobs in America (+ 16); retirement security (+ 15); dealing with rising gas prices (+ 12); creating jobs (+ 10); creating economic security for families like yours (+ 7); fiscal accountability (+ 7); for small businesses (+ 6); and providing economic opportunities (+ 5).[16]

But Democrats shouldn't take too much comfort from these numbers, for, as Texiera writes,

> When you look carefully at the list of economic issues Democrats hold an advantage on, it is striking that they hold a huge advantage on a which-side-are-you-on item like "fighting for the middle class," but rather modest advantages on two items that should be at the heart of what Democrats really stand for: creating economic secur-

ity for families like yours [note the "families like yours" language] (+7); and providing economic opportunities (+5). And on another item that traditionally has shown itself to be an especially good predictor of vote choice—"keeping America prosperous"—Democrats are actually running a small deficit (−3).[17]

In many ways, it's astounding that after eight years of Clinton-Gore economic prosperity and five years of slow growth under the Bush administration, the public trusts Republicans more to keep America prosperous. But on closer examination, it's clear that it's not because Americans are gullible or have been misled, but rather because many see Republicans standing for growing the pie and Democrats standing for slicing it more fairly. Voters trust Democrats to look out for people like them, but they trust Republicans to make them prosperous. But unless things are really bad, prosperity, or at least the promise of it, trumps empathy.

WHERE'S THE ALTERNATIVE GROWTH THEORY FOR THE NEW ECONOMY?

If Democrats are to effectively compete with Republicans in the economic sphere, they will need to do two things. First, they will need to make a much clearer and more convincing argument that an economic policy that consists of nothing more than serial tax cuts for the highest earners does not boost economic growth in the moderate and long term. Part 2 tried to do just that by examining the logic and evidence for supply-side claims that tax cuts boost work, savings, and growth and that tax cuts don't boost inequality or budget deficits.

But, while it's necessary to offer a compelling and well-reasoned critique of the purported growth impacts of supply-side policies, it's not enough. Democrats must also boldly and unambiguously articulate their own growth strategy, and it can't be simply a Keynesian reformulation from a prior era. It's not that Bush doesn't talk about growth; he talks about it constantly. For example, "The best way to make sure economic opportunity reaches throughout our land is to make sure that we have economic growth. My administration has pursued, and will continue to pursue, pro-growth economic policy."[18]

It's not that Democrats have never owned the growth issue. Indeed, in the old economy, liberal Keynesianism was an optimistic doctrine, focusing on growth by getting to full employment. In fact, the Republicans were the party of caution and pessimism, worrying about keeping the deficit down even if growth and full employment suffered. In the old economy, it was the conservative Keynesians who said they would accept less growth for a little more fiscal discipline and a little less inflation. And unless inflation was really high, liberals won. Indeed, like Democrats today, Republicans then had no growth alternative to Keynesianism. All they could do was carp about spending and hope to hold it in check. As Paul Craig Roberts notes in reference to a tax-cutting amendment offered in 1977 by Republican congressman John Rousselot, "With this amendment Republicans were ridding themselves of the albatross of negativism. They had finally found a way to compete with the Democrats spending programs. The supply-side movement was underway."[19] He goes on to note, "Previously Republicans had simply railed against the deficit, voted no, and talked about building a record for that time when the voters would wake up to the ruin being inflicted on them by the Democrats' handouts."[20] If this sounds surprisingly like Democrats today who are convinced that voters will rise up in righteous indignation when they finally grasp the magnitude of the budget deficit and the inequity of the Republican tax policies, it's because it reflected the same underlying conditions facing a minority party looking more to the past than to the future.

While conservatives sought to replace the then dominant Keynesian economic thinking of the mid-1970s with supply-side economics, many on the left have never abandoned it. As the economy has become more global, dynamic, and technology driven, many liberals remain wedded to the demand-side economic policy framework of the post-WWII mass-production corporate era: Keynesian management of the business cycle; big bureaucratic government; economic regulation of key sectors; and policies to redistribute, rather than grow, wealth. Jeff Faux, former head of the liberal Economic Policy Institute, sums up the left's prevailing doctrine, stating, "The Democratic party had crafted a compelling story that was moved by three main ideas: a progressive era idea that the federal government was the only institution powerful enough to challenge the power of big business; a populist idea that income redistribution was a key; and Keynesian economics that said that the key economic role of the federal government was to jump-start consumer demand and through its spending keep it up."[21]

Current liberal economic proposals continue to reflect this orientation. For example, former Clinton administration labor secretary Robert Reich recently proposed that Democrats adopt a "covenant with America," modeled on the Republicans' 1994 Contract with America. However, his ten-point plan is essentially mute on growing the economy, other than to offer vague reassurances that "we will restore the growth of the American middle class and of middle-class incomes." It's not clear just how he proposes Democrats do this, although he hints at a path: repeal the supply-side tax cuts.[22] One can only sputter, "That's it? That's supposed to be their economic plan?"

The 2005 House Democratic plan on jobs and the economy also took a page out of the Keynesian book: extending unemployment benefits, providing fiscal support for states and localities so they can maintain spending levels, and extending tax cuts to the middle class so they will spend more money. Viewing economic prosperity as largely synonymous with worker well-being, many on the left continue to maintain that it's increases in the demand for goods and services that drives growth (rather than innovation and increased productivity of companies) and that the central goal of economic policy is to keep demand high through robust government spending and measures to boost wages (e.g. strong unions, minimum wage laws). In Keynesian fashion, "the Democratic plan will pump money into the economy by helping those who can't find a job because of the sagging economy. It extends unemployment benefits for the five million American workers who are still out of a job despite their continued job search."[23] In a nod to the need to be business friendly, the House plan does support business tax cuts, but only to encourage businesses to hire unemployed workers. But just as supply-side economics is not an effective growth strategy for the New Economy, neither is a Keynesian populist one.

What's striking about this plan is that there is virtually no emphasis on boosting long-term per capita income growth through productivity and innovation—it's all about providing a short-term boost to employment.[24] This is not just by happenstance. Let's face it, many in the Party have had a hard time being full-throated, unabashed, no-holds-barred advocates of growth. Instead, there are too often caveats: what about issues like the environment, job displacement, equality, materialism and the decline of the community? To be sure, these concerns are important, but to the extent that they keep Democrats from standing squarely as the party of growth and embracing, not scoffing at, John Kennedy's statement that "a rising tide lifts all boats," they get in the way of advancing the kinds of policies needed to grow the economy.

Many core constituents of the party, including Naderites, environmentalists, and antiglobalists see growth and technological change as leading to environmental degradation, reduced quality of life, and increased wealth for the rich. They blame the United States for being too rich, consuming too much of the world's resources, and contributing to more than our share of the world's pollution. Their answer is to simplify our lifestyle, or at least to put bumper stickers on their SUVs encouraging us to think globally and act locally. Moreover, some on the left fear that growth creates inequality, at least in the short run, as it benefits the "haves" and corporate interests. But as Benjamin Friedman points out in his recent book *The Moral Consequences of Economic Growth*, "Economic growth—meaning a rising standard of living for the majority of citizens—more often than not fosters greater opportunity, tolerance of diversity, social mobility, commitment to fairness, and dedication to democracy." In contrast, when an economy stagnates, "the resulting frustration generates intolerance, ungenerosity, and resistance to greater openness of individual opportunity. It erodes people's willingness to trust one another, which in turn is a key prerequisite for a successful democracy."[25]

Finally, perhaps the most important reason for Democrat's lack of full-throated enthusiasm for a growth policy is because they have relied so heavily on the advice of liberal and centrist neoclassical economists who tell them that there is little that government can do to grow the economy. Most liberal neoclassical economists who advise Democrats have little to say about productivity, innovation, and growth. While supply-side economists tout the growth miracles that will occur if we just follow their prescription, many liberal economists respond that there is little that can be done to boost growth. For example, the term "productivity" warrants a mention on just three of the 236 pages of Alan Blinder's *Heard Heads, Soft Hearts*. "Innovation" must be even less important, for it does not earn a single mention. As these two factors are the most important in determining an economy's growth rate, it's not surprising that Blinder fails to lay out a growth strategy. This isn't because Blinder is not a good economist; in fact, he's a very fine economist. Rather, it's because, like most liberal neoclassical economists, he largely doesn't believe government can influence growth, except perhaps in the short term on the consumer demand side. Indeed, he argues that "although economics can tell the government much about how to influence aggregate demand, they can tell it precious little about how to influence aggregate supply. Let no supply-sider tell you differently."[26]

For elected officials struggling to figure out what they can do to boost growth, Blinder offers this helpful advice: "Nothing—repeat, nothing—that economists know about growth gives us a recipe for adding a percentage point or more to the nation's growth rate on a sustained basis. Much as we might wish otherwise, it just ain't so."[27] Frustrated with this advice, an inquiring Democratic elected official might decide to turn elsewhere for advice, perhaps to Paul Krugman, figuring that he will surely proffer some useable economic wisdom. But again the official is to be disappointed, since Krugman says that since we don't know why productivity slowed down in the 1970s and 1980s, "that makes it hard to answer the other question. What can we do to speed it up?"[28]

There are two problems with this neoclassical pessimism. First, new research on economic growth suggests that we do know what causes growth and that government can take demonstrable steps to spur growth. Second, since the mid-1970s when productivity growth fell from about 3 percent per year in the postwar period to around 1.2 percent until 1996, the political imperative has been to figure out how to "influence aggregate supply," in other words, how to raise long-term growth rates. By claiming that it's impossible and then scoffing at supply-siders for attempting to do so, Blinder, Krugman, and their neoclassical colleagues pave the way for conservatives to claim the growth issue as their own. While Blinder should be commended for not selling promises he doesn't believe can be kept, I would argue that we can influence aggregate supply and that growth economics policies are intended to do just that.

If economic policy can't help improve most Americans' standard of living by boosting growth, liberal neoclassicalists counsel, at least it should help ensure that the economic pie is sliced a bit more fairly. As liberal economist Frank Levy argues, "We cannot legislate the rate of productivity growth. . . . That is why equalizing institutions are so important."[29] It is this belief that the best government can do is redistribute the pie more evenly that leads Democrats to focus so much on measures like boosting taxes on the wealthy; instituting "living wage" programs; and increasing spending on health insurance, public housing, and other social programs.

Often looking at technology not as something that will boost growth but rather will displace workers, some Democrats actually oppose economic policies that explicitly favor new technology and investment. Indeed, it's become fashionable in Democratic circles to argue that workers play second fiddle to machinery and equipment. Senator Ted Kennedy (D-MA) argues that "often however, whether to purchase new equipment or to create new jobs and upgrade existing jobs is a relatively close choice financially. In those cases, we should not make it more attractive to buy new equipment than to create new jobs. We need a new job creation tax credit that provides several years of tax benefits for a company that invests in an expanded workforce. The analogy is to the tax benefit currently available for depreciating new equipment."[30] Likewise, Gene Sperling, former head of President Clinton's National Economic Council, argues, "New technology will always make it more efficient to replace workers with machines or computers but decisions should be based on relative economic costs, not a tax code that tips the balance against workers."[31]

There are three things wrong with this analysis. First, the proposals that stem from it, in particular job creation tax credits, fail to reflect the fact that—in contrast to decisions to upgrade machines and computers—employers do not make hiring decisions on the basis of tax policy. They base hiring decisions on their expectations of market demand for their product or service. Second, the main public policy driver of overall employment growth, at least in the short run, is federal fiscal and monetary policy. Even if tax incentives were to be effective in driving down unemployment, if that level got too low, the Federal Reserve Bank would simply raise interest rates to get the level to what they consider the right level. Finally, exactly how are workers' incomes supposed to go up if companies do not become more productive? New equipment is a key to boosting productivity.

This aversion to new technology and automation stems in part from some liberals' fear that both are threats to full employment. In his book *The End of Work*, ironically published in 1995 at the beginning of the economic boom, liberal social critic Jeremy Rifkin laments that "[technological change] is now leading to unprecedented levels of technological unemployment, a precipitous decline of consumer purchasing power [the cause of all economic woes according the Keynesian model], and the specter of a worldwide depression of incalculable magnitude and duration."[32] However, history has clearly and consistently refuted the notion that high productivity leads in the moderate to long term to higher unemployment. For example, new technologies (e.g., tractors, disease-resistant crops, chemical fertilizers) boosted agricultural productivity, spurring a decline in agricultural employment. As food became cheaper (American consumers spend less of their income on food than any other nation), consumers spent the money they saved from cheaper food on other things (e.g., cars, appliances, entertainment), creating jobs in other sectors.

When pressed, liberal economic commentators may acknowledge this, but they respond that while this may have been true in the past, things are very different now. Because technology is now displacing jobs not only in agriculture and manufacturing, but also in the service sector, there will be no new job-generating growth sectors to employ all those who lose their jobs. For example, Rifkin alleges that when millions of retail jobs are displaced by e-commerce and a host of other service-sector jobs undergo digital automation, there will be no new jobs to replace them. If we boost productivity in the retail, banking, insurance, and other service sectors that have been strong job generators, where in the world will people find work?

This "Luddite fallacy" that technological change destroys more jobs than are created fails to recognize that savings from a more efficient industry—in this case, for example, the insurance industry—would flow back to the economy in one of three ways: lower prices (e.g., lower rates for policyholders); higher wages for the fewer remaining employees, or higher profits (or a combination of the three). In a competitive insurance market, most of the savings would flow back to consumers in the form of lower prices. Consumers might use the savings from lower premiums to go out to dinner a few times, buy books, or go to the movies. That stimulates demand that companies in other industries (e.g., restaurants, bookstores, movie studios) respond to by hiring more workers.

Moreover, in making this argument, Rifkin and other liberals are succumbing to the same mistake supply-siders make in believing that overall employment levels are largely determined by microeconomic decisions of firms and individuals. While supply-siders argue that policies like the minimum wage hurt hiring, liberal economists argue that automation or the payroll tax hurts hiring. In fact, one major insight of Keynesianism which still holds up is that overall employment is largely determined by total demand for products and services by individuals, companies, and governments, and that, as such, overall monetary and fiscal policies are the major determinant of employment, not the tens of thousands of microdecisions about whether to install new equipment.

It's not that progressives never talk about growth. Some do, and some on the left have pushed a progrowth agenda. But many liberal activists and others are often ambivalent about growth and productivity. Many environmentalists fear that growth will harm the environment. Some in the labor movement fear that productivity will lead to fewer jobs. Some social policy activists think it's better to focus directly on helping the disadvantaged through social policies and programs, believing that a rising tide doesn't lift all boats, or even most boats.

As a result, often what is presented in the name of a growth agenda is really a redistribution agenda. The lead economic policies that Senate Democrats offer under the category "Boost Opportunity" are redistributive measures of restoring overtime protection and boosting the minimum wage. Robert Reich proposes that

> Democrats should offer their own supply-side version—"bubble-up" economics. The surest way to grow the economy is to make everyone in it more productive. This means better schools, affordable child care and early-childhood education, access to college, affordable health care, and cheap and efficient public transportation. Bubble-up economics has the added virtue of being equitable. It gives everyone a stake in the nation's future prosperity.[33]

This proposal may have the virtue of boosting equity, but it's hard to see how it is a growth agenda. In reality, what these proposals reflect is a view that since government can't do much to spur growth, we should at least make incomes more equal and create a better safety net for risk. To be sure, in the new knowledge economy, with disturbingly high rates of inequality coupled with the breakdown of employment-based security (including reduced health insurance and defined benefits retirement coverage), more equitable redistribution and a much stronger safety net are essential. But redistributive policies do not constitute a growth agenda, not even if a growth label is slapped on them. So it's no wonder that many voters find the supply-side story, flawed as it is, more appealing: at least the supply-side story promises a larger pie.

ECONOMIC "GIRLIE MEN"?

The liberal economic story suffers from an additional drawback: in contrast to the decidedly optimistic story that supply-siders tell, liberals all too often convey a message that economic disaster is just around the corner. At the 2004 Republican Convention, California governor Arnold Schwarzenegger had one of the more memorable lines when he called Democrats "economic girlie men." It was a bit of a cheap shot, but it resonated with many Americans because it contained an iota of truth. Too many liberals seem to be pessimists, always looking for dark clouds in the silver economic lining. In contrast, George Bush projects a sunny, if Pollyannaish, optimism: "We're strong and I'm optimistic about the future of this economy."[34]

After the bursting of the stock market and dot-com bubbles at the turn of the century, a cottage industry of liberal New Economy skeptics emerged, brandishing an "I told you so" view that saw the 1990s as an illusion. Former Clinton Council of Economic Advisers chief Joe Stiglitz calls the 1990s an economic "disaster."[35] Liberal economic commentator Jeff Madrick saw the growth of the 1990s as an aberration, with much of what went on in the name of the "New Economy" as no more than hype. As a result, "America may well have to learn to live with slower economic growth indefinitely for the first time since the Civil War."[36] For these liberal pessimists, there is no New Economy, no technology revolution, and no recent surge of growth. Indeed, the great recession is only a mistake away. Like Winnie the Pooh's friend Eeyore, they see only the worst.

Why are so many liberals so down on the last decade and so pessimistic about the future? Why would Stiglitz call a decade in which the economy created over twenty million new jobs, drove homeownership to record levels, reduced poverty and unemployment, and drove up productivity a "disaster"? To understand why, it's worth looking at how conservatives reacted to the economic boom of the post-WWII era. Like today's liberals, as the new postwar economy emerged, many conservatives were the Eeyores of their day, not because they were against growth, but because they saw the new social, organizational, and political order as leading to the rise of big business, big labor, and big government, all threats to what they viewed as the good society made up of small businesses, small government, and yeoman farmers and proprietors. To their dismay, the new postwar economy required a new social and political order based more on collective action than individual atomistic freedom. As management guru Peter Drucker argues, "Government became the appropriate agent for all social problems, in fact non-governmental activity became suspect."[37]

Today, as a new social and political order emerges based more on networks, civic action, and public-private partnerships than own big stable corporations, powerful unions, and protective bureaucracies, many liberals are reacting in a similar manner, viewing these inevitable developments with considerable skepticism and dismay. They see the new global, knowledge-based, hypercompetitive economy as a threat to economic justice and social cohesion. Many blame technology and globalization for the downsizing of good jobs, stagnant wages, the degradation of the quality of work, growing inequality, and environmental destruction. Just as the populists who aligned with the Democratic standard bearer William Jennings Bryan in the 1890s sought to resist the onslaught of industrialism and preserve the small farm- and merchant-based economy, the new populists on the left seek to bring back the glory days of stable jobs at big corporations, blue-collar manufacturing, and strong unions; dominant central cities; a national, as opposed to a global, economy; and a big bureaucratic national government. At the end of the day, their land of milk and honey is the old corporate mass-production economy made up of large organizations with secure employment, stable markets, and limited competition.

Bill Clinton may have proclaimed that "the era of big government is over," but many on the left remain in denial about big government's loss of effectiveness and popularity and continue to fight a rear-guard action to slow its demise, frantically mobilizing for one fight after another to fend off Republican attacks on sacred and hard-fought Democratic accomplishments such as environmental and workplace protections, progressive taxes, Social Security, and an array of social programs. Many hope to take the country back to the high-water mark of liberalism, the Great Society era that saw the expansion of the welfare state. Indeed, much of Howard Dean's 2004 presidential campaign was styled as a protest against the politics of the last twenty years (including the Clinton administration). Dean looked back to the 1960s as "a time of great hope. Medicare had passed. Head Start had passed. The Civil Rights Act, the Voting Rights Act . . . we felt like we were all in it together, that we all had responsibility for the country. . . . That's the kind of country that I want back."[38] Such resistance is not confined to the U.S. left. In Britain, economist and New Labour adviser Anthony Giddens states, "There is something more going on—a willful refusal to face up to the change the left must make to adapt to the world in which we find ourselves. On this topic, many on the British left are in a state of denial."

Many liberals fear that acknowledging that the New Economy has produced a revival of growth and will likely lead to continued strong growth, at least for another decade, requires them to give up their rights to critique the more problematic aspects of the New Economy (e.g., risk, inequality, dynamism). As a result, it's just easier to be pessimists about the entire New Economy.

KEYNES LIVES

The key to understanding liberal economic doctrine is that much of it is still rooted in Keynesian demand-side economics, which at its core was a response to the principal economic challenge of the 1930s: getting people back to work. As a result, full employment was the overriding objective, even if that meant employing people doing unproductive make-work. Indeed, Keynes once wrote,

> If the Treasury were to fill old bottles with banknotes, bury them at suitable depths in disused coal-mines which are then filled up to the surface with town rubbish, and leave it to private enterprises on well-tried principles of laissez-faire to dig the notes up again, . . . there need be no more unemployment and, with the help of the repercussions, the real income of the community, and its capital wealth also, would probably become a good deal greater than it actually is.[39]

He did acknowledge that "it would indeed be more sensible to build houses and the like; but if there are political and practical difficulties in the way of this, the above would be better than doing nothing." Really? Of course Keynes is right that employing people in productive work would be the best solution. But if that's not possible, wouldn't paying people unemployment insurance so that at least if they are going to produce nothing of value they can enjoy doing it while they are fishing be better than having them do makework with no value?[40]

Full employment is the overriding goal of demand-side economics, and boosting consumer demand through the help of government is the instrument for achieving that goal. Liberal economist James Galbraith argues that "consumption is also an important and much maligned policy objective. People should have the incomes they need to be well fed, housed, and clothed—and also to enjoy life. Public services can help: day care, education, public health, culture, and the arts all deserve far more support than they are getting."[41] Former Democratic House leader Dick Gephardt echoes the view, exclaiming that "raising wages does more than help someone buy food or pay for shelter. Remember the Republican nostrum of the 1980s, supply-side economics? I'm a believer in demand-side economics. Raising wages increases the buying power of American workers and that's good for the entire country."[42]

To be sure, during periodic economic slowdowns, government "pump priming" through temporary increases in spending or cuts in taxes can help boost spending and get the economy back to operating at close to full capacity. But these policies do little to boost growth through higher productivity. Demand-side policies can make sure the "economic car" is going at its peak speed of sixty mph instead of forty mph, but they can't build a faster one that can go seventy mph. Yet building an economic car that can go faster is critical to boosting the incomes of all Americans, for over the moderate and long term, changes in wages have been tied to changes in productivity. From 1963 to 1973, business productivity grew 35 percent while wages grew 31 percent. In that decade, average American workers saw their real incomes go up by almost one-third. In contrast, between 1985 and 1995, productivity grew 9 percent, while wages increased just 6 percent.

This is not to say that productivity growth alone is enough to raise all boats. Indeed, there is disturbing evidence that even with the high productivity growth of the last decade, most of the gains are going to the top earners, and average earners' incomes are growing much more slowly than the rate of productivity growth. As a result, higher productivity is a necessary but not sufficient condition for boosting incomes.

The focus on maintaining strong economic demand also explains why the left was so critical of the Clinton administration's efforts to balance the budget and pay down the debt.[43] Many liberals see balancing the budget as a trap laid for Democrats by crafty Republicans who want to end the era of big government and liberal largess. According to this view, balancing the budget, even in the long term, hurts economic growth by reducing consumer demand. Yet in the 1990s it had no such effect, as unemployment was driven down to levels not seen since the boom years of the 1960s.

The Keynesian focus on full employment and avoiding recessions may have made sense in the old economy, when the major challenge was dealing with relatively frequent economic slowdowns and when the economy faced no significant international competition. However, there is considerable evidence that the New Economy has lessened the severity of the business cycle.[44] And in the new global economy, boosting productivity, innovation, and competitiveness have become pivotal challenges that need to be addressed.

Some liberal economists have begun to acknowledge the nature of the new economic challenges and in response to modify Keynesian economics. In their 2000 book *Growing Prosperity: The Battle for Growth with Equity in the Twenty-First Century*, liberal economists Barry Bluestone and Bennett Harrison tried to update the liberal demand-side story for the New Economy by making investment the key to productivity. However, even so, they still put full employment and strong consumer demand at the center of their model, this time because they see these factors as leading companies to invest in new machinery and equipment, which in turn boosts productivity. While their new narrative acknowledges the importance of private-sector actions to boost productivity, at the end of the day it's still a demand-side story. They state that "what initially energized the post-WWII economy boom had less to do with supply-side factors [like technology] and more to do with extraordinary buoyant demand."[45] Overlooking the development of the electromechanical automation systems and science-based corporate research and development that drove productivity after World War II, they go on to say, "There was no great technology breakthrough on the supply side like the steam engine or electrification."[46]

This formulation, however, can't explain the decline in productivity and investment that began in the mid-1970s. Because of demographic factors, employment actually grew faster in the last half of the 1970s than it did in the roaring 1960s, which according to their model should have spurred companies to invest in even more buildings and machinery. Yet investment declined, and productivity growth stagnated.

Something more was at work, and that something was changes in the underlying technology system in the economy. By the 1970s, the technoeconomic production system that had powered the old postwar economy had run its course, and it became exceedingly difficult to find additional productivity opportunity of which to take advantage. It wasn't until the emergence of the digital economy in the 1990s that productivity growth was able to rebound, and that took thirty years of Moore's law of the constant doubling of computer chip speeds for the technology to finally get cheap and powerful enough to drive a $5 trillion economy.[47]

In fact, innovation and productivity are actually driven much more by factors like technological innovation than by changes in spending. To use a prior example, if Marc Andreessen didn't create the Web browser because his taxes were lowered, as the supply-side story would imply, then neither did he create it because he calculated that consumer demand was high enough to enable more people to afford Internet service. He created it because he was driven to find a new way to surf the Internet (and because he could do the research thanks to federal funding granted to the University of Illinois). This isn't to say that consumer demand is unimportant, but without innovation, it can't generate sustained growth.

NEW ECONOMY POPULISTS

One of the most memorable lines from Senator John Kerry's 2004 presidential campaign was his reference to CEOs of companies that moved operations offshore for tax advantages as "Benedict Arnolds." Kerry's political consultants probably thought the term would resonate with voters who saw themselves at risk for losing their jobs from offshoring. But for many voters Kerry's comments simply reinforced their view that Democrats are antibusiness. And indeed, many liberals do view business as the problem, believing, or at least suspecting, that "what's good for GM" is, by definition, probably not good for the nation. It was this same belief that led Al Gore to build his 2000 presidential campaign around the theme of "people versus the powerful." In this view, most economic policies involve zero-sum trade-offs, not between growth and fairness, as supply-siders tell us, but between big rapacious corporations on the one hand and weak consumers and workers on the other.

According to this view, the job of government is not to work in partnership with corporate America to help it be more innovative and more productive; rather, it's to temper corporate America's worst tendencies with a strong government hand. As liberal commentator Harold Meyerson writes, "Time was when the Democrats were the party of economic justice and opportunity, the party that championed emerging constituencies as well as classes: Catholics, blacks, women. They were the party of the many against the powerful, which played a lot better in the electoral arena than being the party of the one against the many."[48]

Notwithstanding this, many on the left realize that to win they need to temper, or at least obscure, their impulses toward populism, since it leads them to be perceived as having no viable growth strategy. One way to avoid being seen as antibusiness is to extol the virtues of small business and small farmers, as if somehow small businesses and small farmers are more moral and more important to prosperity than large businesses and corporate farms. In his recent book, *The Pro-Growth Progressive*, former Clinton National Economic Council head Gene Sperling argues that "small business remains the key driver of American job growth creating about 75 percent of all new jobs."[49] Sperling's not alone; the Kerry-Edwards 2004 platform promised to help "encourage investments by small business."[50] House Democrats promise to "Fight for America's Small Business" because they are "the engine of America's economy."[51] In siding with small business over large, progressives are placing small businesses in the same boat as workers—both need help against the workings of rapacious large corporations. There is no better case of this than in the left's animus toward Wal-Mart. While it's true that Wal-Mart's employment practices have been anything but progressive, to attack Wal-Mart on the grounds that it is unfair to small retailers is to put the interest of a few thousand small-business owners ahead of the interests of tens of millions of consumers who benefit from Wal-Mart's incredible efficiency and

productivity. Fighting for small-business owners per se, as opposed to helping all business become more productive and competitive, is just one more
form of economic redistribution.

While it's true that small firms create more jobs, it's only a small portion
of them (fewer than 5 percent) that are responsible for most of the jobs gained
by small business.[52] Moreover, compared to larger firms, small businesses on
average are less productive, conduct less research and development, pay
lower wages, and provide fewer health and retirement benefits. This isn't to
say that entrepreneurship is not central to prosperity. It is. But while most
entrepreneurs are small businesses (at least initially), most small businesses
are not entrepreneurs. The best path to helping workers prosper is to ensure
that businesses in America boost productivity and become more innovative,
regardless of their size.

To be sure, there are plenty of instances where companies both large and
small violate the law and/or abuse the public trust, including fraudulently
cooking the corporate books, dumping hazardous wastes, building unsafe
products and maintaining dangerous workplaces, discriminating against particular workers, and paying miserly wages and providing no health benefits.
Indeed, it's entirely appropriate for progressives to redouble their efforts to
ensure that government actively limits and punishes corporate misdeeds.
However, it's one thing to say that business must abide by the law and be a
good corporate citizen, and quite another to hold out big business as the
adversary. For while most Americans may have their misgivings about corporations, they also realize that corporate America is the engine of employment
and prosperity. Even at the height of the Enron and other corporate accounting scandals, 76 percent of Americans either fully or partly agreed with the
statement, "The strength of this country today is mostly based on the success
of American business."[53]

This does not mean that the left must accept the current market realities in
Candide-like terms. There is no doubt that the economic system has changed
in the last two decades so that workers have fewer protections, face much
more risk, and get much lower wages relative to top management. However,
while castigating corporate America may pump up the liberal base, it leads
to dead ends in terms of effective solutions. In the new global competitive
economy, with its intense pressures from capital markets for short-term
profits, business leaders have little flexibility in how to respond to these
forces. For a particular CEO not to respond would mean that he would
quickly be shoved out and replaced by a CEO who would respond. As a
result, the focus of progressives' energy should not be to blame individual
companies, unless these companies break the law or engage in unethical
behaviors. Rather, it should be to fight for the creation of rules, regulations,
and supports so that corporations end up taking the kinds of actions that boost
prosperity and security for all Americans.

CAPITAL FUNDAMENTALISTS

If liberal economists advise Democrats to focus on boosting spending and thereby employment, many centrist, neoclassical economists advise Democrats to focus on boosting savings to boost investment. However, unlike supply-siders, who see tax cuts as the lever to lift savings and investment, many centrist economists see fiscal discipline as the tool. These "capital fundamentalists" see more capital (both physical capital and sometimes human capital) as the key to growth.

Based on their neoclassical economics training, many centrist and some liberal economists see high savings rates as the key to growth. Peter Orszag argues that "the fundamental benefit of higher national savings—achieved by preserving a substantial portion of the projected budget surplus—is that it will expand economic output in the future. Higher national saving leads to higher investment, which means that future workers have more capital with which to work and are more productive as a result."[54] In commenting on Gene Sperling's book *The Pro-Growth Progressive*, Jason Furman, who was in charge of economic policy for John Kerry's presidential campaign, argues,

> Economists like to focus on capital and labor as the source of growth. The traditional conservative answer to maximizing growth is simple: eliminate taxes on capital and you will get more of it. Lower taxes on labor and you will get more of it. Your [Sperling] answer is much more nuanced. . . . To encourage capital formation you argue for savings incentives for moderate income families, many of whom save little or nothing today.[55]

Like conservative supply-siders, these centrist neoclassical economists view savings as the key to growth, but instead of helping the rich save by cutting their taxes, they want to help low-income people save by cutting their taxes and help government save by raising taxes on the wealthy. Yet as we saw in chapter 6, increased savings is at best a weak ingredient to spur growth.

When framed as a debate about the best way to boost savings—and with few Americans knowing enough economics to judge which side is right—tax cuts end up sounding better to many voters. Moreover, by casting economic policy in these capital-centric ways, these liberal and centrist neoclassicalists are asking Democrats to play on the supply-side field, where tax rates and capital are the most important matters. As a result, when liberal and centrist neoclassical economists promote fiscal discipline as the *centerpiece* of their economic policy, they weaken the ability of Democrats to offer a compelling critique of supply-side economics. For example, in a response to a letter signed by 450 economists condemning the Bush tax cuts, Martin Feldstein states, "I don't know of anybody who says this is a bad idea because of tax policy. What they say is, this is a bad idea because of the budget."[56] Once the debate is framed this way—we acknowledge that tax cuts boost growth, but because they lead to budget deficits they end up hurting growth—it's easy for conservatives to respond, well let's get the best of both worlds by cutting taxes to spur growth and cutting government to reduce the deficit. To which liberals can only say that they want to cut the budget deficit by repealing tax cuts, understandably a difficult political sell.

This isn't to say that fiscal discipline is not important. It's important for at least three reasons. As we saw in chapter 6, large budget deficits raise interest rates, thereby reducing investment. Moreover, today's large budget deficits also draw in large amounts of foreign capital, keeping the value of the dollar significantly higher than it would be otherwise, eroding the competitive position of firms in the United States, and contributing to the largest trade deficits in American history. Finally, the growing national debt acts as a huge "birth tax" on the next generation, who eventually must repay the debt. Yet, even though fiscal discipline is important for all these reasons, by itself it is not the major factor in driving growth; innovation is. Moreover, if fiscal discipline comes at the expense of needed investments in research, infrastructure, education and training, it's shortsighted.

Neoclassical capital fundamentalists play into the hands of supply-siders in one other way. Like supply-siders, their ideal tax code is a simple one with a low rate. For example, Alan Blinder's second commandment of taxation is "Thou shalt distort economic incentives as little as possible." He goes on to argue that "every tax influences incentives, as supply-siders correctly emphasize. . . . Unless the market is malfunctioning, such tax-induced redirections of resources reduce economic efficiency. They are therefore to be minimized."[57] This leads him to sound like an unreconstructed supply-sider when he argues that we should "tax all sources of income at the same rates and make those rates as low as possible."[58] Blinder believes that the failure to do so will lead to misallocation of resources, the most cardinal of sins among neoclassical economists. In other words, if some activities are taxed at a higher rate than others, consumers will consume less of these than the "market" would otherwise dictate, thus violating Adam Smith's sacred invisible hand. Yet this sounds awfully like the supply-side doctrine of lowering tax rates and getting the government out of "social engineering." Indeed, supply-siders will argue that if what you really want is a simple tax code with low rates and few distortions, why don't you just replace the income tax with a really simple one, like a national sales tax or a flat tax with just a few deductions.

Notwithstanding the views of neoclassicalists on the right and left, growth economics holds that smart use of the tax code to provide incentives for certain kinds of actions is good economic and social policy. Tax policy can advance important goals such as investing in renewable resources, boosting college enrollment, encouraging adoption of children, and increasing saving for retirement. Because in many cases, individuals and business can accomplish collective goals more effectively than inflexible bureaucratic programs, tax incentives can be an effective tool to achieve objectives like boosting workforce training and increasing corporate research and development investments. In these cases, "distorting" behavior by using the tax code to encourage certain actions can boost economic and societal welfare because certain activities have what economists call externalities, where the actions of individuals or organizations affect others, either for good or ill. When I drive my car, I impose negative externalities on others in the form of traffic congestion, public-sector costs like the salaries of the highway patrol, and environmental pollution. Unless these costs are internalized (e.g., through higher gas taxes), I will drive more than is socially optimal. In other cases, actions I take create positive externalities. If I install solar cells on my roof to generate electricity, I consume less polluting electricity, thereby making the environment cleaner. Without a tax credit for installing solar cells, people will install fewer solar cells than is socially optimal. In these cases, tax incentives for individuals and companies to invest in activities that benefit not just themselves but society as a whole make us all better off.

This is not to say that we shouldn't simplify the tax code; there are indeed a host of provisions in the code that are there only because of the effective lobbying of particular interests and have very little legitimate economic or social rationale. But simplifying the code has become the holy grail for neoclassical economists on both the left and the right. At least, they claim, decisions will be made by the market and the tax code. Such a view ignores the fact that individuals and companies are part of a broader society that has a stake in them doing some things more (e.g., investing in technology) and other things less (e.g., using fossil fuels). Radical simplification will come at the cost of using the tax code as an effective economic and social policy tool.

There is one other strain of capital fundamentalism, and that is one that holds that human capital (e.g., more education) is the key. Indeed, it has become fashionable in economic policy circles to fall back on the universal elixir of "more education" as the solution to a host of problems, from income inequality, to slow growth, to lagging international economic competition. For example, when asked what the government should do about rising levels of inequality, former Federal Reserve Bank chairman Alan Greenspan counseled more skills, arguing that "we have not been able to keep up the average skill level of our workforce to match the required increases of increasing technology."[59]

However, simply providing more education and training for workers will not stop lower-paying jobs from growing faster than middle-paying ones, or stop the top earners from capturing a growing share of the growth of the economic pie. It's true that more education can help a particular individual move from being a cashier to an accountant, but it's a mistake to generalize from what's rational for an individual to what's rational for society as a whole. While more education can help, it will not create relatively more higher-paying accountant jobs and relatively fewer lower-paying cashier jobs; rather, it will create more highly educated persons in low-wage jobs. In this case, social outcomes are quite different from individual ones.[60] (It is true that increasing the supply of college-educated workers could reduce inequality by lowering their wages relative to workers with less education. It is also true that if fewer people had low levels of education, there would be less willingness of people to take low-skill jobs, leading employers to find ways to do without them through means like automation and the like.)

The human capital remedy, particularly boosting college education, is also readily applied as the medicine of choice for meeting the new competitiveness challenge. But given that only one other nation in the world has a higher share of its youth graduating from college, it's hard to see how more college education is the answer to companies moving jobs to nations like China, where wage rates are a tenth of American wages. This is not to say that a better education system would not be helpful, or that we do not need to educate more scientists and engineers. However, the "more education" nostrum provides all too easy a solution for many people, allowing more difficult but important challenges (e.g., how to get companies to invest more in innovative activities here in the United States) to be overlooked. Like conservative financial capital fundamentalists who focus on tax cuts to boost savings because it's seen as a relatively easy lever to pull, human capital fundamentalists focus on boosting education because that's seen as a somewhat easy lever to pull (e.g., expand Pell grants, fully fund No Child Left Behind).

CONCLUSION

If forced to choose between these two divergent economic doctrines—conservative supply-side and liberal demand-side—all too often voters will default to the conservative Republican position for a simple reason: Republicans talk about growth, Democrats about redistribution. Republicans tell an optimistic, confident story; Democrats warn of gloom and doom. Republicans talk about unleashing the private-sector engine of economic growth; Democrats talk about shackling it. Fortunately, these are false choices. It is possible to embrace progressive policies that boost opportunity for low- and middle-income Americans while at the same time promoting productivity growth and innovation. However, this requires articulating a forward-looking, optimistic economic plan to grow the economy, not just redistribute its fruits and curb its large and powerful actors.

NOTES

1. Alan S. Blinder, *Hard Heads, Soft Hearts: Tough-Minded Economics for a Just Society* (Reading, MA: Addison-Wesley, 1987), 13.
2. Blinder, *Hard Heads*, 28.
3. Blinder, *Hard Heads*, 31.
4. Blinder, *Hard Heads*, 96.
5. Blinder, *Hard Heads*, 88.
6. Blinder, *Hard Heads*, 64.
7. Blinder, *Hard Heads*, 165.
8. William L. Watts, "Daschle: Democrats Will Press for Middle Class Tax Relief," Tax Policy Center, 3 January 2003, www.taxpolicycenter.org/news/dems_blast_div.cfm (accessed 21 November 2005).
9. CNN, "Daschle Vows Tax Breaks for Middle-class Families," www.cnn.com/2003/ALLPOLITICS/01/04/dems.radio.
10. George W. Bush, "President Discusses Economy and Tax Relief in North Carolina" (Washington, DC: White House, 5 December 2005).
11. Krugman, "Supply-side Virus Strikes Again: Why There Is No Cure for This Virulent Infection," *Slate*, 15 August 1996, http://web.mit.edu/krugman/www/virus.html (accessed 21 November 2005).
12. Blinder, *Hard Heads*, 15.
13. Blinder, *Hard Heads*, 69.
14. Blinder, *Hard Heads*, 87.
15. Blinder, *Hard Heads*, 90.
16. Ruy Texiera, "Public Opinion Watch," Washington, DC: Center for American Progress, 20 July 2005. Also see Celinda Lake and Daniel Gotoff, "Overview of Recent Research on the Economy" (Washington, DC: Campaign for America's Future, 11 July 2005), www.ourfuture.org/docUploads/lake_poll_july2005.pdf (accessed 26 November 2005).
17. Texiera, "Public Opinion Watch."
18. George W. Bush, "President Discusses Strong and Growing Economy," Chicago, 6 January 2006, www.whitehouse.gov/news/releases/2006/01/20060106-7.html (accessed 31 January 2006).
19. Paul Craig Roberts, *The Supply-Side Revolution: An Insider's Account of Policymaking in Washington* (Cambridge, MA: Harvard University Press, 1984), 7.
20. Roberts, *The Supply-Side Revolution*, 10.
21. Jeff Faux, "You Are Not Alone," in *The New Majority*, eds. Stanley Greenberg and Theda Skocpol (New Haven, CT: Yale University Press, 1997).

22. Robert Reich, "A Covenant with America," *The American Prospect*, November 2005, 48.

23. Nancy Pelosi, "On the Issues: Jobs and the Economy," http://democraticleader .house.gov/issues/the_economy/index.cfm (accessed 24 November 2005).

24. House Democrats did however offer an innovation agenda. www.housedemocrats .gov/bigpicture/jobs_and_economy/issue.cfm?level2id = 91.

25. Benjamin Friedman, *The Moral Consequences of Economic Growth* (Cambridge, MA: Harvard University Press, 2005).

26. Blinder, *Hard Heads*, 107.

27. Blinder, *Hard Heads*.

28. Paul Krugman, *The Age of Diminished Expectations* (Cambridge, MA: MIT Press, 1990).

29. Frank Levy, *The New Dollars and Dreams: American Incomes and Economic Change* (New York: Russell Sage Foundation, 1999), 4.

30. Edward M. Kennedy, "Creating a Genuine 'Opportunity Society'" (speech delivered at the City University of New York Graduate Center, 1 March 2004), www.gc.cuny .edu/spotlight/spotlight_kennedy_speech.htm (3 December 2005).

31. Gene Sperling, *The Pro-Growth Progressive* (New York: Simon & Schuster, 2005), 85.

32. Jeremy Rifkin, *The End of Work: The Decline of the Global Labor Force and the Dawn of the Post-Market Era* (New York: Putnam, 1995), 15.

33. Robert Reich, "For Democrats Adrift, Some Fiscal Therapy," *Washington Post*, 10 November 2002, B1, www.robertreich.org/reich/11102002.asp (accessed 23 November 2005).

34. George W. Bush, "President Discusses Strong and Growing Economy."

35. Joseph Stiglitz, *The Roaring Nineties: A New History of the World's Most Prosperous Decade* (New York: W. W. Norton, 2003).

36. Jeffrey Madrick, *The End of Affluence* (New York: Random House, 1995).

37. Peter Drucker, *Post-Capitalist Society* (New York: HarperCollins, 1993), 123.

38. Paul Farhi, "Dean Tries to Summon Spirit of the 1960s: Candidate's Recollections Differ from Historians' Views of a Turbulent Decade," *Washington Post*, 28 December 2003, A5.

39. John Maynard Keynes, *The General Theory of Employment* (New York: Harcourt Brace and World, 1935), 129.

40. It's true that this could lead workers to lose skills and their attachment to the labor force, but the broader point is that simple make-work does not boost economic welfare.

41. James Galbraith, "The Surrender of Economic Policy," *American Prospect*, 1 March 1996.

42. Richard Gephardt, *An Even Better Place: America in the 21st Century* (New York: Public Affairs, 1999), 73.

43. Stiglitz, *The Roaring Nineties*.

44. One reflection of this new stability is the fact that quarter-to-quarter GDP volatility is down significantly since the mid-1980s. In the three decades preceding 1983, approximately 30 percent of quarterly GDP growth rates were in excess of 1.5 percent, while 22 percent were negative. In comparison, the numbers after 1993 were 78 and 10 percent. Economists attribute the reduced cyclicality to several causes, including a decline in the

change in inventory investments and a greater role of the service sector in the economy. For example, as a result of just-in-time inventory practices, the average production lead time for supplies has declined from seventy-two days during the 1961-to-1983 period, to forty-nine days from 1984-to-1998 period. Robert D. Atkinson, *The Past and Future of America's Economy: Long Waves of Innovation That Power Cycles of Growth* (Northampton, MA: Edward Elgar, 2005).

45. Barry Bluestone and Bennett Harrison, *Growing Prosperity: The Battle for Growth with Equity in the Twenty-First Century* (New York: Houghton Mifflin, 2000), 33.

46. Bluestone and Harrison, *Growing Prosperity*, 37.

47. Named after Intel founder Gordon Moore, it refers to the prediction Moore made in the early 1970s that the cost of computing power would decline by half every two years, while the power would double. In fact, Moore was not optimistic enough; computing power has been doubling about every eighteen months.

48. Harold Meyerson, "What Are Democrats About?" *Washington Post*, 17 November 2004, A27.

49. Sperling, *Pro-Growth Progressive*, 86.

50. Kerry-Edwards 2004, *Strong at Home, Respected in the World*, Washington, DC, 2004.

51. www.house.gov/smbiz/democrats/SMALL%20BUSINESS%20FACT%20SHEET %20FINAL%20(2)%20(2).doc.

52. According the National Commission on Entrepreneurship, only 4.7 percent of U.S. businesses that existed in 1991 at least doubled their employment from 1992 to 1997. Cited in Organisation for Economic Co-operation and Development, "Micro-Policies for Growth and Productivity: Final Report" (Paris: OECD, 2005), 17.

53. Pew Research Center for the People & the Press, "Views of Business and Regulation Unchanged by Enron," 21 February 2002, http://people-press.org/reports/print.php 3?PageID – 349 (accessed 23 November 2005).

54. Peter R. Orszag, "Marginal Tax Rate Reductions and the Economy: What Would Be the Long-Term Effects of the Bush Tax Cut?" (Washington, DC: Center on Budget and Policy Priorities, March 2001), 1.

55. Jason Furman, "Comments on the Pro-Growth Progressive," www.tpmcafe.com/ author/jfurman (accessed 3 December 2005).

56. Quoted in Justin Fox, "Here We Go Again: Supply Side Economics Is Back! But This Is Not 1981—and That's Why Bush Tax Plans Don't Quite Cut It," *Fortune* 147, 12 May 2003, 64.

57. Blinder, *Hard Heads, Soft Hearts*, 162.

58. Blinder, *Hard Heads, Soft Hearts*, 164.

59. Alan Greenspan, quoted in Nell Henderson, "Greenspan Says Workers' Lack of Skills Lowers Wages," *Washington Post*, 22 July 2004, A1.

60. Robert D. Atkinson, "Inequality in the New Knowledge Economy," in *The New Egalitarianism*, eds. Anthony Giddens and Patrick Diamond (New York: Polity, 2005).

Chapter Eleven

Growth Economics: A Policy for Today's Economy

The way we're really going to grow the economy is to invest in people, to invest in innovation, to have the federal government put money in the kind of research that will create the new high-technology . . . industries that will create the millions of new jobs.

—Senator Joseph Lieberman

Both conservative supply-side economics and liberal demand-side economics are flawed doctrines for growing the twenty-first-century economy, in large part because they both look back for guidance to prior eras. Crafting an effective growth strategy requires a pragmatic approach based on the realities of today's global, knowledge-based economy. This means adopting a growth economics framework that recognizes that productivity growth through innovation is the key determinant of our standard of living.

Where supply-side economics places freedom as its overarching goal, and demand-side economics places fairness as its, growth economics places fast and widely shared growth as its. Ensuring robust productivity growth—the amount of economic output per hour worked—will be essential over the next two decades if the workforce is able to support the escalating number of baby-boom retirees without seeing its own standard of living go down. To do so, we will need to use every policy tool available to help make the nation more productive and to restore the relatively broad-based income growth enjoyed during the mid- and late 1990s. Indeed, growth is a key social policy, since as John Kennedy reminded us, a "rising tide lifts all boats." If we can put in place the growth economics policies to boost productivity by just one percentage point more than the expected trend, and if everyone shares in that growth, the average working American will be making $4,300 more per year in ten years than they are now, and over $10,000 more in twenty years. That's how to let Americans have more of "their money."

Instead, both liberal and conservative economic doctrines want to take a shortcut to growth, focusing less on productivity and more on redistribution. Conservatives want to raise after-tax income by cutting taxes—taking from public expenditures to boost private incomes—and by having workers work harder in response to lower taxes. Indeed, this increase in after-tax incomes (with decreases in pretax incomes) is a major talking point for President Bush in his recent stump speeches. Yet cutting taxes in the face of deficits and at the expense of needed public investments is the wrong answer. Nor is working harder an option. Americans already work harder than workers in any advanced industrial nation. We should be doing more, not less, to help Americans better balance work and family life.

Liberals want to tax the rich more and funnel the proceeds to programs and policies to benefit "working families." While efforts to redistribute the pie more fairly can help provide a one-time increase in incomes for many Americans, without robust productivity growth such efforts will fall short of the goal of allowing most Americans to enjoy sustained and robust increases in their standard of living.

Growth economics takes a different route to raising wages and incomes: it seeks to boost productivity while at the same time working to ensure that the benefits are broadly shared. To achieve this, income growth and innovation need to be at the center of economic policy. In fact, we should set an explicit national goal of doubling productivity in twenty-five years (this would require an annual rate of productivity growth of 3 percent per year) while at the same time reducing voluntary work time 10 percent. Toward that end, we should embrace investment, regulatory, tax, and trade policies that advance that goal, and we should reject those policies that do not. If we did double productivity, Americans would enjoy 80 percent higher incomes with 10 percent less work.

Growth economics is grounded in an understanding that economic prosperity is principally driven not by a small set of Promethean investors seeking to maximize their portfolios, as conservatives would have us believe, nor by government seeking to redistribute a fixed pie from higher-income Americans to lower-income Americans, as liberals tell us. Rather, the keys to growth are in some ways profoundly simple. As an OECD report on the knowledge economy states, "Long-term growth and employment depend less on short-term allocative efficiency measures . . . than on a set of long-term policies aimed at enhancing the knowledge base . . . through increased investment in the knowledge infrastructure, the knowledge distribution system, and the human knowledge component."[1] Leading economists now acknowledge that without change we cannot grow, that increases in knowledge and competition drive growth and change, and that government has a key role to play in that process.[2] In short, they are saying that the best macroeconomic policy is microeconomic policy, not individual tax cuts as supply-siders push, but factors such as support for research, innovation, investment in new equipment, skill building, and promotion of competitive markets.

Growth economics recognizes that it is only through actions taken by workers, companies, industry consortia, entrepreneurs, research institutions, civic organizations, and governments that an economy's productive and innovative power is enhanced. As a result, when examining how the New Economy creates wealth, growth economics is focused on a different set of questions: are entrepreneurs taking risks to start new ventures? Are workers continually upgrading their skills, and are companies organizing production in ways that utilize those skills? Are companies in America investing in technological breakthroughs, and is government supporting the technology base (e.g., funding research and the training of scientists and engineers)? Are regional clusters of firms and other institutions fostering innovation? Are policy makers avoiding erecting protections for companies against more innovative competitors? Are research institutions transferring knowledge to companies? And are policies supporting the ubiquitous widespread adoption of advanced information technologies and e-commerce? In short, growth economics recognizes the fundamental insight that innovation takes place in the context of institutions. This shifts the focus of economic policy away from the supply-siders' focus on wealthy individuals toward creating an institutional environment that supports technological change, entrepreneurial drive, and higher skills.

So is growth economics a demand-side or a supply-side doctrine? The answer is that it is both. On the one hand, growth economics focuses on supply-side factors like knowledge, skills, and investment. But unlike supply-side economics, it does not focus principally on the effect of marginal tax rates on the willingness and ability of individuals to work, save, and invest.

But growth economics is also focused on the demand side of the equation in the sense that it seeks to increase the demand by organizations for the factors that boost growth and innovation: new knowledge, new skills, and new capital equipment (including software and information technology equipment). In other words, it's less about boosting consumer demand for products and services and more about boosting the demand of companies for more knowledge, more investment in new equipment and software, and more skilled workers. As a result, whereas supply-side economics and demand-side economics focus principally on individuals—with the former focusing on permanent cuts in individual tax rates and the latter on boosting wages, benefits, and government-funded benefits to individuals—growth economics focuses on helping organizations be more productive and innovative. Because organizations (for-profit, nonprofit, and government) generate the lion's share of the wealth in advanced knowledge economies, and most of this is from business, it's impossible to be progrowth and antibusiness. At the same time, growth economics is not blindly probusiness; but it is proinnovation and pro-productivity.

GROWTH ECONOMICS PRINCIPLES

Growth economics is guided by fifteen key principles. Some of these principles, such as the focus on growth and ensuring that markets are competitive, may be seen by some as conservative. Others, such as the belief that government action is a key component in ensuring growth, may be seen by some as liberal. In fact, these are pragmatic principles designed to produce robust and widely shared growth in the new global and innovation- and knowledge-based economy of the twenty-first century. And these are principles that can and should be embraced by both political parties.

Growth Economics Focuses More on Boosting Productivity and Innovation and Less on "Allocative Efficiency"

Growth economics rejects the neoclassical notion that just getting the allocation of factors right is enough. Supply-siders and neoclassical economists generally focus on ensuring that the allocation of factors (capital, labor, and goods and services) is determined by individuals making free choices in the market not distorted by regulations or taxes. However, there are two problems with this. First, their model assumes that markets get it right most of the time, and that even when they don't, governments will get it wrong. They believe that the pretax marketplace is efficient and that taxes, regulation, and spending distort Adam Smith's invisible hand. But as economist F. M. Scherer stated, this model "assumes perfect competition, constant returns to scale, and the absence of externalities. All three assumptions have been questioned, often convincingly, by new growth theorists."[3] Indeed, while markets are important tools in determining what is produced and how, there is a host of ways in which markets fail or at least don't completely succeed. One is externalities, where the effects of actors in the marketplace affect others, either for good or ill. In this case, without government intervention, there will be too much or too little production of an activity. For example, market forces left alone will lead to an underinvestment in research, since the results of scientific research "spill over" to other companies, preventing the company doing the research from completely capturing all the economic benefits. There are other kinds of market failures, including "network effects," where actions by private actors will succeed only if other actors take similar steps. For example, enabling the use of personal-health-information smart cards requires that PCs come with smart-card encoders, that doctors' offices and other health providers have smart-card readers, that all smart cards have a comparable standard, that medical information codes are standardized, that the millions of public and private health providers agree to use the system, and that privacy issues be dealt with. Individual actors in the marketplace can find it hard, although not impossible—witness how Visa and MasterCard created standards for the credit card industry—to solve these coordination problems without the assistance of smart public policies.

Second, as we saw in section 2, in a new knowledge- and innovation-driven economy, allocative efficiency is not the major factor in driving growth. Rather, the lion's share of growth is determined by what economists call productive efficiency and adaptive efficiency. Productive efficiency is the ability of organizations to reorganize production in ways that lead to the greatest amount of output with the fewest inputs, including labor inputs. Adaptive efficiency is the ability of economies and institutions to change over time to respond to successive new situations, in part by developing and adopting technological innovations. Economist Douglas North explains:

> Adaptive efficiency . . . is concerned with the kinds of rules that shape the way an economy evolves through time. It is also concerned with the willingness of a society to acquire knowledge and learning, to induce innovation, to undertake risk and creative activity of all sorts, as well as to resolve problems and bottlenecks of the society through time. We are far from knowing all the aspects of what makes for adaptive efficiency, but clearly the overall institutional structure plays a key role to the degree that the society and the economy will encourage the trials, experiments and innovations that we can characterize as adaptively efficient. The incentives embedded in the institutional framework direct the process of learning by doing and the development of tacit knowledge that will lead individuals in decision-making processes to evolve systems that are different from the ones that they had to begin with.[4]

In a world where allocation efficiency is all that matters and where market failures are few, one can make a compelling case for limited government, except perhaps to address issues of equity. But in a world in which productive and adaptive efficiency is what matters, the role for explicit and effective growth economics policies is more compelling.

Active, Smart Government Policies to Boost Innovation and Competition Foster Growth

Relying on the market alone and consigning government to a role of enforc-ing contracts and protecting property is a path to suboptimal growth. All else being equal, economies that forge smart public-private partnerships will always outperform economies in which government abdicates its role and leaves most actions up to private actors. Markets get many things right, and if forced to choose between an economy with strong markets and limited gov-ernment or one with limited markets and strong government, we should chose the former. But in contrast to what supply-siders warn, that's a false choice—we can walk and chew gum at the same time. In other words, we can have policies that are promarket and pro–public policy intervention.

Growth economics is based on the principle that government action, including investments in science, technology, infrastructure, education, and skills, provides a foundation upon which productivity growth depends. In this sense, it rejects the ideological fixation of the right that holds that government failure is always worse than market failure. Indeed, supply-side economics is based on an ideological view that governmental action is not only never complementary to markets but is always inferior. As President Bush tells us, "The role of government is not to try to create wealth; that's not the role of government."[5]

But it's not as if government spends and people invest; indeed, the lion's share of the Bush tax cuts have gone to consumption. Just witness the recent housing boom, certainly not a development that leads to higher productivity or innovation. Moreover, not all private-sector investments benefit the econ-omy, since a not insignificant share are made for the zero-sum activity of gaining market share, not boosting productivity.[6]

Growth economics holds that the public sector can help boost innovation. Yet supply-siders argue that government only gets in the way of the private sector innovating. Yet even a rudimentary history of innovation clearly dem-onstrates that government policies have played a key role in stimulating tech-nological innovation. The list of recent innovations that can trace their origins to government support of research is long and impressive, including bar codes, Web browsers, computer-aided manufacturing, magnetic resonance imaging, fiber optics, and tissue engineering, to name just a few.[7] And of course the Internet, which underpins so much current economic activity, and the mapping of the human genome, which will be the basis of so much of our future innovation, would not have been developed without an active govern-ment role. This suggests that we should expand government support for research—not just basic undirected research, but also applied research in areas of key national need (e.g., boosting productivity, reducing fossil-fuel energy consumption, etc.). (See appendix.)

Our Collective Prosperity Depends on Our Willingness to Embrace Change

Too often progressives want growth without risk, discomfort, or displacement. Yet growth depends upon what economist Joseph Schumpeter called "creative destruction," the sweeping away of less productive firms, industries, and occupations. As a result, growth economics unequivocally favors progress and innovation, not special interests from business, labor, and the civic sector fighting innovation in favor of holding on to the status quo. This does not mean unreflectively embracing all innovations or all developments in the marketplace. It does, however, mean that the default position should be in favor of innovation. America didn't get to be the most prosperous nation on earth by saying, "Wait until the innovation is proven and completely safe." Breakthroughs never occur without risk and uncertainty.

Innovation and change are disruptive. They displace workers and make some skills obsolete; they cause firms, and even entire industries, to fail; they lead to industrial and economic restructuring in cities and sometimes even whole regions; they upset traditional ways of doing things; and they lead to wholly unexpected developments, impossible to predict ahead of time. Who would have predicted in the late 1980s that a government network run by the National Science Foundation would evolve into the Internet and be used for everything from online dating, to buying an array of goods and services, to blogging. Because innovation is disruptive, it tends to spark strong political demands to insulate affected segments of the economy and slow down economic change.

But while innovation is disruptive and often frightening, it is also almost always good, creating new opportunities and increased incomes for Americans. As a result, demands to slow down change, boost friction, and preemptively regulate nascent innovations, while understandable, inherently deny opportunities to less politically powerful interests in the guise of "protecting" those with clout. As a result, to effectively promote growth in the New Economy, government must not give in to these protectionists, but rather should facilitate the processes of innovation and change. Government must be on the side of policies that boost innovation and foster higher productivity and be against policies that seek only to divide a slowly growing pie, protect or reward special interests at the expense of overall economic progress, slow down the process of change, or place innovation in a stranglehold of well-meaning but often misguided regulatory constraints. In particular, this means not giving in to special interests fearful of change. These protectionists need to be rebuffed in a host of areas—from their opposition to bioengineered foods that promise dramatic increases in agricultural productivity; to mergers that promise heightened efficiencies; to new business entrants in markets that threaten incumbent organizations and existing business models; and to new information technologies, such as placement of radio frequency identification devices (RFID) on consumer products, on grounds that they erode privacy.

While Some Companies Compete Internationally, All Countries Do

When it comes to international trade, supply-siders and neoclassical economics generally hold that firms compete but countries do not. As a result, there is little need to put in place policies to help boost national competitiveness. According to this view, if a high-value-added, innovative firm like Boeing, for example, goes out of business, as long as America maintains flexible labor and capital markets, these resources will flow into other industries, including into expanding or new firms and sectors. In this market environment, policies are needed only to facilitate the transition of resources from losing to winning companies, including making sure that losing companies are not protected from this tough but necessary discipline and that workers get reemployed quickly. As a result, holders of this neoclassical view believe that as long as we have a good education system and don't restrain creative destruction, then all should be well.

This conventional view may have accurately described the United States before the emergence of the era of globalization in the last two decades. During the old-economy era, if firms couldn't compete and went out of business, the only issue was making sure that the assets, including the workers, were quickly redeployed to other companies that could compete successfully. However, in the new global economy, this framework no longer sufficiently explains industrial and economic change in the new global economy in which knowledge is increasingly the major factor of production. In contrast to the neoclassical view, knowledge is not a free-flowing commodity. Workers have context-specific knowledge whose value declines significantly when the context is lost. Moreover, there are significant spillovers from firm activities and significant first-mover advantages, including learning effects, which let firms translate early leads into dominant positions. There are also significant network effects that mean that advancement in one industry (e.g., broadband telecommunications) can lead to advancement in a host of others (e.g., Internet video).

As a result, for many parts of the U.S. economy exposed to international competition, if you lose it, you can't easily reuse it. In these cases, foreign imports may end up substituting for the defunct U.S. product. This framework—what some have termed a neo-Schumpetarian framework, after economist Joseph Schumpeter—better describes a growing share of the U.S. economy, particularly those sectors focused on technology- and knowledge-based production, than does the neoclassical adjustment model.

This means that losing international competitions in knowledge-based industries leads to losing much more than just the firms. It means losing much of the value from these dispersed pieces of value now represented by unemployed workers, vacant offices, surplus machines, and underutilized suppliers. If a firm using highly trained scientific and technical talent cuts production, it's often not easy to put the workers and the training they embody into use in other sectors. Take a hypothetical example. If a technology-based company like Boeing were to go out of business because of government-subsidized competition from its European competitor Airbus, in all likelihood the nation could not rely on market forces, including a dramatic drop in the value of the dollar, to recreate a domestic aviation industry. For, to recreate domestic production, Boeing would have to recreate all the talent that was lost, not just the talent of individual workers, but the collective knowledge embedded in Boeing and in the entire Boeing supply chain of parts suppliers. Supply-siders and other neoclassical economists will claim that losing Boeing doesn't really matter as long as resources, including workers, flow to new activities. But many of the resources—for instance, the organizational knowledge embedded in the company—will simply vanish. Moreover, the resources embedded in mobile factors of production (e.g., workers' skills, machines, buildings) may just as easily flow to new activities that are in lower-value-added activities that pay lower wages. For example, many of the tens of thousands of Boeing workers who combine their knowledge to produce the world's most advanced passenger jet airplanes could easily end up working in organizations that produce much less value per worker, leading to a lower national standard of living. Supply-siders will also claim that even having this conversation implies some kind of heavy-handed industrial policy of picking winners and losers, à la European subsidies for Airbus. But recognizing that high-value-added, innovation-based companies are important to the future prosperity of the United States does not imply that public policy should pick individual companies or even individual industries for support. As discussed in the appendix, it does imply that it should take steps to make it more likely that such companies will invest and prosper in the United States, by taking steps such as boosting the R&D tax credit, for example.

This suggests that economic policy must do more than focus on enhancing skills, boosting education, and funding programs to help dislocated workers more easily get new jobs, although clearly these must play a part in any solution. A robust national competitiveness policy must do more. It must be grounded in a simple understanding that in the twenty-first-century global economy, nations can no longer be indifferent to the industrial and value-added mix of their economy. With the sole exception of the United States, virtually all nations have consciously adopted national policies to "intervene in the market"—in this case to make it easier for corporations to invest in higher-value-added activities that create higher-wage jobs in their nation. These nations are not content to sit idly by to observe how the market will allocate production, for they know that it could just as easily allocate production to low-wage T-shirt factories and call centers instead of to higher-wage semiconductor factories and software companies. And while the profitability of both kinds of activities might be similar, the impacts on standards of living are not.

There is one group of elected officials in the United States who understand the necessity of going beyond letting firms alone determine the location of high-value-added economic activities. Since the mid-twentieth century, most governors—whether Republican or a Democrat—have put in place policies to tilt the playing field so that corporations create higher-value-added jobs in their states. Like the neoclassical economists who dictate which economic policies are acceptable and which are not in Washington, most governors also recognize that markets generally create prosperity. But unlike the Washington economic mandarins, governors have the real-world understanding borne of political necessity that markets don't always generate that prosperity for their citizens. The next one thousand high-value-added jobs could just as easily be created in another state or another nation. That's why both Republican and Democratic governors "intervene" in their economies with activist economic development policies. It's certainly true that some of what states do in the name of economic development is zero-sum (in other words, doesn't lead to increased national prosperity), but much of what they do—such as investing in workforce development, funding includes university-industry research centers, expanding infrastructure, and supporting early-stage venture capital—positive-sum activities that help not just the state economy but the national economy.

Now that the U.S. economy has become in essence a large state (in the sense that a large share of the economy is traded internationally and competes against other nations the way states have long had to compete), the United States no longer has the choice of whether to "intervene"; our choice is how we will intervene. Leaving it up to the results of market competition alone will lead the United States increasingly to lose out on global competitions for high-value-added technology and knowledge-intensive production. This means federal policy makers need to develop a national competitiveness policy focused on ensuring that innovation, and not just innovative people, stays and grows in the United States. This doesn't mean picking individual companies for support. It does mean adopting policies, like expanding the R&D tax credit and boosting federal support for research, that makes it more likely that companies will innovate here at home.

Growth Economics Distinguishes between Subsidizing Industries and Helping Them Become More Innovative and Productive

Supply-siders would have us believe that any governmental effort that helps business (excluding indiscriminate tax cuts and regulatory relief) is industrial policy: unproductive subsidies that substitute for the wisdom of the market. Many liberals would call any such efforts corporate welfare. As a result, the current economic policy debate in Washington makes almost no distinction between policies that help companies do something socially beneficial that they would not otherwise do or do as much of (e.g., hiring welfare workers, investing in energy-efficient technology, training workers in broader skills, spending more on research and development) and simple subsidies that do nothing to help make a company more productive or innovative. The former would include programs that raise the capacity of companies to be more productive and innovative, like the National Institute of Standards and Technology's (NIST) Manufacturing Extension Partnership (a program to provide technical assistance to help small and medium-size manufacturers), or that help companies develop new technology, like NIST's Advanced Technology Program.[8] The latter would include programs and policies that give money to companies with no increase in productive or innovative potential, such as agricultural subsidies and price supports that postpone needed market adjustments while propping up inefficient farm producers; protections that subsidize a particular activity, such as federally subsidized flood insurance (an incentive for more homeowners and companies to locate in flood plains); tariffs on particular products in response to political pressures from particular industries; and generalized tax cuts not tied to particular desirable corporate behaviors. Government must strive to reduce or eliminate the array of government protections and subsidies that protect entrenched interests without increasing the economy's innovative or productive capacity, while at the same time expanding government investments (both direct spending and tax incentives) to help companies be more innovative and productive.

For Government to Be an Effective Agent of Growth Economics, It Must Be as Fast, Responsive, and Flexible as the Economy and Society with Which It Interacts

Conservative supply-siders throw up their hands at the prospect of government being an agent for growth and innovation and instead claim that we can rely almost exclusively on the private sector to maximize wealth creation. Yet they do little to ensure that government works better and that programs are rigorously and fairly evaluated and in response expand effective programs (they are usually ready, however, to cut less effective, and sometimes more effective, programs). In contrast, many liberal demand-siders are reluctant to embrace a strong reinventing government agenda in part because that agenda has to start with reforming civil service and moving to increased pay-for-performance and more flexible personnel management systems. Such steps will almost always engender resistance from public-sector unions. Moreover, many are loath to embrace initiatives that bypass the bureaucratic status quo, even when it is not working.

Growth economics recognizes that government can best work in a strategic partnership with business, the civil sector, and workers if it does not have to rely on inflexible, rule-driven, hierarchical, and slow bureaucratic organizations. As a result, the new model of governing should be decentralized, non-bureaucratic, catalytic, results oriented, and empowering. In many cases we should replace big, slow bureaucratic agencies with more flexible entities like Performance-Based Organizations (PBOs) or even quasi-public corporations. Moving along a continuum, if a PBO allows government agencies more flexibility and accountability, the next step on the continuum is nonprofit corporations that are not government agencies but are imbued with a public mission and are governed by a government-appointed board. Many nations and U.S. states seeking to reinvent and bring entrepreneurial flexibility to government have transferred a wide range of operational (as opposed to regulatory) tasks from large, bureaucratic agencies to more flexible, smaller, and results-oriented public or private nonprofit corporations.

These organizations would be exempt from many of the stifling personnel and contracting rules that currently hamstring government agencies, and in the case of quasi-public corporations, they would be led by a CEO whose tenure and compensation would be based on achieving results. For example, we should create new nonbureaucratic organizations to boost innovation (American Innovation Foundation), skills (National Skills Corporation), and regional economic development (Rural Prosperity Corporation) (see appendix).

In the old economy, bureaucracy was how we addressed many major public policy problems. In the new knowledge economy, we must rely on a host of new public-private partnerships and alliances. In this new economy, boundaries of all sorts have blurred. In what has been described as "coopetition," companies are entering into partnerships and alliances of all forms. Direct competitors in one market may well collaborate on research and development in another market. Similarly, rather than acting as the sole funder and manager of bureaucratic programs, government needs to coinvest and collaborate with other organizations—networks of companies, research institutions, nonprofit community organizations, and other civic organizations—to achieve a wide range of public policy goals. Compared to government, these organizations have a number of advantages. They are usually closer to the customer and tend to have greater capacity to solve problems because they can be more flexible, they can leverage additional resources, and they can face bottom-line pressures to boost performance. In short, growth economics cannot be implemented without government, but federal government agencies, especially as currently structured, alone can't implement it.

Digital Transformation Is Key to Productivity Growth

Productivity growth in the last 150 years was driven largely by farmers and factory workers getting new, more mechanized tools (farmers got chemical-based fertilizer, better seeds, mechanized farm equipment; factory workers got machine tools, continuous-flow processing, forklifts, and other similar tools). Future advances in productivity will depend on whether we can match these productivity gains in the over 80 percent of the economy that does not involve growing food or making goods: our stores, offices, hospitals, and schools. But the technology system that will get us there is not mechanization; it is digitization—the widespread use of information technology to transform whole sectors and economic functions. That's why growth economics places such a central focus on spurring the transformation to a digital economy.

The information technology revolution is transforming virtually all industries and is central to increased productivity. Indeed, economists have found that one of the major reasons why productivity growth has rebounded from its slow growth rates in the 1970s and 1980s was the spread of the IT revolution.[9] By automating a large share of functions involving the routine processing of information, including face-to-face, phone, and paper transactions, the digital economy promises to continue to be the major engine of productivity. Information technology is allowing companies to automate and make more efficient a host of processes, including replacing paper checks with e-banking, replacing manual ticket functions with kiosks, enabling people to communicate through voice recognition systems, filling out forms online, and generally eliminating a large share of routine information-based tasks. As recently as five years ago, checking into an airport meant going to the airline counter, waiting in line for your boarding pass, and then turning it in upon boarding, where it was then mailed to a location for the data to be key-punched into a database. Now a person can go online or to a self-serve kiosk and get her own boarding pass that is read automatically upon check-in. The savings from IT-enabled transactions go way beyond the savings from elimi-nating paper or automating face-to-face transactions; they allow whole cate-gories of economic functions to be eliminated. For example, e-commerce could cut the cost of buying a house in half by allowing consumers to use the Web to substitute for much of what real estate agents do.

As a result, growth economics pays special attention to developing a robust national e-commerce strategy to foster digital transformation. This means crafting a legal and regulatory framework that supports the growth of the digital economy in such areas as taxation, privacy, digital signatures, tele-communications regulation, and industry regulation (in banking, insurance, and securities, for example). It also means using procurement and other direct government tools to help break digital "chicken-or-egg" logjams around issues like broadband, smart cards, and other network-dependent technolo-gies. It means fighting the efforts of brick-and-mortar middlemen to erect all manner of laws and regulations to thwart e-commerce competitors. It means working to spur e-transformation in sectors where the government has a large presence as a customer, regulator, or funder (e.g., health, education, transpor-tation, banking and securities, and housing) by working with industry to develop sector transformation strategies. It means funding cutting-edge research in advanced information technologies. It means aggressively deploy-ing customer-centric e-government applications while making sure that all aspects of government—federal, state, and local—use information technolo-gies where possible to lower costs and boost service quality.

Commercialization of Knowledge and Research Drive Innovation

Knowledge, technology, and innovation are central to growth. The twenty-first-century economy grows not because we do more of the same, but because we do things differently and better, and this requires generating and applying knowledge. Whether the knowledge is from an entrepreneur with a new idea for selling a service or product over the Internet,[10] a researcher inventing a new product, an engineer designing changes to factory production processes, a programmer coming up with new software, an entrepreneur designing a new e-commerce business model, or an office worker gaining skills to do her job better, it all produces knowledge that drives growth.

Supply-siders claim that with the exception of modest investments in basic science and some mission-specific research like defense, space, and health, government should leave research and innovation to the private sector. But a global, hypercompetitive economy with equity markets demanding that companies generate profits in the current quarter has made it increasingly difficult for business to maintain its investments in research, particularly earlier-stage basic and applied research. Boosting funding for this kind of research, which if successful may not produce profits for five to ten years, is particularly difficult for companies to justify. Moreover, even if shareholders rewarded such long-term investments, companies would still underinvest in research because companies cannot capture all of the benefits of the research they perform. The private sector underinvests in research because much of the returns to investments in knowledge spill over and cannot be completely captured.[11] An entrepreneur develops a new business model that others copy. A university transfers discoveries from the lab to the marketplace. A company makes a breakthrough that forms the basis of innovations that other companies can use. This is why studies have found that the rates of return to society from corporate R&D are at least twice the estimated returns that the company itself receives.[12] As a result, a strong public role for direct funding for science, technology, and research and its commercialization is needed. Moreover, tax incentives for the private sector to invest more in research are critical to fueling a high-powered knowledge economy.[13] In fact, economists have found that publicly supported research is a key driver of economic growth. For example, over 30 percent of U.S. patents are based on research supported by the public sector, and that share is increasing.

Unfortunately, government investment in knowledge has been falling. As a share of GDP, government support for basic and applied research (not including development) has dropped from around 0.60 percent of GDP in the 1960s, to 0.45 percent in the 1980s, to 0.38 percent in 2000. Federal funding for non–defense or health-related research and development has fallen even more, plummeting from 1.41 percent of GDP in 1970 to just 0.21 percent in 2003. As a result, R&D as a share of GDP is now higher in South Korea and Finland and is rising in Sweden, Japan, Canada, and Australia. One of the main reasons is because the federal government's share has fallen so much. Moreover, the tax incentives given to companies to invest in research and development are significantly lower in the United States than in many other nations.

Studies of academic research consistently show a significant rate of return (RoR). Mansfield found a 28 percent RoR from federally funded academic research.[14] Publicly funded agricultural research has shown a consistent rate of return of around 40 percent.[15] A study of a sample of fourteen research projects funded by the Department of Commerce's National Institute of Standards and Technology showed a median RoR of 144 percent.[16] Economists Leyden and Link conclude that government funding of research spurs additional private funding.[17]

As a result, increased government support of research is a key pillar of growth economics. Government should increase its investments in science and technology by at least $10 billion a year, with much of the money devoted to new industry-university research partnerships. Moreover, private-sector research should be encouraged by doubling the R&D tax credit and providing an even more generous flat credit for collaborative R&D conducted by firms in research consortia or partnerships with federal labs, universities, or other research institutions.

Higher Skills Boost Productivity

While technological innovation is the major driver of productivity growth, having a workforce with up-to-date skills also plays an important role. Indeed, new technology and new kinds of business models require not so much more skills, but new skills. Yet, in spite of the increased importance of skills, competitive pressures have meant that American companies invest less in training as a share of GDP than they did ten years ago. One reason for this decline is that as Americans spend less time at any one job, companies that train workers risk seeing that investment walk out the door before it pays for itself. Moreover, while higher-skilled workers enable companies to restructure work in more productive ways, unless companies first restructure work to take advantage of higher skills (and pay workers more because of it), individuals have less incentive to get more skills. Both of these factors lead to less skill development than is optimal.

As a result, it's incumbent upon government to provide the kinds of incentives and programs that will encourage organizations and workers to boost their skills. But like federal support for research, federal support for training has also fallen dramatically, from 0.19 percent of GDP in 1980 to 0.05 percent in 2004, with significant cuts from the Bush administration. It's time to reverse this cut in funding by allocating an additional $1 billion per year for training efforts to support the establishment of a new National Skills Corporation that would work with industry and unions to boost training. In addition, we should create a new knowledge tax credit that would allow companies to take a 40 percent tax credit on increases in training expenses. Finally, there's a special challenge to ensure an adequate supply of scientists and engineers.

Our nation needs reinvigorated efforts to boost this supply, both by enhancing science and math education and by making it easier for foreign scientific and engineering talent to move here and stay here.

Investment in New Equipment and Software Extends Innovation throughout the Economy

Supply-side economics argues that lower taxes stimulate investment, but companies' decisions to invest in new capital equipment have almost nothing to do with personal income tax rates. Moreover, even if tax cuts were to lead to more savings, the money is just as likely to be spent on houses, vehicles, or other consumer items bought on credit that do little to boost productivity. Demand-siders argue that companies invest in response to growing consumer demand so they can expand output. This ignores the fact that what's most important is not more capital equipment, but new generations of capital equipment, as that is largely how innovation is diffused through the economy.

Growth economics holds that companies invest in new equipment so that they can produce better (e.g., cheaper, faster, different), not just more. Moreover, it holds that investment is important, not to generate more capital equipment, but to induce the adoption of new capital equipment. In other words, it's not the amount of capital equipment that matters to growth; it's the refreshment rate of it. Whether it's a $1,000 personal computer or a $1 million milling machine for an auto-parts supplier, a major way in which technological innovation is diffused through the economy is through investments in new machinery, equipment, and software. New innovations like faster computers or high-speed telecommunications requires enormous amounts of investment to realize the benefits of these innovations.

Both demand-siders and supply-siders argue that investment is driven by independent factors—consumer demand in the former and saving in the latter—and therefore that there is no need for specific government investment policies. But this ignores the fact that just as with research, investment in new capital often produces total benefits that exceed the benefits the companies making the investments receive.[18] Left to its own, the market will lead to an underinvestment in new capital equipment (including machines, computers, and software). One reason is that investment followers can benefit from the learning that investment leaders have done. As U.C. Berkeley economist Brad DeLong found, investment in equipment "appears to yield social benefits to the economy in terms of higher productivity that dwarf the profits that owners of the capital goods installed are able to privately appropriate."[19]

Therefore, incentives to stimulate capital investment, even when output is not rapidly growing, will boost productivity growth. By lowering the cost of equipment, investment incentives encourage more investment by making it turn the corner of profitability earlier than it otherwise would.[20] It also changes the cost-benefit ratio of replacing old equipment before it wears out with new and better equipment that not only has productivity-enhancing effects but that is also safer for the workers involved and less environmentally damaging.

Clearly, macroeconomic policy efforts such as keeping inflation low and the deficit under control to keep interest rates low help spur investment, but this spurs spending both on items that boost productivity (e.g., new machines) and on those that don't (e.g., more housing). But tax policy can spur investment specifically in those things that boost productivity. One way is to let companies expense (write off) all of the cost of investment in machinery and equipment in the first year instead of being able to deduct only a part of the cost of the equipment each year until it is fully depreciated as required under current tax law. Allowing companies to expense in the first year all investments in new equipment and software would raise the after-tax rate of return on those investments, spurring more of them.[21] In addition, it would make companies in the United States more competitive with companies in other nations, since they would be using the latest equipment and software.[22]

While such tax changes will boost investment, other more direct initiatives can help as well, particularly to help small and midsized companies who are likely to have less information about the best avenues for investment. For example, the Department of Commerce's Manufacturing Extension Partnership supports regionally based, industry-led efforts to help small manufacturers adopt more productive shop floor technologies and techniques.

Place Matters

Innovation and productivity are driven by companies and other institutions, but these do not just exist independently, divorced from the real physical world. They exist in three-dimensional space, and interactions between physically proximate organizations matter. In fact, in regional economies, the whole is often greater than the sum of the parts. In other words, firms in related industries often cluster together in a particular region, allowing them to take advantage of common resources (e.g., a workforce trained in particular skills, technical institutes, a common supplier base). Moreover, in a knowledge-based economy, having knowledge is not enough; it must be shared, and in many regions, clusters of firms that network and communicate are able to raise the overall knowledge levels that they can draw upon more than if they were isolated and separate. Perhaps the best known cluster is

Northern California's Silicon Valley, where a large agglomeration of high-tech firms, research universities like Stanford, technical colleges to train high-tech workers, venture capitalists, and other supporting institutions makes it the world's most vibrant technology region. But Silicon Valley is not the only region with industry clusters: from the furniture cluster in Tupelo, Mississippi, to the jewelry cluster in Rhode Island and southern Massachusetts, to the biotech clusters in places like Boston, Philadelphia, and San Diego, regional industry clusters abound. And as these examples show, clusters are not only made up of "high-tech" firms; in many cases "low-tech" firms benefit from the learning and knowledge generated in clusters. As a result, growth economics focuses on supporting regional industrial clusters and encouraging rich interorganizational learning environments, in part through working with the federal government in partnerships with state and local governments to support their own technology-based economic development policies.

Broadly Shared Prosperity Requires Full Employment

High levels of productivity and innovation are necessary but not always sufficient factors to ensure broadly shared prosperity. The experience of the 1990s showed that low unemployment levels that many economists objected to for fear of higher inflation were a key factor in ensuring that the decade's growth was widely shared. During the 1990s, full employment helped to boost the real wages of many workers, particularly those at the lower end of the wage scale.[23] Tight labor markets mean that companies must bid up wages, leading to more equal growth in incomes. But tight labor markets are not just a tool for a fairer distribution of the fruits of growth; they are also a spur to growth. When companies must compete more to attract scarce workers, in part by paying higher wages, they are also more likely to invest in new technology and automation as a way to cut costs and produce more output. If macroeconomic policy is strongly expansionary and places achieving full employment ahead of a hawkish focus on keeping inflation very low, employment will grow and the productivity benefits will be spread more widely.

Growth Economics Supports Helping Americans to Equip Themselves to Cope with Change

While growth economics seeks to boost the "animal spirits of innovation," it also seeks to calm the "animal fears of innovation." If people feel they are working without a safety net, they are less likely to engage in new entrepreneurial endeavors or embrace exuberant growth. In the last decade, a growing body of research has pointed to the importance of "social capital" in boosting growth.[24] It turns out that the more we feel we are all in it together, the more likely we are to do what it takes to grow the economy.[25] Moreover, the more we believe that we can afford to take risks, the more likely it is we will take steps that collectively lead to more growth. If workers see themselves adrift in a turbulent economy without support while seeing corporate CEOs getting golden parachutes, their willingness to "make change their friend" plummets. However much we might want to, we can't roll back the clock to the era when workers relied on large stable organizations for security. We can, however, make workers better agents of their own success and managers of their own security. To do so, we need to make a commitment to equip workers with new tools for success. (See appendix.)

Yet if liberals too often want to help Americans cope with change by resisting change, conservatives want to tell people to just get over it. But the answer is to promote change while at the same time helping Americans cope with its consequences. If we are to ask Americans to embrace the New Economy with its continuous change and robust competition, government needs to ensure that workers have access to portable employee benefits, a state-of-the-art system of rapid reemployment, a more effective unemployment insurance system, continuous and affordable lifelong education, expanded opportunities for capital ownership, more universal health insurance. Moreover, with the dramatic growth in pre- and post-tax inequality in the last two decades, the tax code needs to more strongly lean into the wind of this divisive trend. We can start by repealing the Bush tax cuts benefiting the wealthiest Americans earning more than $200,000 per year.

Finally, inequality is not just about differences in individual income; it's about the growing gap in economic prosperity between places. Many communities, particularly rural ones and smaller, older industrial metropolitan areas, are struggling because of economic dislocation. As a result, a key to growth economics is establishing robust national policies to help more places thrive. One way to do this would be to establish a quasi-public Rural Prosperity Corporation focused on helping rural communities prosper, funded by transferring funding now going to wasteful farm subsidies and existing rural development programs in federal agencies (see appendix).

Competitive Markets Drive Innovation and Productivity

Boosting knowledge and investment is not enough. Robust, competitive markets are also needed. Otherwise, existing enterprises will be less motivated to innovate and be more productive, and new enterprises that want to try will be shut out. In fact, innovation is not just the result of increases in knowledge, but of competitive, seemingly destructive forces that determine how companies produce good and services.

Growth economics supports competitive markets and entrepreneurship. It's based on the fact that demanding consumers who are able to buy what they want from whom they want (subject to appropriate health and safety regulations) create an environment that forces companies to improve or die. This means that growth economics embraces open markets, both abroad and at home.

At home, growth economics means removal of a whole host of protections and subsidies for domestic producers, including protections guarding incumbent producers against more robust e-commerce competitors. Rather than compete fairly in the marketplace, a host of middlemen in a variety of service, retail, and professional industries have worked to erect all manner of legal and regulatory barriers, particularly at the state level, to hobble competitors. For example, car dealers have worked successfully to get legislation enacted in all fifty states prohibiting car dealers from selling cars directly to consumers. If consumers could configure and buy cars online directly from car manufacturers the way they can buy computers from companies, they could save thousands of dollars per car. But it's not just car dealers that have hindered e-commerce competition; a host of industries and professions have, including optometrists (opposing online contact-lens sales), travel agents, real estate agents, brick-and-mortar education (teachers unions opposing online charter schools), and even morticians (opposing online purchases of caskets). In fact, it is in the nature of firms and unions to resist competition. Government must actively and aggressively fight against these pressures, since these protectionists threaten consumer welfare by limiting consumer choice and keeping more efficient competitors from the market. Moreover, such restraints often have regressive effects, hurting lower-income consumers more. In a free-market economy, consumers, not vested interests colluding and using the political process to impede competition, should decide how commerce is structured. As a result, the federal government should engage in a systematic effort to root out impediments to fair competition, including using its powers to press states to abolish protectionist rules and laws.

Globally, growth economics means embracing international trade. Trade can boost growth by allowing our economy to specialize in higher-value-added activities. Moreover, because it increases the relevant market size, bringing in new competitors, trade also increases economic competition, keeping prices down and fostering innovation. However, these benefits of trade are fully realized only if the global trading system is based on open markets and limited government distortions. Markets, not governments, should decide trade patterns. Unfortunately, many U.S. trading partners, particularly in Asia, engage in a host of market-distorting actions designed to unfairly gain longer-term economic advantage, including currency manipulation, requirements for foreign firms to produce domestically if they are to have access to domestic markets, rampant theft of intellectual property, tariff and nontariff barriers to accessing their markets, discriminatory tax and regulatory policies, and distortions of standards to shut out nondomestic competitors.[26] To fully realize the benefits of globalization, the U.S. government needs to much more actively use the World Trade Organization process to ensure that foreign markets are competitive, fair, and open. In particular, it means that all countries, not just the United States, must open their markets, respect intellectual property rights, and not manipulate their currency for mercantilist competitive advantage.

Growth economics also embraces entrepreneurship, not in the way supply-siders often do, by simply cutting taxes and regulations for business of all sizes, but in the way that economist Joseph Schumpeter meant when he referred to new and innovative economic activities, whether from a large corporation introducing a new service or a lone inventor developing a new idea in his garage. As Schumpeter put it, "The function of entrepreneurs is to reform or revolutionize the pattern of production by exploiting an invention or, more generally, an untried technological possibility for producing a new commodity or producing an old one in a new way, by opening up a new source of supply of materials or a new outlet for products, by reorganizing an industry and so on."[27] As a result, growth economics does not focus on helping any particular size class of business, but rather on creating a climate conducive to entrepreneurial activity that brings true innovation to the economy.

Finally, growth economics also means developing a modern understanding and application of antitrust law to prevent anticompetitive practices. Too often antitrust has been used by business threatened by change to try to protect incumbents and hobble competitors. In other cases, in their fear of any type of collusive behavior, holders of conventional antitrust doctrine often reflexively oppose business collaboration, fearing that companies will engage in anticompetitive practices. Yet there are cases where collaboration between firms, for example on precompetitive research and development or on developing industry standards, can boost innovation. Indeed, such "coopetition" (where companies both compete and collaborate with one another) is a central driver of innovation in the New Economy.

Fiscal Discipline Underpins Growth Economics

While a cornerstone of growth economics involves significantly increasing investments in science, technology, skills, and education, it also focuses on maintaining fiscal discipline and expeditiously paying down the debt. Growth economics does not worship at the altar of tax cuts or a balanced budget, but it does recognize that fiscal discipline is important. Fiscal discipline is important not just because it lowers interest rates, but because it's just the right thing to do so that we do not pass on a huge "birth tax" to the next generation. Moreover, the huge increase in the budget deficit in the last five years has contributed to a higher value of the dollar than otherwise would be the case, making companies in the United States less competitive in international trade.[28]

Because innovation is the most important factor in boosting growth, fiscal discipline should not come at the expense of needed public investments and tax incentives to companies to spur innovation and productivity. However, there are ways to regain fiscal discipline that don't shortchange needed investments. A first step in implementing growth economics should be to repeal the Bush tax cuts for the wealthy (e.g., dividend tax, capital gains, and top income tax rate reductions). Equally important will be reining in growth in entitlement spending. One way to do that would be to institute progressive indexing for Social Security, which would mean that benefits for higher-income recipients would grow at the rate of inflation, while benefits for lower-income recipients would grow in real terms at the rate of average income growth. There are also a host of areas where spending could be cut with little negative social or economic cost. For example, we should phase out over ten years the $20 billion plus in annual subsidies going to farm businesses.[29]

What about the Budget, "Industrial Policy," and Jobs?

Some on both the right and the left may raise a number of objections to a growth economics agenda, including that it's too expensive, it's picking winners and losers, and it puts capital ahead of workers.

Can We Afford a Growth Economics Agenda?

Implementing a growth economics agenda will require new investments by government, both through direct spending and tax incentives for companies. However, such investments need not boost the deficit. The spending increases could be accompanied by offsetting spending cuts, such as cutting farm subsidies. The tax incentives could be paid for by implementing a modest "business activity tax" (BAT) that businesses would pay on the amount of "value added" they add during the production process.[30] Combining a BAT with a refundable income tax credit for lower-income Americans would allow government to raise this additional revenue in a way that is progressive but also boosts domestic investment in skills, research, and equipment. Moreover, because it would be used to pay for additional corporate tax incentives (e.g., letting companies "expense" their investments in equipment in the first year) and expanding the R&D tax credit, it would be revenue neutral. Some companies might pay more if they did little research, training, or investment, but this would be offset by tax cuts on companies who did more research, training, and investment. A BAT provides an additional advantage in that, under the World Trade Organization rules, it is border adjustable, meaning that the tax would not be applied to exports, while it would be applied to imports, making companies in the United States more competitive, like the majority of our major trading partners that already have in place border-adjustable taxes.

Isn't This Just Industrial Policy and "Picking Winners and Losers"?

Supply-siders are fond of arguing that since "uncertainty is pervasive in the modern economy a centralized strategy to create growth is not feasible. Growth must be left to the entrepreneurs."[31] As a result, many supply-siders will object that a growth economics agenda amounts to industrial policy and "picking winners and losers." Yet supply-siders don't frame economic policy as a choice between some strategic public action and no public action. For them, the choice is between free markets and communism, free choice and totalitarianism. For example, in dismissing the need for federal government actions to help boost U.S. competitiveness in the face of new challenges, especially from Asia, Greg Mankiw framed the choice this way: "Policymakers should not try to determine precisely which jobs are created, or which industries grow. If government bureaucrats were capable of such foresight, the Soviet Union would have succeeded as a centrally planned economy. It did not, providing the best evidence that free markets are the bedrock of economic prosperity."[32]

But this kind of "black-and-white" framing poses a false choice. It does not follow that any kind of government strategy to solve pressing problems, even if done in ways that foster competition, relies on market tools and is industry led; is "industrial policy"; or, even worse, is state socialism. Even so, supply-siders are likely to view any economic agenda that gives government a more active role, even one that explicitly doesn't favor particular industrial sectors, as industrial policy. Growth economics does not focus on helping particular companies or even particular industries, but it does focus on increasing government support for key generic inputs to growth and higher-value-added economic activities on the public and private side, including research, skills, and investment.

In contrast, some on the left will view any effort to help companies be more productive and innovative, especially if it involves tax incentives, as unfair corporate welfare. Indeed, the left is fond of pointing out that corporations pay fewer taxes as a share of GDP today than they did a generation ago. But this view overlooks the fact that corporations aren't people and that in a competitive marketplace higher corporate taxes are ultimately paid for principally by consumers in the form of higher prices. Moreover, paying for corporate tax incentives through a business activity tax means that, overall, corporations will pay the same amount of taxes as before.

What About Jobs and Workers?

Finally, some on the left may be ambivalent toward a growth economics agenda because they fear that a dynamic, high-productivity economy will mean increased risks and fewer jobs. But while innovation and productivity could lead some workers to lose their jobs (because companies can produce more with fewer workers), by no means does it mean that unemployment will be higher. Indeed, during the postwar boom, the nation enjoyed robust productivity growth and high levels of employment. Without strong productivity growth and robust innovation, sustained income growth for working Americans is impossible. The key is not trying to throw sand in the gears of the productivity and innovation machine to slow it down to a more "human pace," as some on the left want to do, but to ensure that the benefits of robust productivity and innovation flow to all Americans and that all Americans have tools to successfully navigate a dynamic labor market.

CONCLUSION

In the New Economy, innovation and knowledge are the most important factors driving economic growth. If we are to boost both, government cannot consign its role to simply redistributing resources to the needy (or even the middle class), as liberals advocate, or to funneling resources to rich investors, as conservatives advocate. Rather, government needs to invest in research, innovation, and skills while supporting competition, all in a way that both preserves fiscal discipline for future generations and helps workers manage increased risk. By putting knowledge and innovation at the center of our nation's economic policies, we can ensure robust economic growth and rising standards of living for all Americans.

Growth economics implies a fundamentally different approach to growing the economy than the Bush administration's single-minded efforts to slash taxes and shrink government. But the difference goes beyond economics and speaks to attitudes about the very nature of our American community. Utilizing government to achieve public goals beyond national defense and public order is seen by conservatives as a violation of individual liberty. But government incentives to spur actions that will result in benefits for all of us do not represent an infringement of personal liberty. No company, for example, would be forced to take a tax credit for training their workers or for conducting R&D in partnership with a university. No laid-off worker would be forced to take a tax credit for health insurance expenditures.

When the United States broke away from the British Empire, they formed a loose confederacy with a relatively weak central government. Flaws in that approach were such that the founders were moved to revamp their system of government. But they chose neither to return to the strictures of being royal subjects nor to abandon the idea of central government. Instead, they reinvented their government to better take advantage of the power to both protect individual liberty and foster collective prosperity.

Today, America is still more than simply a collection of self-sufficient individuals interacting in the market to satisfy their wants. There are collective goals that we can all support which can be accomplished only through working together: a clean environment; livable communities; employment, retirement, and health security; a growing body of scientific and technical knowledge; dignifying and satisfying workplaces; great public universities; an effective transportation system; and more time to spend with families, to name a few. Reaching these collective goals does not mean rejecting markets, but it also does not mean rejecting effective public action. Just like the best sports teams are ones with competitive, hardworking, and talented players who also have a coach and work together as a team, the best society is one in which individuals pursue more than their short-term individual self-interest. A great society grows from a blend of individual talent and teamwork. When we only act alone, we fail to produce the kinds of things that working as a team can produce.

Team members have a mutual responsibility to each other. But such mutual responsibility is not a hair shirt we must wear to be "just" or "fair." It is, in fact, what helps us as individuals excel. A good society depends on freedom, justice, *and* collective action. Even noted economist Friedrich Hayek, the primary source of inspiration for conservative supply-siders, argued, in a passage overlooked by today's conservatives, "that there are common needs that can be satisfied only by collective action."[33] Growth economics means rejecting both the supply-side and demand-side doctrines whose time has passed, and instead enlisting both the power of public action and of competitive markets in a modern strategy to give all Americans the best chance of realizing the American dream.

NOTES

1. Luc Soete, "Globalization, Employment, and the Knowledge-Based Economy," in *Employment and Growth in the Knowledge-based Economy* (Paris: Organisation for Economic Co-operation and Development, 1996), 387.

2. For example, see Charles I. Jones, "Sources of U.S. Economic Growth in a World of Ideas," *American Economic Review* 92, no. 1 (2002): 220–39.

3. Jonathan Temple, "The New Growth Evidence," *Journal of Economic Literature* 37 (March 1999): 112–156.

4. Douglas C. North, *Institutions, Institutional Change, and Economic Performance* (Cambridge, MA: Cambridge University Press, 1990), 80–81.

5. George W. Bush, "President Highlights Importance of Small Business in Economic Growth," 19 January 2006, www.whitehouse.gov/news/releases/2006/01/20060119-2.html (accessed 21 January 2006).

6. Some studies find that only a small share of capital is spent to boost productivity. In contrast, a large share is spent by companies on things like automated databases in order to gain market share from their competitors. While the latter helps the individual company, from a collective sense it is at best a zero-sum activity that transfers resources from one company to another.

7. National Science Foundation, "Nifty Fifty" (Washington, DC: National Science Foundation), www.nsf.gov/od/lpa/nsf50/nsfoutreach/htm/home.htm (accessed 24 November 2005).

8. The Manufacturing Extension Partnership is a highly effective program that was a semifinalist for a 2004 Innovations in American Government award sponsored by Harvard University's Kennedy School of Government. Likewise, the ATP program has been shown to be a highly effective program. See Charles W. Wessner, ed., *Government-Industry Partnerships* (Washington, DC: Board on Science, Technology, and Economic Policy, National Research Council, 2001).

9. For example, Federal Reserve Bank economists Steven Oliner and Daniel Sichel found that the use of computers and the production of computers added two-thirds of the 1 percentage point step-up in productivity growth between the first and second half of the decades. Steven D. Oliner and Daniel Sichel, "The Resurgence of Growth in the Late 1990s: Is Information Technology the Story?" Federal Reserve Bank of San Francisco, *Proceedings*, 2000.

10. David B. Audretsch and Max Keilbach, "Entrepreneurship Capital and Economic Performance" (discussion paper no. 3678, Max Planck Institute of Economics, Centre for Economic Policy Research [CEPR], London, 2003), http://papers.ssrn.com/paper.taf?abstract_id=371801 (accessed 23 November 2005).

11. Charles I. Jones and John Williams, "Measuring the Social Return to R&D," *Quarterly Journal of Economics* 113 (1998): 1119–35.

12. Council of Economic Advisers, *1995 Economic Report of the President* (Washington, DC: U.S. Government Printing Office, 1996).

13. Kenan Patrick Jarboe and Robert D. Atkinson, "A Case for Technology in the New Economy" (Washington, DC: Progressive Policy Institute, 1998).

14. Edwin Mansfield, "Basic Research and Productivity Increase in Manufacturing," *American Economic Review* 70, no. 4 (1980): 863–73.

15. Zvi Griliches, "The Search for R&D Spillovers," *Scandinavian Journal of Economics* 94 (1992): 29–47.

16. Greg Tassey, "The Economics of a Technology-Based Service Sector," planning report, 98–2 (Washington, DC: National Institute of Standards and Technology, 1998).

17. D. P. Leyden and A. N. Link, "Why Are Government R&D and Private R&D Complements?" *Applied Economics* 23 (1991): 1673–81.

18. See Christian Keuschnigg, "Business Formation and Aggregate Investment," *German Economic Review* 2, no. 1 (2001): 31–55; and Bradford DeLong and Larry H. Summers, "Equipment Investment and Economic Growth," *Quarterly Journal of Economics* 106 (1991): 445–502.

19. Bradford J. DeLong, "Productivity Growth, and Investment in Equipment: A Very Long Run Look," *Growth and Equipment*, August 1995, 31, www.j-bradford-delong.net/pdf_files/JEH_Machinery.pdf (accessed 24 November 2005).

20. F. M. Scherer, *New Perspectives on Economic Growth and Technological Innovation* (Washington, DC: Brookings Institution Press, 1999).

21. Equipment includes industrial equipment and information processing equipment and software.

22. For example, semiconductor factories in Japan can depreciate 88 percent of their cost in the first year, compared to just 20 percent in the United States.

23. Jared Bernstein and Dean Baker, *The Benefits of Full Employment: When Markets Work for People* (Washington, DC: Economic Policy Institute, 2003), 2.

24. R. Quentin Grafton, Stephen Knowles, and P. Dorian Owen, "Social Divergence and Productivity: Making a Connection" (Ottawa: Centre for the Study of Living Standards, 2004), www.csls.ca/repsp/2/graftonetal.pdf (accessed 23 November 2005).

25. Jonathan Temple, "Growth Effects of Education and Social Capital in the OECD Countries," Department of Economics, University of Bristol, UK, 19 June 2001, www.nuff.ox.ac.uk/Users/Temple/abstracts/edfinal2.pdf (accessed 22 November 2005).

26. U.S. Trade Representative, *2005 National Trade Estimate Report on Foreign Trade Barriers*, www.ustr.gov/Document_Library/Reports_Publications/2005/2005_NTE_Report/Section_Index.html (accessed 23 November 2005).

27. Joseph A. Schumpeter, *Capitalism, Socialism, and Democracy* (1942; repr., New York: Harper Perennial, 1975), 132.

28. Even though some conservatives and the Bush administration claim that budget deficits don't affect trade, they sang a different tune during the Clinton administration. At that time, prominent conservative economists, such as Martin Feldstein, Greg Mankiw, John Taylor, and Alan Meltzer, argued that cutting the budget deficit would help reduce the value of the dollar and boost U.S. competitiveness.

29. Robert D. Atkinson, "Reversing Rural America's Economic Decline: The Case for a National Balanced Growth Strategy," Washington, DC: Progressive Policy Institute, 2004.

30. This variation of a VAT is based in part on the tax described in Gary Clyde Hufbauer and Paul L. E Greico, "Comprehensive Reform for U.S. Business Taxation," sub-

mitted to the President's Advisory Panel on Federal Tax Reform (Washington, DC: Institute for International Economics, 21 April 2005).

31. Chris Edwards, "Entrepreneurs Creating the New Economy" (Washington, DC: Congressional Joint Economic Committee, November 2000), www.cato.org/research/articles/edwards11-00.pdf (accessed February 4, 2006).

32. Gregory Mankiw, "Remarks at the Annual Meeting of the National Association of Business Economists Washington Economic Policy Conference," 25 March 2004, www.whitehouse.gov/cea/mankiw-032404.html (accessed 2 December 2005).

33. Friedrich A. Hayek, *The Constitution of Liberty* (Chicago: University of Chicago Press, 1960, paperback edition 1978), 257.

Appendix

Growth Economics Policy Proposals: Support the Innovation Nation

A major part of supply-side economics' appeal is that it has a message that can be put on a bumper sticker: "Lower taxes boosts growth." It's a bit harder to boil down the growth economics message to a bumper sticker, but "Support the Innovation Nation" might be a good first start.

Bumper sticker or not, growth economics does lead to specific policy steps that government can take to boost growth. While the agenda outlined here is by no means intended to be complete, it does suggest some of the steps government could take.

BOOST FEDERAL SUPPORT FOR RESEARCH AND DEVELOPMENT WHILE CREATING A NATIONAL INNOVATION FOUNDATION

Because innovation drives growth, the federal government needs to make the promotion of innovation a central component of its economic policies. While the Department of Commerce has this as one of its missions, its efforts are too limited and too diffuse. Therefore, we should transfer the National Telecommunications Information Administration; the Technology Administration, including NIST; and the National Science Foundation to a new American Innovation Foundation, while boosting their combined budgets from $5 billion to $15 billion over the next five years.[1] The goal of the foundation would not be to direct innovation or own patents, but rather to work in partnership with universities and other research institutions and the private sector to support innovation. The increased funds would be used to do the following:

1. Enhance the nation's research infrastructure (the equipment, facilities, and installations needed to undertake leading-edge research and

develop advanced technologies).[2] Such infrastructure might include DNA analysis equipment for cancer research, nanoengineering research facilities for new materials and systems, and supercomputers to create new media and virtual reality environments. One core component of this new research infrastructure is an advanced cyberinfrastructure program to build more ubiquitous, real-time, and collaborative digital research environments.[3]

2. Support scientific research that offers direct economic benefits, including increased manufacturing competitiveness and higher productivity. This means: (1) boosting funding by $1 billion annually for NSF's Division of Design, Manufacture, and Industrial Innovation, which focuses on fundamental research in design, manufacturing, and industrial engineering; (2) allocating $1 billion per year to a Productivity Enhancement Research Fund to fund early-stage research at universities or joint industry-university projects focused on increasing the efficiency of industrial or service processes in technologies such as robotics, machine vision, expert systems, and voice recognition—the fund would support early-stage research in processes with broad applications to boost productivity in a range of industries, not late-stage research focused on particular companies; (3) investing $1 billion annually in up to one hundred industry-university American Ingenuity Research Alliances[4]—the fund would support early-stage research in processes with broad applications to boost productivity in a range of industries, not late-stage research focused on particular companies; (4) boosting renewable energy research by at least $2 billion annually; and (5) investing $1 billion to match state government investments in technology-based economic development. States would be required to match the federal funds at a ratio of at least one to one and invest in joint university-industry or other collaborative industry-based innovation programs. Industry would be required to match all federal funds one to one. Thus, $1 billion in federal funds would be leveraged into at least $3 billion in additional R&D funding, much of it conducted at non-top-tier universities with small and medium-size firms as partners. The additional cost for these research initiatives would be $10 billion per year.

BOOST INCENTIVES FOR THE PRIVATE SECTOR TO INVEST IN R&D BY EXPANDING AND REFORMING THE R&D TAX CREDIT

While reversing the relative decline in public funding of research (particularly nondefense, non–health related research) is essential, it's equally important to encourage business to invest more in R&D. Business investment in R&D increased through the 1990s but has fallen since as a share of GDP.[5] As a result, federal tax policy should provide greater rewards for companies that invest in R&D in the United States.[6] Congress should do the following:

1. Make the research and development tax credit permanent.[7]
2. Double the credit from 20 to 40 percent.
3. Create a flat, nonincremental, 40 percent credit for company expenditures for collaborative research at universities, federal laboratories, or research consortia or for support for education and training in American schools and universities.[8]
4. Make it easier for small and start-up companies to claim the credit by letting them claim for calculation of their R&D base, gross receipts equal to at least $1 million.
5. Make expenditures on global standards setting and patenting eligible for the credit.[9]
6. Boost the alternative minimum credit to 10 percent of qualified research (and training) expenses over 60 percent of the taxpayer's qualified research expenses.[10]

There is general agreement that the R&D tax credit has been a cost-effective policy tool. For example, the former Congressional Office of Technology Assessment concluded that "for every dollar lost in tax revenue, the R&D tax credit produces a dollar increase in reported R&D spending, on the margin."[11] Other studies have found even greater benefits, with the economic benefit to tax-cost ratio between 1.3 and 2.0.[12]

The additional cost for this knowledge credit would be approximately $20 billion per year, leading to at least $20 billion more in private sector R&D. Boosting the R&D credit to 40 percent would cost approximately $5 billion, expanding the base credit to 10 percent would cost approximately $5 billion, and creating the flat collaborative credit would cost approximately $2.5 billion.

ENCOURAGE INVESTMENT IN NEW
EQUIPMENT, TECHNOLOGY, AND SOFTWARE

Government can play a key role in encouraging companies to invest in new equipment and machinery. Congress should do the following:

1. Let companies expense investment in machinery and equipment in the first year instead of only being able to deduct part of the cost of the

equipment each year until it is fully depreciated. Allowing companies to expense in the first year all investments in new equipment and software would raise the after-tax rate of return on those investments, spurring more of them.[13] In addition, it would make companies in the United States more competitive with companies in other nations.

2. Triple funding for the Department of Commerce's Manufacturing Extension Partnership (MEP) to $300 million per year. MEP should also establish sector-based modernization centers in particular industrial sectors. In addition, the federal government should extend these kind of industrial extension programs to include select service industries.

ACCELERATE DIGITIZATION
OF THE ECONOMY

Widespread use of computers, the Internet, telecommunications, and other information technologies will be a key to continued productivity growth. Government should take a number of steps, including the following:

1. Boost broadband supply. America continues to fall behind other nations in broadband adoption, falling from third in the world in 2000 to sixteenth in 2004. Currently, fewer than thirty million households subscribe to broadband, and for those that do, most get what can be called "skinny broadband," with speeds of around 1 megabit per second.[14] To truly accelerate the digital revolution and enable things like telemedicine, distance learning, telecommuting, and Internet video downloads, broadband speeds will need to be much faster, at least as fast as ten to twenty megabits per second. In contrast to nations such as Japan and South Korea, which have moved aggressively to roll out next-generation high-speed broadband (e.g., twenty to thirty megabits), U.S. telecommunication companies are only just now beginning to roll out faster services. While the private sector will build most, if not all, of this network, government can help speed the process. All levels of government can remove regulatory and tax barriers to deployment, such as charging high fees for right-of-way access. But they can and should go beyond this to provide financial incentives to spur rollout of next-generation high-speed Internet access. Broadband services should be made exempt from federal, state, and local taxation and from requirements to pay into the Universal Service Fund for at least the next five years until many more Americans subscribe to higher speed broadband services. More-

over, Congress should consider putting in place tax incentives for the deployment of new broadband networks, including allowing telecommunications companies to expense new broadband investments in the first year. This is the model many other nations have used to successfully spur deployment of advanced telecommunications infrastructures. For example, the Japanese government allowed NTT to rapidly write-off the cost of its new fiber broadband networks. The Korean government did the same. The Canadian government recently boosted by 50 percent its tax incentives for investments for broadband, Internet, and other data network infrastructure equipment.

2. Boost broadband demand. The federal government could take a number of steps to do this, including the following:
   a. Fund PBS to put its television programs online so that people would be able to go online and download content films like Ken Burns's *Civil War*.
   b. Jump-start the e-book marketplace and broadband by establishing a national digital lending library through the Library of Congress.[15]
3. Spur e-transformation of sectors. Where government has a large presence as a customer, regulator, or funder (e.g., health, education, transportation, banking and securities, law enforcement, and housing), it should work with industry to develop sector e-transformation strategies. The executive branch should have all government agencies examine how their procurement, regulatory, and other actions can speed the digitization of sectors they influence. It should task federal agencies with working with technology developers and users to help formulate IT reinvention road maps for a variety of industries, with a particular focus on how government policies, including procurement and regulations, can help speed digital transformation.[16] Health care is a prime example. The Bush administration has begun an initiative to help develop standards for exchanging medical information, including patient records, but more could be done to spur systemic change.

BOOST SKILLS

1. Transform the R&D tax credit into a knowledge tax credit by allowing companies to take a 40 percent tax credit on incremental increases in training expenses. The training tax credit would cost approximately $8.5 billion.
2. Create a new quasi-public National Skills Corporation. Funds and responsibility would be transferred from employment and training pro-

grams managed by the Department of Labor and adult education programs at the Department of Education. This quasi-governmental corporation would have a board of directors made up of business and labor leaders, educators, and local elected officials appointed by the president and Congress. The corporation would do the following:

a. Cofund in partnership with industry and/or unions regional and/or sectorial skills alliances.[17]

b. Establish a nationwide network of easy-to-find "learning stores," staffed by friendly professionals. Individuals should be able to consult with a learning specialist and/or serve themselves at a kiosk and get what they need: including assessing their skills; locating courses, degree programs, and certificate programs; and determining qualifications for financial assistance.

c. Establish Learn.gov, a state-of-the-art online learning and worker reemployment Web portal with information on jobs; training and education courses available; financial assistance; self-administered skills assessment and career counseling; the ability to apply online for education and training benefits; and most importantly, a wide range of free, Internet-based courses and training materials.

3. Expand funding for the NSF Advanced Technical Education program, a program to fund curriculum development for advanced technical education in community and technical colleges.

4. Boost the supply of workers with math, science, and engineering skills.

a. Foster the creation of 250 public charter high schools focused specifically on math, science, engineering, and computing. Increased technical skills are critical to future growth. However, relatively fewer American college students are getting degrees in math, science, and engineering. In contrast, virtually all other advanced nations and a host of developing nations such as China and India are increasing science and engineering graduates. Moreover, fewer foreign students—until now an important source of science and engineering graduates—are coming to the United States for their degrees, and fewer are staying in the nation after they graduate. Unless more students come to college with an interest in and skill for science and engineering, it will be difficult to significantly boost science and engineering college graduates. As a result, we need to foster the creation of a system of public charter high schools focused specifically on math, science, engineering, and computing, modeled on schools like Thomas Jefferson Math and Science Academy in Alexandria, Virginia. A significant share of these academies should be focused on serving disadvantaged populations.[18]

b. Provide full funding for math and science education partnerships, including the Noyce scholarship program and the Science, Technology, Engineering, and Math Talent Expansion ("Tech Talent") program.

c. Make it easier for those talented foreign students getting a doctorate in math, science, or engineering to stay in the United States by exempting them from the H1-B cap and also expediting the process by which they can qualify for a green card.

PROMOTE COMPETITION, NOT PRIVILEGE

1. Create a White House position of competition ombudsman whose responsibility it is to identify, analyze, and advocate for cases where proposed or current government rules and laws unfairly impede competition and innovation, including the emergence of new e-commerce business models.

2. Charge federal agencies, including the Federal Trade Commission, the Securities Exchange Commission, the Federal Communications Commission, and other agencies overseeing commerce with aggressively rooting out protectionist laws and regulations, particularly those applying to e-commerce competitors.

3. The federal government should continue to push for expanded global market integration. But at the same time, it should work more actively to enforce trade agreements and WTO and IMF rules. The U.S. government needs to be much more vigilant and energetic in working within the existing international institutions to create a more open and market-based global trading system, including getting tougher on currency manipulation, intellectual property theft, closed markets, standards manipulation, and a host of other protectionist and mercantilist practices.[19]

GIVE AMERICANS MORE TOOLS
TO MANAGE RISK

1. Do a better job helping workers who have lost their jobs.
   a. Reform the federal unemployment insurance (UI) system: (1) all workers who lose their job through no fault of their own should be eligible to receive UI benefits, even if they have only been working a short time or are making low wages; (2) provide for an additional

thirteen weeks of UI benefits for workers who are engaged in a certified skills training program; (3) establish a federal floor for the level of cash UI benefits above which all states must operate.[20]

b. Allow companies to take a credit of 65 percent on expenditures related to health care for their current and retired workers.[21] This would encourage significantly more companies to provide health care for their workers. Moreover, it would also reduce the cost differential with nations that provide government-supported health care (e.g. Canada), making companies in the United States more competitive.

c. Provide transitional health insurance benefits to unemployed workers by expanding the 65 percent refundable tax credit to help workers collecting unemployment insurance purchase health coverage, either through COBRA (continuing coverage from ex-employers), a purchasing pool or other state-sponsored health plan, or individual coverage.

d. Institute "New Economy Scholarships" for workers losing their jobs through no fault of their own. These scholarships would make access to training for dislocated workers who are collecting unemployment insurance as universally available as access to college by providing dislocated workers with a scholarship worth up to $4,000.[22]

2. Establish a new Rural Prosperity Corporation (RPC) focused on helping rural communities prosper economically, funded by transferring funding now going to ineffective existing rural development programs in federal agencies. The RPC would be governed by a board of directors appointed by the president and Congress, and composed of business and labor leaders, state and local elected officials, and rural development experts. The corporation would have three missions: (1) to make performance-based matching grants to catalyze and support state rural development efforts, (2) to support research on rural economic growth and evaluation of best practices in rural economic development, and (3) to fund research in technologies that would support industries locating in rural areas (e.g., wind energy).

RESTORE FISCAL HEALTH

1. Generate additional revenues.
   a. Eliminate the Bush tax cuts for the wealthy (e.g., dividend tax, capital gains, and top income tax rate reductions).
   b. To pay for the array of growth economics tax incentives proposed

here, establish a 5 percent "business activity tax" that businesses would pay on the amount of "value added" they add during the production process. Combining a BAT with a refundable credit for lower-income Americans would allow government to raise this additional revenue in a way that is both progressive and consistent with the overarching goal of promoting domestic corporate investment and enhancing the competitiveness of companies in the United States.[23]

2. Rein in unnecessary spending.

   a. Create a nonpartisan Corporate Welfare Elimination Commission to examine all industry-specific spending and tax provisions. This commission would recommend a package of reforms and cuts for those subsidies serving no overriding national purpose, and, like the base-closing effort, Congress should be required to vote the package up or down without amendment.

   b. Limit the growth of entitlement spending. This should start by instituting progressive indexing for Social Security, which would limit the growth of benefits for higher-income recipients to the rate of inflation. In addition, steps should be taken to limit the growth of Medicare spending, in part by working to boost the efficiency of the current medical care system.

NOTES

1. Adding $10 billion to the nation's research enterprise would restore the ratio of federal R&D to GDP that the nation enjoyed in the early 1990s.

2. As the National Science Board reports, "Over the past decade, the funding for academic research infrastructure has not kept pace with rapidly changing technology, expanding research opportunities, and increasing numbers of users."

3. The National Science Foundation Blue Ribbon Committee on CyberInfrastructure recently concluded that our nation's science, engineering, and educational enterprises would dramatically benefit from major advances in information technology.

4. Industry-led research alliances of at least ten firms would be eligible for matching federal funds, provided the firms agree to develop midterm technology road maps that identify generic science and technology needs that firms share and then invest the funds through a competitive selection process in these research areas in universities and federal laboratories.

5. While it's not clear why funding declined, one cause may be the offshoring of research by U.S. firms to other nations. Between 1994 and 2001, R&D by U.S. firms increased 70 percent faster overseas than it did in the United States. Major U.S. companies such as Microsoft, General Electric, and Cisco have made significant investments in R&D facilities overseas, particularly in developing countries. One reason is the growing

number of talented, low-cost researchers in nations like China and India. But another reason is that the tax treatment of R&D in the United States is relatively unfavorable compared to other nations. For example, the Canadian government provides a flat, nonincremental, 20 percent R&D credit for large companies, and up to a 35 percent credit for small companies. Provincial government credits can be taken on top of these. In contrast, U.S. companies can take only a 20 percent credit on increases in R&D, and few states have significant credits.

6. Studies, including by the former Congressional Office of Technology Assessment, have shown that the R&D credit is effective at boosting private-sector research.

7. The official name is the research and experimentation tax credit.

8. One reason for this more generous collaborative R&D credit is that more of the benefits of such collaborative R&D spill over to the economy than proprietary in-house R&D.

9. Corporate investments to participate in global standard-setting processes are an important component to ensuring U.S. competitiveness. But because of the free-rider problem where companies benefit from the actions of other companies, U.S. companies appear to underinvest in standards-settings activities, just as they do in R&D.

10. This would include the average of qualified research expenses over the last three years.

11. U.S. Congress, Office of Technology Assessment, "The Effectiveness of Research and Experimental Tax Credits" (Washington, DC: Office of Technology Assessment, 1995).

12. Coopers and Lybrand, "Economic Benefits of the R&D Tax Credit," January 1998.

13. Equipment included is industrial equipment and information processing equipment and software.

14. www.yankeegroup.com/public/products/decision_note.jsp?ID = 13117.

15. Robert D. Atkinson, Shane Ham, and Brian Newkirk, "Unleashing the Potential of the High-Speed Internet: Strategies to Boost Broadband Demand" (Washington, DC: Progressive Policy Institute, 2002).

16. Robert. D. Atkinson, "What's Next?" *Public CIO*, February 2005, www.public-cio .com/story.php?id = 2005.01.31-92922 (accessed 23 November 2005).

17. Robert Atkinson, "Building Skills for the New Economy: A Policymaker's Handbook" (Washington, DC: Progressive Policy Institute, 2001).

18. This is similar to a recommendation made by the National Academy of Sciences' report "Rising above the Gathering Storm," to expand statewide specialty high schools focused on science, technology, and mathematics.

19. In the case of nations like China that peg their currencies to another currency (in this case, the dollar), the appropriate solution may be for them to revalue their currency upward to better reflect their trade surplus. One way this could be done would be for the IMF to convene a panel of experts who would agree on the extent to which the nation's currency is undervalued.

20. Robert D. Atkinson, "Modernizing Unemployment Insurance for the New Economy and the New Social Policy" (Washington, DC: Progressive Policy Institute, 2002).

21. This could work by setting a base credit amount that companies could take per worker. If companies spent more than that on health care for their workforce, they would be able to deduct it as they currently do, but not take the more generous credit.

22. Red tape would be reduced by allowing workers to apply for aid directly from certified training providers rather than government agencies. To protect workers, training providers would have to be certified and report results on an annual report card to help workers identify the best lifelong learning programs. Paul Weinstein Jr., "New Economy Work (NEW) Scholarships: Universal Access to Training for Dislocated Workers" (Washington, DC: Progressive Policy Institute, 2002).

23. In order to limit compliance costs, only firms with revenues of $10 million or more would be subject to the BAT. Because the BAT is border adjustable under WTO rules, whereas general corporate taxes are not, it will help reduce the trade deficit, including promoting U.S. exports. Currently, virtually every major trading partner (with the exception of Australia) has some kind of VAT/BAT, and that means they are able to subject imports to the VAT tax and exempt their exports—an advantage our companies don't enjoy.

Bibliography

'Abd-ar-Rahmân Abû Zayd ibn Khaldûn. *The Muqaddimah: An Introduction to History*. Translated by Franz Rosenthal, edited by N. J. Dawood. Princeton, NJ: Princeton University Press, 1967, 23.

Akhtar, M. A., and Ethan S. Harris. "The Supply Side Consequences of U.S. Fiscal Policy in the 1980s." New York: Federal Reserve Bank of New York, 1991.

Alesina, Alberto, Edward Glaeser, and Bruce Sacerdote. "Work and Leisure in the U.S. and Europe: Why So Different?" Cambridge, MA: Harvard University, 2005.

Alesina, Alberto, and Dani Rodrik. "Distribution Politics and Economic Growth." *Quarterly Journal of Economics* 109 (1994): 465–90.

Allen, Mike. "A Deficit, Yes, But Few Regrets." *Washington Post*, 9 June 2003.

Armey, Richard. *The Flat Tax*. New York: Ballantine Books, 1996.

Arthur, Brian W. "On the Evolution of Complexity." Sante Fe, NM: Santa Fe Institute, 1993.

Atkinson, Robert D. "Building Skills for the New Economy: A Policymaker's Handbook." Washington, DC: Progressive Policy Institute, 2001.

———. "The Bush 'New Balance' UI Plan: Lower Taxes for Employers, Fewer Benefits for Workers." Washington, DC: Progressive Policy Institute, 2002.

———. "Inequality in the New Knowledge Economy." In *The New Egalitarianism*, edited by Anthony Giddens and Patrick Diamond (New York: Polity, 2005).

———. "Modernizing Unemployment Insurance for the New Economy and the New Social Policy." Washington, DC: Progressive Policy Institute, 2002.

———. *The Past and Future of America's Economy: Waves of Innovation that Power Cycles of Growth*. Northampton, MA: Edward Elgar, 2005.

———. "Reversing Rural America's Economic Decline: The Case for a National Balanced Growth Strategy." Washington, DC: Progressive Policy Institute, 2004.

———. "What's Next?" *Public CIO*, February 2005.

Atkinson, Robert D., Shane Ham, and Brian Newkirk. "Unleashing the Potential of the High-Speed Internet: Strategies to Boost Broadband Demand." Washington, DC: Progressive Policy Institute, 2002.

Audretsch, David B., and Max Keilbach. "Entrepreneurship Capital and Economic Performance." Discussion paper 3678, Max Planck Institute of Economics, Centre for Eco-

nomic Policy Research, London, 2003. http://papers.ssrn.com/paper.taf?abstract_
id = 371801 (accessed 23 November 2005).

Auerbach, Alan J. "Flat Taxes: Some Economic Considerations." California Policy Semi-
nar Brief Series, March 1996. www.ucop.edu/cprc/auerbach.html (accessed 25 November 2005).

Auten, Gerald E., Charles T. Clotfelter, and Richard L. Schmalbeck. "Taxes and Philanthropy among the Wealthy." In *Does Atlas Shrug?* edited by Joel B. Slemrod. Cambridge, MA: Harvard University Press, 2000.

Autor, David H., Lawrence F. Katz, and Melissa S. Kearney. "Trends in U.S. Wage
Inequality: Re-Assessing the Revisionists." Working paper 11627, National Bureau of
Economic Research, Cambridge, MA, September 2000.

Averett, Susan L., Edward N. Gamber, and Shelia Handy. "William E. Simon's Contribution to Tax Policy." *Atlantic Economic Journal* 31, no. 3 (September 2003).

Barro, Robert J. "Bush's Tax Cuts: Reaganomics Redux." *Business Week*, 20 January
2003.

———. "Economic Growth in a Cross Section of Countries." *Quarterly Journal of Economics* 106, no. 2 (May 1991): 407–43.

Bartlett, Bruce. "Bush Is Laying the Foundation for Fundamental Tax Reform." Dallas:
National Center for Policy Analysis, 2003. www.ncpa.org/edo/bb/2003/bb020503.html
(accessed 21 November 2005).

———. *Reaganomics: Supply Side Economics in Action*. Westport, CT: Arlington House
Publishers, 1981.

Bell, Daniel. *The Cultural Contradictions of Capitalism*. New York: Basic Books, 1976.

Bernheim, Douglas B. "Taxation and Saving." In *Handbook of Public Economics*, edited
by A. J. Auerbach and M. Feldstein. North Holland: Elsevier Science Publishers, 2002.

Bernstein, Jared, and Dean Baker. *The Benefits of Full Employment: When Markets Work
for People*. Washington, DC: Economic Policy Institute, 2003.

Blahous, Chuck. "Ask the White House." 8 June 2005. www.whitehouse.gov/ask/
20050608.html (accessed January 24, 2006).

Blinder, Alan S. *Hard Heads, Soft Hearts: Tough-Minded Economics for a Just Society*.
Reading, MA: Addison-Wesley, 1987.

Bluestone, Barry, and Bennett Harrison. *Growing Prosperity: The Battle for Growth with
Equity in the Twenty-first Century*. New York: Houghton Mifflin, 2000.

Blumenthal Sidney. "Seeking Insolvency: The Strange Career of Supply-Side Economics." *World Policy Journal*, 22 June 1997.

Bosworth, Barry, and Gary Burtless. "Effects of Tax Reform on Labor Supply, Investment
and Savings." *Journal of Economic Perspective* 6, no. 1 (Winter 1992): 3–25.

Brimelow, Peter. "It's the Taxes Stupid." *Forbes*, 12 February 1996, 157.

Broder, David. "A Price to Be Paid for Folly." *Washington Post*, 11 September 2005,
A22.

Burke, Edmund. *Reflections on the Revolution in France*. 1790.

Bush, George W. "A Blueprint for New Beginnings: A Responsible Budget for America's
Priorities." Message to Congress, White House, Washington, DC, February 2001.

———. "President Bush Closes the White House Economic Conference." 16 December
2004. www.whitehouse.gov/news/releases/2004/12/20041216-8.html (accessed 21
November 2005).

———. "President Discusses Economy and Tax Relief in North Carolina." Washington, DC: White House, 5 December 2005.

———. "President Discusses Strong and Growing Economy." Chicago, 6 January 2006. www.whitehouse.gov/news/releases/2006/01/20060106-7.html (accessed 31 January 2006).

———. "President Highlights Importance of Small Business in Economic Growth." 19 January 2006. www.whitehouse.gov/news/releases/2006/01/20060119-2.html (accessed 20 January 2006).

———. "President Honors Milton Friedman for Lifetime Achievements." Remarks by the president in tribute to Milton Friedman, Eisenhower Executive Office Building, May 2002.

———. "President Outlines Economic Growth Agenda." White House Office of the Press Secretary, 26 October 2005.

———. "Remarks by the President in Tax Cut Bill Signing Ceremony," 7 June 2001.

———. "Remarks by the President to Future Farmers of America," July 2001.

———. "Remarks by the President to the Employees of the Department of Labor," Washington, DC, 4 October 2001. www.yale.edu/lawweb/avalon/sept_11/president_052.htm (accessed 21 November 2005).

———. "Speech in Green Bay, WI," 28 September 2000.

———. "Speech in Scranton, PA," 6 September 2000.

Business Week. "Dole's Gamble." 19 October 1996. www.businessweek.com/1996/34/b34891.htm (accessed 22 November 2005).

———. "The Real Economic Legacy of Ronald Reagan: There's Much More to It Than Tax Cuts and Small Government." 21 June 2004, 154.

Carroll, Christopher D. "Why Do the Rich Save So Much?" In *Does Atlas Shrug?* edited by Joel B. Slemrod. Cambridge, MA: Harvard University Press, 2000.

Carroll, Robert, Douglas Holtz-Eakin, Mark Ridder, and Harvey S. Rosen. "Entrepreneurs, Income Taxes, and Investment." In *Does Atlas Shrug?* edited by Joel B. Slemrod. Cambridge, MA: Harvard University Press, 2000.

Center for American Progress. "A Fair and Simple Tax System for Our Future: A Progressive Approach to Tax Reform." Washington, DC: January 2005.

Chernow, Ron. *The House of Morgan*. New York: Simon & Schuster, 1990.

Clinton, Hillary. Remarks made at the Democratic Leadership Council's National Conversation, Columbus, Ohio, July 2005.

CNN, "Daschle Vows Tax Breaks for Middle-class Families," www.cnn.com/2003/ALL POLITICS/01/04/dems.radio.

Congressional Budget Office. "An Analysis of the President's Budgetary Proposals for Fiscal Year 2004." Washington, DC: CBO, March 2003.

———. "Budget Options." Washington, DC: CBO, February 2001.

———. "Economic Stimulus: Evaluating Proposed Changes in Tax Policy." Washington, DC: CBO, January 2002.

———. "Effective Marginal Tax Rates on Labor Income." Washington, DC: CBO, November 2005.

———. "Effective Tax Rates, 1979–1997." Washington, DC: CBO, October 2001.

———. "Effects of the Federal Estate Tax on Farms and Small Businesses." Washington, DC: CBO, July 2005.

————. "Historical Budget Data." Washington, DC: Congressional Budget Office, 2005.

Coolidge, Calvin. "Address before the National Republican Club at the Waldorf-Astoria," New York, 12 February 1924.

————. "State of the Union Message." 3 December 1924.

Costa, Dora. "The Wage and the Length of the Work Day: From the 1890s to 1991." *Journal of Labor Economics* 18, no. 1 (January 2000): 156–81.

Council of Economic Advisers. *1995 Economic Report of the President*. Washington, DC: U.S. Government Printing Office, 1996.

————. *2005 Economic Report of the President*. Washington, DC: Government Printing Office, 2005.

Cox, Michael W., with Richard Alm. *Myths of Rich and Poor: Why We're Better Off Than We Think*. New York: Basic Books, 1999.

Daniels, Mitch. "Press Briefing on the Budget by OMB Director Mitch Daniels." 3 February 2003. www.whitehouse.gov/omb/speeches/daniels_04budget.html (accessed 26 November 2005).

Darda, Michael. "Keynesian Sleights-of-Hand." *National Review Online*, 22 July 2005. www.nationalreview.com/nrof_comment/darda200507220844.asp (accessed 21 November 2005).

DeLong, Bradford J. "Productivity Growth and Investment in Equipment: A Very Long Run Look." *Growth and Equipment*, August 1995, www.j-bradford-delong.net/pdf_files/JEH_Machinery.pdf (accessed 24 November 2005).

DeLong, Bradford J., Claudia Goldin, and Lawrence F. Katz. "Sustaining U.S. Growth." In *Agenda for the Nation*, edited by H. Aaron, J. Lindsay, and P. Nivola, 17–60. Washington, DC: Brookings Institution, 2003.

DeLong, Bradford J., and Lawrence H. Summers. "Equipment Investment and Economic Growth." *Quarterly Journal of Economics* 106, no. 2 (1991): 445–502.

Dew-Becker, Ian, and Robert J. Gordon. "Where Did the Productivity Growth Go? Inflation Dynamics and the Distribution of Income." Paper presented at the 81st meeting of the Brookings Panel on Economic Activity, Washington, DC, 8–9 September 2005.

Donovan, William. *The Future of the Republican Party*. New York: New American Library, 1964.

Drago, Robert, David Black, and Mark Wooden. "The Existence and Persistence of Long Work Hours." Bonn, Germany: Institute for the Study of Labor, August 2005.

Drucker, Peter. *Post Capitalist Society*. New York: HarperCollins, 1993.

Dunham, Richard, Howard Gleckman, and Lee Walczak. "Gambling on Growth." *Business Week*, 17 February 2003. www.businessweek.com/magazine/content/03_07/b3820001_mz001.htm (accessed 21 November 2005).

Du Pont, Pete. "Flattery Will Get You Everywhere: On Tax Reform, Steve Forbes Has the Right Idea." *Wall Street Journal*, Wednesday, 31 August 2005. www.opinionjournal.com/columnists/pdupont/?id = 110007183 (accessed 26 November 2005).

Dynan, Karen E., Jonathan Skinner, and Stephen P. Zedes. "Do the Rich Save More?" *Journal of Political Economy* 112, no. 2 (2004): 397–444.

Easterly, William. *The Elusive Quest for Growth: Economists' Adventures and Misadventures in the Tropics*. Cambridge, MA: MIT Press, 2002.

Easterly, William, and Ross Levine. "It's Not Factor Accumulation: Stylized Facts and Growth Models." *World Bank Economic Review* 15 (2001): 177–219.

Easterly, William, and Sergio Rebelo. "Fiscal Policy and Economic Growth." *The Journal of Monetary Economics*, no. 32 (1993): 417–58.

Evans, Michael K. *The Truth about Supply-Side Economics*. New York: Basic Books, 1983.

Farhi, Paul. "Dean Tries to Summon Spirit of the 1960s: Candidate's Recollections Differ from Historians' Views of a Turbulent Decade." *Washington Post*, 28 December 2003, A5.

Faux, Jeff. "You Are Not Alone." In *The New Majority*, edited by Stanley Greenberg and Theda Skocpol. New Haven, CT: Yale University Press, 1997.

Federal Reserve Bank of Cleveland. *Annual Report*. 2003.

Feenberg, Daniel R., and James M. Poterba. "Income Inequality and the Incomes of Very High Income Taxpayers: Evidence from Tax Returns." Working paper, National Bureau of Economic Research, Cambridge, MA, 1993.

Feldstein, Martin. "Supply Side Economics: Old Truths and New Claims." Working paper 1792, National Bureau of Economic Research, Cambridge, MA, January 1986.

Fink, Richard H. *Supply-Side Economics: A Critical Appraisal*. Frederick, MD: University Publications of America, 1982.

Forbes, Steve. *Flat Tax Revolution: Using a Postcard to Abolish the IRS*. Washington, DC: Regnery Publishing, 2005.

Fox, Justin. "Here We Go Again: Supply Side Economics Is Back! But This Is Not 1981—and That's Why Bush Tax Plans Don't Quite Cut It." *Fortune* 147 (12 May 2003): 64.

Frank, Robert H. "Frames of Reference and the Quality of Life." *American Economic Review* 79, no. 2 (1989): 80–85.

———. "Progressive Taxation and the Incentive Problem." In *Does Atlas Shrug?* edited by Joel B. Slemrod. Cambridge, MA: Harvard University Press, 2000.

Frank, Robert H., and Philip J. Cook. *The Winner-Take-All Society*. New York: Free Press, 1995.

Friedman, Benjamin. *The Moral Consequences of Economic Growth* (Cambridge, MA: Harvard University Press, 2005).

Friedman, Joel, and Aviva Aron-Dine. "Extending Expiring Tax Cuts and AMT Relief Would Cost $3.3 Trillion through 2016." Washington, DC: Center on Budget and Policy Priorities, 2006.

Furman, Jason. "Comments on the Pro-Growth Progressive." www.tpmcafe.com/author/jfurman (accessed 3 December 2005).

Galbraith, James. "The Surrender of Economic Policy." *American Prospect*, 1 March 1996.

Galbraith, John Kenneth. *The New Industrial State*. New York: Signet Books, 1968.

Gale, William. "Economic Growth through Tax Cuts." Testimony before the Joint Economic Committee, 4 March 1999. www.brookings.edu/views/testimony/gale/19990304.htm (accessed 21 November 2005).

Gale, William, and Peter Orszag. "Bush Administration Tax Policy: Effects on Long Term Growth." *Tax Notes*, 18 October 2004.

———. "Bush Administration Tax Policy: Short-Term Stimulus." *Tax Notes*, 1 November 2004.

———. "Bush Administration Tax Policy: Summary and Outlook." *Tax Notes*, 29 November 2004: 1281–83.

Garvin, Glenn. "He Was Right: Looking Back at the Goldwater Moment." *Reason Online*, October 2002. www.reason.com/0203/cr.gg.he.shtml (accessed 29 November 2005).

Gentry, William M., and R. Glenn Hubbard. "Tax Policy and Entrepreneurial Entry." New York: Columbia University School of Business, 2000.

Gephardt, Richard. *An Even Better Place: America in the 21st Century*. New York: Public Affairs, 1999.

Gilder, George. *Wealth and Poverty*. New York: Bantam Books, 1981.

Glassman, James K. "Secular Politics." *Washington Post*, 22 August 1995, A18.

Goldstein, Morris. "Currency Manipulation." *JoongAhn Daily*, 11 December 2003.

Goolsbee, Austan. "Evidence on the High-Income Laffer Curve from Six Decades of Tax Reform." *Brookings Papers on Economic Activity* 1 (Fall 1999).

———. "It's Not about the Money: Why Natural Experiments Don't Work on the Rich." In *Does Atlas Shrug?* edited by Joel B. Slemrod. Cambridge, MA: Harvard University Press, 2000.

Grafton, R. Quentin, Stephen Knowles, and P. Dorian Owen. "Social Divergence and Productivity: Making a Connection." Ottawa: Centre for the Study of Living Standards, 2002. www.csls.ca/repsp/2/graftonetal.pdf (accessed 23 November 2005).

Graham, Otis L. *Toward a Planned Society*. New York: Oxford University Press, 1976.

Gray, Robert T. "President Reagan's Call for Continuing the Free-Enterprise Revolution." *Nation's Business* 76, no. 7 (July 1988): 63.

Greenberg, David. "Tax Cuts in Camelot?" *Slate*, 16 January 2004. www.slate.com/id/2093947 (accessed 22 November 2005).

Greenspan, Alan. "Antitrust." In *Capitalism: The Unknown Ideal*, edited by Ayn Rand. New York: Signet, 1964.

———. "The Assault on Integrity." In *Capitalism: The Unknown Ideal*, edited by Ayn Rand. New York: Signet, 1964.

———. "Gold and Economic Freedom." In *Capitalism: The Unknown Ideal*, edited by Ayn Rand. New York: Signet. 1964.

———. "Testimony before the Committee on the Budget, U.S. Senate," 25 January 2001, 107th Cong., 1st Sess., www.federalreserve.gov/BoardDocs/Testimony/2001/2090 10125.htm (accessed 22 November 2005).

Greenspan, Stanley I. "Child Care Research: A Clinical Perspective." *Child Development*, 74 (2003): 1064.

Greider, William. "The Education of David Stockman." *Atlantic Monthly*, December 1981, 46–47.

Griffith, Robert. "Dwight D. Eisenhower and the Corporate Commonwealth." *American Historical Review* 87, no. 2 (1982): 87–122.

Griliches, Zvi. "The Search for R&D Spillovers." *Scandinavian Journal of Economics* 94 (1992): 29–47.

Gross, Daniel. "Field of Dreams." *Slate*, 2 February 2004. www.slate.com/id/2094801 (accessed 25 November 2005).

———. "The Maestro Is a Hack: How Alan Greenspan Has Become a Bush Puppet." *Slate*, 21 November 2002. http://slate.msn.com/id/2074429 (accessed 22 November 2005).

———. "Address to a joint meeting of the American Machine Tool Distributors Association and the Association for Manufacturing Technology." Washington, DC, 4 October 2005.

Gwartney, James D. "Supply-Side Economics." In *The Concise Encyclopedia of Economics.* www.econlib.org/library/Enc/SupplySideEconomics.html (accessed 21 November 2005).

Hailstones, Thomas. *A Guide to Supply-Side Economics.* Reston, VA: Reston Publishing Company, 1982.

Hall, Robert E., and Charles I. Jones. "Why Do Some Countries Produce So Much More Output Per Worker Than Others?" *Quarterly Journal of Economics*, February 1999, 85–116.

Hassett, Kevin. "Rich Man, Poor Man: How to Think about Income Inequality (Hint: It's Not as Bad as You Think)." Washington, DC: American Enterprise Institute, May 2003.

Hassett, Kevin, and R. Glenn Hubbard. "Where Do We Put the Surplus?" *Wall Street Journal*, 29 January 2001, 26.

Hayek, F. A. *The Road to Serfdom.* 1944. Chicago: University of Chicago Press, 1994.

Hazlitt, Henry. *Economics in One Lesson.* 1946. New York: Arlington House Publishers, 1979.

Heim, B. T. "The Incredible Shrinking Elasticities: Married Female Labor Supply, 1979–2003." Working paper, Duke University, 2004.

Heller, Walter. "The Kemp-Roth-Laffer Free Lunch." *Wall Street Journal*, 12 July 1978, 20.

Helpman, Elhanan. *The Mystery of Economic Growth.* Cambridge, MA: Belknap Press, 2004.

Henderson, David R. *Contemporary Economic Policy* 7, no. 4 (1989): 116–28.

Henderson, Nell. "Greenspan Says Workers' Lack of Skills Lowers Wages." *Washington Post*, 22 July 2004, A1.

Hetherington, Marc. *Why Trust Matters: Declining Political Trust and the Demise of American Liberalism.* Princeton, NJ: Princeton University Press, 2004.

Hoover, Herbert. "Inaugural Address." 4 March 1929.

Hubbard, R. Glenn. "Commentary on Chapter 13." In *Does Atlas Shrug?* edited by Joel Slemrod. Cambridge, MA: Harvard University Press, 2000.

———. "Economic Outlook and Economic Policy." Remarks at the Macroeconomic Advisers Conference, Washington, DC, 19 September 2002. http://www0.gsb.columbia.edu/faculty/ghubbard/speeches/9.19.02.pdf (accessed 26 November 2005).

———. "A Framework for Economic Policy." Remarks at the Ronald Reagan Presidential Library, 15 February 2002. http://www0.gsb.columbia.edu/faculty/ghubbard/speeches/2.15.02.pdf (accessed 21 November 2005).

———. "Measure Tax-Cut 'Fairness' over a Lifetime." *Wall Street Journal*, 8 January 2003.

———. *Money, The Financial System, and the Economy.* 4th ed. Reading, MA: Addison-Wesley, 2001.

———. "Tax Code Revision." Testimony to the House Ways and Means Committee, 8 June 2005. http://www0.gsb.columbia.edu/faculty/ghubbard/speeches/6.8.05.pdf (accessed 21 November 2005).

———. "The Tax-Cut Debate." *Wall Street Journal*, 28 July 1999. http://www0.gsb.columbia.edu/faculty/ghubbard/Articles%20for%20Web%20Site/Wall%20Street%20Journal/07.28.99%20The%20Tax-Cut%20Debate.pdf (accessed 21 November 2005).

———. "Testimony before the Special Committee on Aging." United States Senate, 4

February 2003. http://aging.senate.gov/public/_files/hr92gh.pdf (accessed 21 November 2005).

Hufbauer, Gary Clyde, and Paul L. E. Greico. "Comprehensive Reform for U.S. Business Taxation." Submitted to the President's Advisory Panel on Federal Tax Reform. Washington, DC: Institute for International Economics, 21 April 2005.

Hughes, Kent. *Building the Next American Century: The Past and Future of Economic Competitiveness*. Washington, DC: Woodrow Wilson Press, 2005.

Hulton, Charles R., and Isabel Sawhill. *The Legacy of Reaganomics*. Washington, DC: Urban Institute Press, 1984.

Hunter, Lawrence A., and Stephen J. Entin. "A Framework for Tax Reform." Dallas: Institute for Policy Innovation, 2005.

Jarboe, Kenan Patrick, and Robert D. Atkinson. "A Case for Technology in the New Economy." Washington, DC: Progressive Policy Institute, 1998.

Johnston, David Cay. "The Richest Are Leaving Even the Rich Far Behind." *New York Times*, 5 June 2005.

Joint Economic Committee. "The Reagan Tax Cuts: Lessons for Tax Reform." Washington, DC: U.S. Congress, April 1986. www.house.gov/jec/fiscal/tx-grwth/reagtxct/reagtxct.htm (accessed 21 November 2005).

Jones, Charles I. "Sources of U.S. Economic Growth in a World of Ideas." *American Economic Review* 92, no. 1 (2002): 220–39.

Jones, Charles I., and John Williams. "Measuring the Social Return to R&D." *Quarterly Journal of Economics* 113 (1998): 1119–35.

Judis, John B. *The Paradox of American Democracy: Elites, Special Interests, and the Betrayal of the Public Trust*. New York: Pantheon Books, 2000.

Kamin, David, Richard Kogan, and Robert Greenstein. "Deficits and the Mid-Session Review: The Administration's Efforts to Make Harmful Deficits Appear Benign." Washington, DC: Center for Budget and Policy Priorities, 1 October 2004.

Kemp, Jack. "Democrats Should Embrace JFK Supply-Side Economics." *Investors Business Daily*, 5 November 2003, A16.

Kennedy, Edward M. "Creating a Genuine 'Opportunity Society.'" Speech delivered at the City University of New York Graduate Center, 1 March 2004. www.gc.cuny.edu/spotlight/spotlight_kennedy_speech.htm (accessed 3 December 2005).

Kerry-Edwards 2004. *Strong at Home, Respected in the World*. Washington, DC, 2004.

Keuschnigg, Christian. "Business Formation and Aggregate Investment." *German Economic Review* 2, no. 1 (2001): 31–55.

Keynes, John Maynard. *The General Theory of Employment*. New York: Harcourt Brace & World, 1935.

Kilgore, Ed. "Starving the Beast." *Blueprint Magazine*, 30 June 2003.

Kim, Kyoo-il, and José Carlos Rodríguez-Pueblita. "Are Married Women Secondary Workers? The Evolution of Married Women's Labor Supply in the U.S. from 1983 to 2000." Washington, DC: Congressional Budget Office, December 2005.

Kinsey, Michael. "A Beast of an Idea: Can Big Deficits Starve the Government Down to Size? Not in This Universe." *Time*, 12 January 2004, 163.

Kirk, Russell, and James McClellan. *The Political Principles of Robert A. Taft*. New York: Fleet Press Corporation, 1967.

Klenow, Peter J., and Sergio T. Rebelo. "The Neoclassical Revival in Growth Economics: Has It Gone Too Far?" *NBER Macroeconomics Annual 1997* 12 (1997): 73–103.

Knack, S., and P. Keefer. "Does Social Capital Have an Economic Payoff? A Cross-Country Investigation." *Quarterly Journal of Economics* 112, no. 4 (1997): 1252–88.

Kotlikoff, Laurence J. "The Case for the 'Fairtax.'" *Wall Street Journal*, 7 March 2005, A18.

Krugman, Paul. *The Age of Diminished Expectations*. Cambridge, MA: MIT Press, 1990.

———. "Supply-Side Virus Strikes Again: Why There Is No Cure for This Virulent Infection." *Slate*, 15 August 1996. http://web.mit.edu/krugman/www/virus.html (accessed 21 November 2005).

Kudlow, Larry. "Bush's Disappointment." *National Review Online*, 1 December 1999. www.nationalreview.com/kudlow/kudlow120199.html (accessed 21 November 2005).

———. "Bush's Walk on the Supply-Side." *National Review Online*, 21 February 2000. www.nationalreview.com/kudlow/kudlow022100.html (accessed 22 November 2005).

———. "Cheney the Supply Sider." *National Review Online*, 24 July 2000. www.natio nalreview.com/kudlow/kudlow072400.html (accessed 21 November 2005).

———. "Coolidge Redux." *National Review Online*, 28 July 2000. www.nationalreview .com/kudlow/kudlow072800.shtml (accessed 21 November 2005).

———. "Looking Up, Down the Road." *National Review Online*, 29 May 2001. www .nationalreview.com/kudlow/kudlow052901.shtml (accessed 24 November 2005).

———. "The Supply Side of Karl Rove." *National Review Online*, 29 July 2005. www .nationalreview.com/kudlow/kudlow200507290839.asp (accessed 21 November 2005).

———. "W. Holds His Ground." *National Review Online*, 28 February 2001. www.natio nalreview.com/kudlow/kudlow022801.shtml (accessed 25 November 2005).

———. "W. Slams a Homer for Growth." *National Review Online*, 20 October 2000. www.nationalreview.com/kudlow/kudlow102100.shtml (accessed 21 November 2005).

Laffer, Arthur B. "The Laffer Curve: Past, Present, and Future." *Laffer Associates*, 6 January 2004.

Lake, Celinda, and Daniel Gotoff. "Overview of Recent Research on the Economy." Washington, DC: Campaign for America's Future, 11 July 2005. www.ourfuture.org/ docUploads/lake_poll_july2005.pdf (accessed 26 November 2005).

Laubach, Thomas. "New Evidence on the Interest Rate Effects of Budget Deficits and the Debt." Federal Reserve working paper, Board of Governors of the Federal Reserve System, Washington, DC, May 2003.

Lee, Susan. "The Unmanaged Economy." *Forbes*, 17 December 1984, 147.

Leibfritz, Willi, John Thornton, and Alexandra Bibbee. "Taxation and Economic Performance." Paris: Organisation for Economic Co-operation and Development, 1997.

Leyden, D. P., and A. N. Link. "Why Are Government R&D and Private R&D Complements?" *Applied Economics* 23 (1991): 1673–81.

Leuchtenburg, William E. *Franklin D. Roosevelt and the New Deal: 1932–1940*. New York: Harper & Row, 1963.

Levy, Frank. *The New Dollars and Dreams: American Incomes and Economic Change*. New York: Russell Sage Foundation, 1999.

Li, Wenli, and Pierre-Daniel Sartre. "Growth Effects of Progressive Taxes." Washington, DC: Board of Governors of the Federal Reserve System, November 2001.

Lindsey, Lawrence B. *The Growth Experiment: How the New Tax Policy Is Transforming the U.S. Economy*. New York: Basic Books, 1990.

———. "Remarks by Dr. Lawrence B. Lindsey at the Federal Reserve Bank of Philadel-

phia." Washington, DC: White House, 19 July 2001. http://www.whitehouse.gov/news/
releases/2001/07/20010719-4.html (accessed 12 February 2006).

———. "The Seventeen-Year Boom." Washington, DC: American Enterprise Institute,
2000.

———. "A Tax Code for the Future: The Growth Experiment Revisited." New York:
Manhattan Institute, January 1995.

———. "Why We Must Keep the Tax Cut." *Washington Post*, 18 January 2002, A25.

MacAvoy, Paul. "Treasury Secretary W. E. Simon and Congress on the Business Cycle."
In *A Tribute to William E. Simon*, 10–17. Rochester, NY: William E. Simon Graduate
School of Business Administration, 2001.

Madrick, Jeffrey. *The End of Affluence*. New York: Random House, 1995.

Makin, John. "The Mythical Benefits of Debt Reduction." Washington, DC: American
Enterprise Institute, 2000.

Mandel, Michael. *Rational Exuberance: Silencing the Enemies of Growth*. New York:
HarperCollins, 2004.

Mankiw, Gregory N. "Ask the White House." 8 October 2004. www.whitehouse.gov/ask/
20041008.html (accessed 21 November 2005).

———. "Ax Taxes for Xers!" *Fortune*, 16 March 1998. www.economics.harvard.edu/
faculty/mankiw/columns/mar98.html (accessed 24 January 2006).

———. "Bush Is a Leader the Economy Can Trust." *Fortune*, 13 November 2000. http://
post.economics.harvard.edu/faculty/mankiw/columns/nov00.html (accessed 22 November 2005).

———. "Candidates Need Clues, Not Tax Plans." *Fortune*, 20 March 2000. http://post.ec
onomics.harvard.edu/faculty/mankiw/columns/mar00.html (accessed 22 November
2005).

———. "Deficits and Economic Priorities." *Washington Post*, 16 July 2003. http://post.ec
onomics.harvard.edu/faculty/mankiw/columns/washpost.pdf (accessed 22 November
2005).

———. "The Economic Agenda." International Tax Policy Forum. Washington, DC:
American Enterprise Institute, 2 December 2004. http://post.economics.harvard.edu/
faculty/mankiw/columns/AEIspeech.pdf (accessed 22 November 2005).

———. *Principles of Macroeconomics*. 3rd ed. Mason, OH: Thompson, 2004.

———. "Professor Mankiw Interview Questions: The Marshall Society Interview."
2004–2005. http://post.economics.harvard.edu/faculty/mankiw/columns/marshall.pdf
(accessed 23 November 2005).

———. "Remarks at the National Bureau of Economic Research Tax Policy and the
Economy Meeting." Washington, DC: National Press Club, 4 November 2003. www.
whitehouse.gov/cea/NPressClub20031104.html (accessed 23 November 2005).

———. "Remarks at the Annual Meeting of the National Association of Business Economists." Atlanta, GA, 15 September 2003. http://post.economics.harvard.edu/faculty/
mankiw/columns/nabe.pdf (accessed 25 November 2005).

———. "So Who Do We Thank for This Boom?" *Fortune*, 11 October 1999. http://post
.economics.harvard.edu/faculty/mankiw/columns/oct99.html (accessed 25 November
2005).

Mansfield, Edwin. "Basic Research and Productivity Increase in Manufacturing." *American Economic Review* 70, no. 4 (1980): 863–73.

Mariger, Randall. "Labor Supply and the Tax Reform Act of 1986: Evidence from Panel Data." Washington, DC: Board of Governors of the Federal Reserve System, June 1994.

McIntyre, Robert S. "Down Is Up (Or So Some Say)." *American Prospect*, August 2005.

McKinley, William. "First Inaugural Address." 4 March 1897.

Meese, Ed. *With Reagan: The Inside Story*. Washington, DC: Regnery Gateway, 1992.

Mellon, Andrew W. *Taxation: The People's Business*. New York: Macmillan, 1924.

Meyerson, Harold. "What Are Democrats About?" *Washington Post*, 17 November 2004, A27.

Milligan, Kevin. "Tax-Preferred Savings Accounts and Marginal Tax Rates: Evidence on RRSP Participation." University of Toronto, Department of Economics, 8 May 2001.

Mitchell, Daniel J. "Reducing Tax Rates across the Board: A Cornerstone of Pro-Growth Tax Relief." Washington, DC: Heritage Foundation, 2001.

———. Supplement to "The Impact of Government Spending on Economic Growth." Washington, DC: Heritage Foundation, 15 March 2005.

Moffitt, Robert A., and Mark O. Wilhelm. "Taxation and the Labor Supply Decisions of the Affluent." In *Does Atlas Shrug?* edited by Joel B. Slemrod. Cambridge, MA: Harvard University Press, 2000.

Moore, Stephen. "Real Tax Cuts Have Curves the Economy Booms, and Arthur Laffer Has the Last Laugh." *Wall Street Journal*, 19 June 2005. www.opinionjournal.com/extra/?id = 110006842 (accessed 25 November 2005).

———. "Think Twice about Gregory Mankiw: This Harvard Economist Does Not Belong on the Bush Economic Team." *National Review Online*, 28 February 2003. www.nationalreview.com/moore/moore022803b.asp (accessed 25 November 2005).

Moore, Stephen, and Lincoln Anderson. "Great American Dream Machine." *Wall Street Journal*, 21 December 2005, A18.

Nash, George T. "Modern Tomes." *Policy Review* 84, no. 6 (July–August 1997). www.policyreview.org/jul97/thnash.html (accessed 22 November 2005).

National Science Foundation. "Nifty Fifty." Washington, DC: National Science Foundation. www.nsf.gov/od/lpa/nsf50/nsfoutreach/htm/home.htm (accessed 24 November 2005).

Nelson, Richard R. *Technology, Institutions, and Economic Growth*. Cambridge, MA: Harvard University Press, 2005.

Niskanen, William A. *Reaganomics: An Insider's Account of the Policies and the People*. New York: Oxford University Press, 1988.

———. "'Starving the Beast' Will Not Work." *Cato Handbook on Policy*, 6th ed. Washington, DC: Cato Institute, 2005, 114.

Niskanen, William A., and Stephen Moore. "Supply Tax Cuts and the Truth about the Reagan Economic Record." Cato Policy Analysis no. 261, Cato Institute, Washington, DC, 1996.

Norquist, Grover. "Step-by-Step Tax Reform." *Washington Post*, 9 June 2003, A21. www.washingtonpost.com/ac2/wp-dyn?pagename = article&contentId = A32629-2003Jun8&notFound = true (accessed 21 November 2005).

———. Interview on *Frontline*, 12 October 2004. www.pbs.org/wgbh/pages/frontline/shows/choice2004/interviews/norquist.html (accessed 21 November 2005).

North, Douglas C. *Institutions, Institutional Change, and Economic Performance*. Cambridge, MA: Cambridge University Press, 1990.

———. "Poverty in the Midst of Plenty." Stanford, CA: Hoover Institution, October 2000. www.hoover.stanford.edu/pubaffairs/we/current/north_1000.html (accessed 23 November 2005).

Novak, Robert. "Father of Supply-Side." *Town Hall.com*, 1 September 2005. www.town hall.com/opinion/columns/robertnovak/2005/09/01/155310.html (accessed 21 November 2005).

Oliner, Steven D., and Daniel Sichel. "The Resurgence of Growth in the Late 1990s: Is Information Technology the Story?" Federal Reserve Bank of San Francisco, *Proceedings*, 2000.

Organisation for Economic Co-operation and Development. "Micro-Policies for Growth and Productivity: Final Report." Paris: OECD, 2005, 17.

Orszag, Peter R. "Marginal Tax Rate Reductions and the Economy: What Would Be the Long-Term Effects of the Bush Tax Cut?" Washington, DC: Center on Budget and Policy Priorities, 16 March 2001. www.cbpp.org/3-15-01tax.htm (accessed 21 November 2005).

Parker, Richard. *John Kenneth Galbraith: His Life, His Politics, His Economics*. New York: Farrar, Straus and Giroux, 2005.

Passel, Peter. "Do Tax Cuts Raise Revenue? The Supply Side War Continues." *New York Times*, 16 November 1995, D2.

Pelosi, Nancy. "On the Issues: Jobs and the Economy." http://democraticleader.house .gov/issues/the_economy/index.cfm (accessed 24 November 2005).

Persson, Torsten, and Guido Tabellini. "Is Inequality Harmful for Growth? Theory and Evidence." *American Economic Review* 84 (1994): 600–21.

Peterson, Peter G. *Running on Empty: How the Democratic and Republican Parties Are Bankrupting Our Future and What Americans Can Do about It*. New York: Farrar, Straus & Giroux, 2004.

Petska, Tom, and Mike Studler. "Income, Taxes, and Progressivity: An Examination of Recent Trends in the Distribution of Individual Income and Taxes." Washington, DC: Internal Revenue Service, Statistics of Income Division.

Pew Research Center for the People & the Press. "Views of Business and Regulation Unchanged by Enron." 21 February 2002. http://people-press.org/reports/print.php3?- PageID = 349 (accessed 23 November 2005).

Piketty, Thomas, and Emmanuel Saez. "Income Inequality in the United States, 1913– 1998." *Quarterly Journal of Economics* 118, no. 1 (February 2003): 1–39.

Pinkerton, James P. *What Comes Next: The End of Big Government—and the New Paradigm Ahead*. New York: Hyperion, 1995.

Plosser, Charles I. "The Search for Growth." In *Policies for Long Run Economic Growth: A Symposium Sponsored by the Federal Reserve Bank of Kansas City*. 1992.

Polanyi, Karl. *The Great Transformation*. Boston: Beacon Press, 1944.

Prescott, Edward C. "Why Do Americans Work So Much More Than Europeans?" *Federal Reserve Bank of Minneapolis Quarterly Review* 28, no. 1 (July 2004): 2–13.

Price, Lee. "The Boom That Wasn't." Washington, DC: Economic Policy Institute, December 2005. www.epi.org/briefingpapers/168/bp168.pdf (accessed 3 February 2006).

Putnam, Robert D. *Bowling Alone: The Collapse and Revival of American Community* (New York: Simon & Schuster, 2000).

Raum, Tom. "Bush Economic Team under Fire over Jobs." *Associated Press*, 20 February 2004.

Reagan, Ronald. *An American Life*. New York: Simon & Schuster, 1990.

———. "Economic Recovery Program." Speech delivered 28 April 1981. www.townhall.com/documents/recovery.html (accessed 22 November 2005).

———. "Great Quotes from President Reagan." The Reagan Information Page. www.presidentreagan.info/speeches/quotes.cfm (accessed 22 November 2005).

———. "White House Report on the Program for Economic Recovery." 18 February 1981. www.reagan.utexas.edu/archives/speeches/1981/21881c.htm (accessed 22 November 2005).

Reed, Lawrence W. "Why Limit Government?" Washington, DC: Heritage Foundation, June 2004.

Reich, Robert. "A Covenant with America." *The American Prospect*, November 2005, 48.

———. "For Democrats Adrift, Some Fiscal Therapy." *Washington Post*, 10 November 2002, B1. www.robertreich.org/reich/11102002.asp (accessed 23 November 2005).

Rifkin, Jeremy. *The End of Work: The Decline of the Global Labor Force and the Dawn of the Post-Market Era*. New York: Putnam, 1995.

Roach, Brian. "Read My Lips: More Tax Cuts—the Distributional Impacts of Repealing Dividend Taxation." Working paper 03-01, Global Development and Environment Institute, Tufts University, February 2003.

Roberts, Paul Craig. "My Time with Supply-Side Economics." *Independent Review* 7, no. 3 (Winter 2003): 393–97. www.vdare.com/roberts/supply_side.htm (accessed 21 November 2005).

———. *The Supply-Side Revolution: An Insider's Account of Policymaking in Washington*. Cambridge, MA: Harvard University Press, 1984.

Roboy, David. "Norman B. Ture on Supply-Side Economics." *Enterprise*, June 1980.

Romer, Paul M. "Beyond Classical and Keynesian Macroeconomic Policy." *Policy Options*, July–August 1994.

———. "Implementing a National Technology Strategy with Self-Organizing Industry Boards." *Brookings Papers on Economic Activity* 2 (1993): 345–97.

Roosevelt, Franklin Delano. "Second Inaugural Address." 1937.

Roubini, Nouriel. "Supply Side Economics: Do Tax Rate Cuts Increase Growth and Revenues and Reduce Budget Deficits? Or Is It Voodoo Economics All Over Again?" http://pages.stern.nyu.edu/~nroubini/SUPPLY.HTM (accessed 25 November 2005).

Saez, Emmanuel. "Do Taxpayers Bunch at Kink Points?" University of California at Berkeley and National Bureau of Economic Research, 13 June 2000. http://emlab.berkeley.edu/users/saez/bunch.pdf (accessed 22 November 2005).

———. "Reported Incomes and Marginal Tax Rates, 1960–2000: Evidence and Policy Implications." In *Tax Policy and the Economy*, edited by James M. Poterba, 117–71. Cambridge, MA: National Bureau of Economic Research, 2004.

Sammartino, Frank, and David Weiner. "Recent Evidence on Taxpayers' Response to the Rate Increases of the 1990s." *National Tax Journal* 50 (3 September 1997): 683–705.

Sawhill, Isabel, and Alice Rivlin. "Restoring Fiscal Sanity: How to Balance the Budget." Washington, DC: Brookings Institution, 2004.

Say, Jean-Baptiste. *Treatises of Political Economy*. Trans. C. R. Princep, ed. Clement C.

Biddle. 4th ed. Philadelphia: Lippencott, Grambo. www.econlib.org/library/Say/sayT41.html (accessed 21 November 2005).

Scherer, F. M. *New Perspectives on Economic Growth and Technological Innovation.* Washington, DC: Brookings Institution Press, 1999.

Schiller, Robert. *The New Financial Order: Risk in the 21st Century.* Princeton, NJ: Princeton University Press, 2003.

Schmidt-Hebbel, Klaus, and Luis Serven. "Does Income Inequality Raise Aggregate Saving?" *Journal of Development Economics* 61 (April 2000): 417–46.

Schumpeter, Joseph A. *Capitalism, Socialism, and Democracy.* 1942. New York: Harper Perennial, 1975.

Shafer, Jack. "Two-Headed Newt." *Slate,* 25 June 1997. http://slate.msn.com/id/1000029 (accessed 29 November 2005).

Shapiro, Isaac, and David Kamin. "Concentrating on the Wrong Target." Washington, DC: Center for Budget and Policy Priorities, 5 March, 2003.

Slemrod, Joel B. "The Economics of Taxing the Rich." In *Does Atlas Shrug?* edited by Joel B. Slemrod. Cambridge, MA: Harvard University Press, 2000.

Slemrod, Joel, and Jon Bakija. *Taxing Ourselves: A Citizen's Guide to the Debate over Taxes.* Cambridge, MA: MIT Press, 2004.

Slemrod, Joel, William G. Gale, and William Easterly. "What Do Cross-Country Studies Teach about Government Involvement, Prosperity and Economic Growth?" *Brookings Papers on Economic Activity* 2 (1995): 373–431.

Smith, Adam. *The Wealth of Nations.* New York: Penguin Classics, 2000.

Soete, Luc. "Globalization, Employment, and the Knowledge-Based Economy." In *Employment and Growth in the Knowledge-based Economy.* Paris: OECD, 1996.

Sperling, Gene. "Bush's Job Record Belies Much-Touted Recovery." *Bloomberg News,* 13 August 2004.

———. *The Pro-Growth Progressive.* New York: Simon & Schuster, 2005.

Sperry, Peter B. "The Compelling Case for Tax Cuts Now: Growing Surplus, Shrinking Debt." *Capitalism Magazine,* 12 February 2001. www.capmag.com/article.asp?ID=306 (accessed 22 November 2005).

———. "Growing Surplus, Shrinking Debt: The Compelling Case for Tax Cuts Now." Washington, DC: Heritage Foundation, 7 February 2001.

Stein, Herbert. *What I Think: Essays on Economics, Politics, and Life.* Washington, DC: American Enterprise Institute Press, 1998.

Steinmo, Sven. "The Evolution of Policy Ideas: Tax Policy in the 20th Century." Boulder, CO: University of Colorado, Department of Political Science, 16 January 2002.

Stiglitz, Joseph. *The Roaring Nineties: A New History of the World's Most Prosperous Decade.* New York: W. W. Norton, 2003.

Sullivan, Martin A. "Do Economists Matter?" *Tax Notes,* 15 January 2001, 280.

Sullum, Jacob. "A Flood of Red Ink: The Fiscal Fallout from Hurricane Katrina." *Reason Online,* 23 September 2005. www.reason.com/sullum/092305.shtml (accessed 25 November 2005).

Suskind, Ron. "The Price of Loyalty, the Bush Files: Economy, Fundamental Tax Reform; the Bush Plan," http://thepriceofloyalty.ronsuskind.com/thebushfiles/archives/000093.html (accessed 26 November 2005).

Taft, William Howard. "The Anti-Trust Law." Authentic History Center, Beverly, MA, 1

October 1912. www.authentichistory.com/audio/1900s/19121001_William_H_Taft-The_Anti-Trust_Law.html (accessed 27 November 2005).

Tanzi, V., and H. Zee. "Tax Policy for Emerging Markets: Developing Countries." *National Tax Journal*, June 2000, 299–322.

Tassey, Greg. "The Economics of a Technology-Based Service Sector." Planning report, 98–92. Washington, DC: National Institute of Standards and Technology, 1998.

Temple, Jonathan. "Growth Effects of Education and Social Capital in the OECD Countries." Department of Economics, University of Bristol, UK, 19 June 2001. www.nuff.ox.ac.uk/Users/Temple/abstracts/edfinal2.pdf (accessed 22 November 2005).

———. "The New Growth Evidence." *Journal of Economic Literature* 37 (March 1999): 112–156.

Texiera, Ruy. "Public Opinion Watch." Washington, DC: Center for American Progress, 20 July 2005.

Tobin, James. "Fiscal Policy: Its Macroeconomics in Perspective." Working paper, Yale University, Cowles Foundation for Research in Economics, New Haven, CT, May 2001.

U.S. Department of the Treasury, Office of Tax Analysis. "The Federal Estate and Gift Tax: Description, Profile of Taxpayers and Economic Consequences." Washington, DC: Office of Tax Analysis, 1998.

U.S. Office of Management and Budget. *FY 2002 Economic Outlook, Highlights from FY 94 to FY 2001, FY 2002 Baseline Projections*. Washington, DC: Office of Management and Budget, 16 January 2001.

U.S. Trade Representative. *2005 National Trade Estimate Report on Foreign Trade Barriers*. www.ustr.gov/Document_Library/Reports_Publications/2005/2005_ NTE_Report/Section_Index.html (accessed 23 November 2005).

Wall Street Journal. "John Maynard Domenici." 16 April 1981.

Wanniski, Jude. "SSU Spring Lesson #7: The Kennedy Tax Cut." www.wanniski.com/showarticle.asp?articleid = 4213 (accessed 22 November 2005).

———. *The Way the World Works*. Washington, DC: Regnery, 1978

Watts, William L. "Daschle: Democrats Will Press for Middle-Class Tax Relief." Tax Policy Center, 3 January 2003. www.taxpolicycenter.org/news/dems_blast_div.cfm (accessed 21 November 2005).

Weinstein, Paul, Jr. "Family Friendly Tax Reform." Washington, DC: Progressive Policy Institute, 2005.

———. "New Economy Work (NEW) Scholarships: Universal Access to Training for Dislocated Workers." Washington, DC: Progressive Policy Institute, 2002.

www.ppionline.org/ppi_ci.cfm?knlgAreaID = 107&subsecID = 175&contentID = 250586 (accessed 23 November 2005).

Wesbury, Brian S. "Taking the Voodoo Out of Tax Cuts." 2 June 2003. www.econlib.org/library/Columns/y2003/Wesburytaxcuts.html (accessed 22 November 2005).

Wessner, Charles W., ed. *Government-Industry Partnerships*. Washington, DC: Board on Science, Technology, and Economic Policy, National Research Council, 2001.

White House. "President Bush's Agenda for Job Creation and Economic Opportunity." 6 January 2006. www.whitehouse.gov/infocus/economy (accessed 24 January 2006).

White, Kirk. "Marginal Tax Rates and the Tax Reform Act of 1986: The Long-Run Effect on U.S. Wealth Distribution." Working paper, Duke University, Department of Economics, 15 November 2001.

Wiebe, Robert H. *Businessmen and Reform: A Study of the Progressive Movement.* Chicago: Ivan R. Dee, 1989.

Winik, Lyric Wallwork. "The Economic Impact of the Bush and Congressional Democratic Economic Stimulus Plans." Economy.com, February 2003.

———. "Intelligence Report." *Parade*, 4 January 2004.

Zandi, Mark. "The Economic Impact of the Bush and Congressional Democratic Economic Stimulus Plans." Economy.com, February 2003.

———. "Testimony before the Subcommittee on Economic Policy, Senate Banking, Housing and Urban Affairs Committee," 22 May 2003.

Index

About the Author

Robert D. Atkinson, Ph.D., is President of the Information Technology and Innovation Foundation, a Washington, DC–based technology policy think tank. He is the author of *The Past and Future of America's Economy: Long Waves of Innovation that Power Cycles of Growth* (2005). He has an extensive background in technology policy having conducted groundbreaking research projects on technology and innovation. Before coming to ITIF, Atkinson was vice president of the Progressive Policy Institute and director of PPI's Technology & New Economy Project. He previously served as executive director of the Rhode Island Economic Policy Council and as project director at the former Congressional Office of Technology Assessment. In 2002, he was awarded the Wharton Infosys Business Transformation Award Silver Medal. *Government Technology* magazine and the Center for Digital Government named him one of the 25 top "Doers, Dreamers and Drivers of Information Technology." In 2006, *Inc.* magazine listed Atkinson as one of "19 friends" of small business in Washington. Atkinson received his Ph.D. in City and Regional Planning from the University of North Carolina at Chapel Hill in 1989. He lives in Chevy Chase, Maryland.